"Anne Dyson's myriad admirers will find these case studies by her international research team both delightfully typical and importantly unique: typical in vividly describing eight emerging writers; unique in analyzing the supports or constraints —material or ideological—that they encounter in and out of school across five continents. At the end, Dyson has wise words for teachers anywhere about 'the worlds we negotiate with children in the classroom.'"

Courtney B. Cazden, Harvard Graduate School of Education, USA

"No other book in early childhood writing brings together such a combination of experts with understanding drawn from a wide range of contexts. Senior scholars in the field of children's writing have come together from across the globe to compare their case studies with a view to theorizing the central issues in children's writing. The global inclusiveness of the project will not only speak to a wide audience, but will push the thinking in the field."

Hilary Janks, University of the Witswatersrand, South Africa

"*Child Cultures, Schooling, and Literacy* presents a group of stellar researchers who bring to life the authorial lives of children across the globe. It is masterfully designed, the writing is sophisticated, engaging, lyrical. Elegantly theorized, respectful of children, provocative, the book helps us to see young children's writing as an agentive, playful and complex practice—a powerful antidote to the acultural depiction that is often used from a purely developmental point of view."

Beth Graue, University of Wisconsin–Madison, USA

CHILD CULTURES, SCHOOLING, AND LITERACY

Through analysis of case studies of young children (ages 3 to 8 years), situated in different geographic, cultural, linguistic, political, and socioeconomic sites on five continents, this book examines the interplay of childhoods, schooling, and literacies. Written language is situated within particular childhoods as they unfold in school. A key focus is on children's agency in the construction of their own childhoods.

The book generates diverse perspectives on what written language may mean for childhoods. Looking at variations in the complex relationships between official (curricular) visions and unofficial (child-initiated) visions of relevant composing practices and appropriate cultural resources, it offers, first, insight into how those relationships may change over time and space as children move through early schooling and, second, understanding of the dynamics of schools and the experience of childhoods through which the local meaning of school literacy is formulated. Each case—each child in a particular sociocultural site—does not represent an essentialized nation or a people but, rather, a rich, processual depiction of childhood being constructed in particular local contexts and the role, if any, for composing.

Anne Haas Dyson is Faculty Excellence Professor, College of Education, University of Illinois at Urbana-Champaign, USA and American Educational Research Fellow.

CHILD CULTURES, SCHOOLING, AND LITERACY

Global Perspectives on Composing Unique Lives

Edited by
Anne Haas Dyson

Routledge
Taylor & Francis Group

NEW YORK AND LONDON

First published 2016
by Routledge
711 Third Avenue, New York, NY 10017

and by Routledge

2 Park Square, Milton Park, Abingdon, Oxon, OX14 4RN

Routledge is an imprint of the Taylor & Francis Group, an informa business

Library of Congress Cataloging-in-Publication Data
Child cultures, schooling, and literacy: global perspectives on composing
   unique lives / edited by Anne Haas Dyson.
   pages cm
   Includes bibliographical references.
   1. Language arts (Elementary)—Case studies. 2. Children—Social
   conditions—Case studies. I. Dyson, Anne Haas.
   LB1575.8.C47 2016
   372.6—dc23
   2015027905

ISBN: 978-1-138-83152-0 (hbk)
ISBN: 978-1-138-83154-4 (pbk)
ISBN: 978-1-315-73651-8 (ebk)

Typeset in Bembo and Stone Sans
by Florence Production Ltd, Stoodleigh, Devon, UK

For young children and their teachers,
who are writing
their own stories of schooling
all over the globe

BRIEF CONTENTS

CONTENTS

ACKNOWLEDGMENTS

This book, like all texts, is floating on "a sea of talk," and before that sea, it stayed afloat on the steady stream of a dream (Britton, 1970, p. 29). The dream has played and replayed in my mind's eye since I was a young teacher in the 'seventies. Research on children's writing was burgeoning then, and linear descriptions of "writing development" were published here and there. But a cultural tool like written language is not tied to some biological imperative. To understand children's composing, one would need to study that writing within a diversity of cultural, historical, and political settings. This was not something "I" could do.

And so my first big thankyou is to the book's contributors for turning my "I" into a "We." I thank Barbara Comber and co-researcher Lyn Kerkham, Sophie Dewayani, Celia Genishi, Esther Mukewa Lisanza, Jackie Marsh, Peggy Miller, Iliana Reyes and Urvashi Sahni. These friends and colleagues had roots all over the globe but each agreed, with enthusiasm and graciousness, to undertake this collective project. They kept up this kindness—and my spirits—even as I sent one editorial request and then another to them as the book took final shape.

The contributors' "sea of talk" first flowed in a working conference that brought us together to tell stories of young children and composing, based on detailed qualitative case studies. As the stories accumulated, discussions comparing cases filled in the spaces around the stories and common themes emerged, all developed in chapters to come. Because of the central importance of the case studies to this project, heartfelt thanks are also offered to the many educators and administrators who made those studies possible. Depending on the institutional setting, school district representatives, school principals or directors of early childhood centers, and classroom teachers themselves were all involved in allowing the project to go forth. Parents had to consent too, signing university human subject committee forms. All these people must remain anonymous, but they must also know they were critical to the project reported herein.

I acknowledge with a warm heart the case study children who allowed us into their worlds with all our accoutrements, among them notebooks, recorders, and even cameras. The children will not hear my voice but we honor them by sensitively listening to theirs.

None of this work would have been possible without the support of the Spencer Foundation. Although I am a huge fan of the foundation, it is, of course, not responsible for my findings and perspectives. Nonetheless, Spencer provided the support that allowed participants to travel to the working conference and, also, allowed me superb assistants.

Jennifer Raskauskas, a terrific graduate student at the University of Illinois, was the project's main—and very busy—assistant. Jenn monitored the endless details that allowed participants to travel to central Illinois, to have a lovely place to stay, and appropriate (and delicious) food. She arranged transportation, even driving participants herself to and from the airport and out for an evening meal (reservations arranged by her). Jenn taped the working conference, especially the comparative discussions, and then transcribed them. (Tired yet?) After the conference, she provided an additional reading of the formally written case studies and the knitting-the-book-together thematic chapters. She handled correspondence when, for example, national or state curricular guidelines were missing, figures needed redoing, or a fact had to be double-checked. Jenn did all this work with enthusiasm and graciousness, for which we are forever grateful.

A book project like this, involving so many people, generates reference lists that must be double-checked and corralled into a common form. For this seemingly endless task, I must thank another great graduate student here at Illinois, Wendy Maa. Wendy did all this—plus she blended all the references into one long list to avoid duplication (and save space) . . . and then undid that compilation when it did not meet publisher requirements. She did all this with a "no-problem" attitude, contacting participants when references were missing or a tad confusing. I so appreciate Wendy.

Finally, I thank our editor, Naomi Silverman, whose belief in this project helped me sustain my own.

And now I am ready to tell you, dear readers, the story of our collective project and what we have learned. I ask that you sit back, relax, and enjoy the journey to come.

Reference

Britton, J. (1970). *Language and learning*. Harmondsworth, Middlesex, England: Penguin.

SECTION 1

Stories of Composing in Childhoods

1

INTRODUCTION: GATHERING TEXTUAL CHILDREN

Anne Haas Dyson

Late March in the upper Midwest is not, it must be said, gloriously appealing to outsiders. However, to Midwesterners (at least this one) it is indeed glorious—the snow and ice are melted (with a little luck), the sidewalks and roads are not health-hazards, one's breath does not condense in the air. It is a time of anticipation, the trees anxious for their leaves, the ground ready for brave crocuses, the grass promising to turn green any day. To outsiders from milder climates, though, the trees are bare, the grass brown, the yards colorless expanses—and all those farm fields just so much dirt.

So it was when the visitors arrived in my current university town—academic friends, travelers with roots in varied places across the globe (see Figure 1.1) I worried a bit about the scenery, or its lack. I needn't have. The visitors arrived in good humor, with warm grins, all in sync with the season, as they were full of anticipation of what we would do. Moreover, each traveler brought a textual child, that is, a story of a young child (three to eight years), in early schooling, faced with new possibilities—and challenges—of composing. The children hailed from Australia, India, Indonesia, Kenya, Mexico, the UK, and the United States, particularly New York City and right here in central Illinois. Listening to these stories of children enacting their entry into school composing, situated in sometimes startling different places, and analytically comparing individual experience—these were the tasks we would do together (along with enjoying each other's presence).

Below I explain the inquiry that fueled our collective work and then turn to the specifics of the working conference that brought the visitors together.

FIGURE 1.1 Conference Participants

On the Relevance of Writing in Childhoods

> Writing should be . . . relevant to [a child's] life.
>
> *(Vygotsky, 1978, p. 118)*

Going to school is the official work of young children, at least ideally, although gender, poverty, and war may complicate or deny children their place in the schoolroom. Children are to become literate and, thereby, productive citizens. All around the world, literacy is part of contemporary childhoods, although enacted to different degrees and in varied ways in diverse political, sociocultural, and economic conditions (UNICEF, 2012).

Children's writing is particularly interesting in this regard. As a curricular area, it is a window to societies' ways of socializing children into literacy through schooling. As a symbolic tool, it is also a potential window to experienced childhoods themselves. To build on the Vygotsky quote above, any symbolic tool, to be viable, must assume a niche in the symbolic repertoire of a particular sociocultural group, including those consisting of children. Indeed, some kind of graphic symbol-making is an aspect of children's play throughout the world, whether children are creating images and words using sticks in the mud, No. 2 pencils on primary grade paper, or a finger and a touch screen (Matthews, 1999).

The question arises, then, does and how does composing become "releva.. to children who, as small bundles of energy, are drawn, as children are, to each other, to play, and to create some sense of meaning and control in their worlds (Corsaro, 2011; Nelson, 2007)? Herein, we ask this question about children in particular geographic, cultural, linguistic, and socioeconomic circumstances. The responses are due to that international group of scholars, brought together for a working conference on young children's composing. The goal undergirding the conference was a desire for understandings of child composing that are globally responsible and responsive, grounded, as they would be, in those case studies accompanying each participant; that is, in the lives of unique children in diverse home places.

In this chapter, I describe in more detail the work that began in the conference. In the process, I note the project's assumptions about the nature of literacy, the multimodality of composing, and the variability of childhoods. In the closing pages, I provide an overview of the chapters to come. Through those chapters, we will thematically knit together the distinctive cases and, thereby, provide insight into the sociocultural, economic, and institutional factors that support and constrain children's pathways as composers of texts, of relationships the texts mediate, and, indeed, of selves as participants in their worlds. I begin below with the importance of case studies themselves, calling on some "Numberly" children to help me explain our work.

Experiencing Child Diversity through Case Studies

"Everyone liked numbers" in what we might call Numberly Land, a world detailed in a picture book by William Joyce and Christina Ellis (2014, n.p.). Like many administrators and politicians influencing schools, the residents of this Numberly Land live in a world of numbers. That world is orderly, neat, easily grasped. In a similar way, numbers provide an orderly way to understand the progress of nation states toward an educated populace, or the progress of one kindergartener on the designated tests that describe progress along some linear pathway of skills and knowledge.

Now in this Numberly Land, there are disgruntled children, five friends, who know something is missing. Through their hard work and play with what they were given—numbers—they construct letters. And those letters form words, and the words transform their world. By the end of the book, the five Numberly friends are colorful individuals linked in relationship to each other.

I have retold this Numberly story because it is, I think, an allegory for how we understand children and their entry into written language use. Be our attention on the statistics UNICEF (United Nations International Children's Emergency Fund) reports, providing percentages of young children on the literacy track for this country or that one, or on the results of a school's testing regimen, measuring if this child or that one has stepped up to the next level of "literacy skill," one way we "know" children is through numbers. Such numbers are useful for monitoring and comparing literacy in broad terms. But composing is often left out of the numberly report and, moreover, children are left out too—the intentional little ones with worries and joys, resources and relationships, and particular familiarities with the squiggles and images on buildings, paper, and perhaps screens that may (or may not) be part of the practices of their every-day life.

Moreover, in schools across the globe, young children are viewed primarily from the point of view of the official curriculum; they do, or do not, do as they are told. Herein the emphasis is on the agency of children themselves, or what Sherry Ortner calls "embedded agency" (1996, p. 13): individuals interact within, and respond to, the sociocultural, economic, and power structures embedded in their daily lives. Thus, childhoods are socially constructed by societal institutions, including schools designed for children by adults; however, those institutions do not dictate children's experienced lives (Olwig & Gullov, 2003). In schools, where children greatly outnumber adults, relations and semiotic practices inevitably evolve in child places underneath, overlapping, and outside of the official curriculum (e.g., lunch time, recess, before- and after-school play).

Hence, participants in the conference brought detailed stories of children and composing. The cases themselves were of children who, in their local school places, would be deemed "at risk" or some equivalent term. Children deemed "at risk" reveal a society's ideological notions of the "proper" childhood and, at the same time, the kinds of resources, including languages, deemed of most use for school success. Such identification is specific to a geographic and institutional site. Still, variation in economic support, social class structures, gendered and racialized inequities—all are evident if we compare across and within global sites. We, however, are not comparing sites. We are comparing individual children's situated experiences. And children, like those five numberly peers, have needs for making sense and making friends that may lead them down paths not imagined by school (Corsaro, 2011; Dyson, 2003, 2013).

These case studies, presented in Chapter 2, embody the understanding that composing is, from the beginning, multimodal in its representation and communication (Dyson, 1989; Kress, 1997) and situated in culturally and socially meaningful practices (Collins & Blot, 2003; Street, 1984). That is, young children's composing may consist of some combination of drawing, talking, gesturing, singing, and writing; and all that semiotic activity may be within a playful context enacted with other children. Thus, our interest is not only in official curricula but also in child-reinterpretations of official tasks and, moreover, in child-initiated occasions for composing. Indeed, in some of their official school worlds, there was no composing. The children might, for example, copy words from the board; but this did not mean composing as a form of imagination and play never occurred, as readers will see. Conversely, a curriculum that encouraged "composing" could leave a child voiceless, if, for example, a child's experiential or linguistic resources were deemed without academic value. All is not always as it might first appear.

Within the cases, then, children are seen through an official curricular lens: How did children measure up to their school's expectations? However, they are also seen through an unofficial lens grounded in children's social relations and practices. How did school appear when viewed from a child's perspective? In the latter view, companions, avenues for play, and unanticipated cultural resources appeared. For example, Esther Lisanza studied in the former English colony, Kenya; in her village school, children were denied the use of their home language in favor of English, but they sometimes "smuggled" their language in through songs and through unofficial church-related drawing and talking.

The case studies are better conceived of as "cross-contextual" rather than "cross-cultural" (Gillen & Cameron, 2010, p. 14). That is, each case—each child in a particular sociocultural site—does not represent an essentialized nation or a people but, rather, a rich, processual depiction of an experienced childhood in particular local contexts and the role, if any, for composing. Those rich case studies made apparent diverse perspectives on what "writing" may mean in official school worlds, how children's visions of relevant composing practices may relate to official views, how those relationships may change over time and space as children move through early schooling, and, ultimately, into how children may experience the local meaning of school literacy. Below I provide a brief description of how we proceeded.

Working (and Playing) in the Working Conference on Composing in Childhoods

When conference participants gathered for their first full day together, the task at hand was storytelling. We heard case studies of young children in particular physical, cultural, and institutional circumstances enacting their entry into written language use with teachers and peers (see Table 1.1). A case study of a child and her or his composing entails much more than marks on a page. Each child was in a particular institution regulated in varied ways by government guidelines for curriculum and testing, and informed by a particular ideology of childhood, literacy, and progress.

Moreover, the case studies took shape within political histories in which colonialism and oppression, articulated through the complexities of race, gender, and social class, continued to echo in contemporary provisions for education (Wells, 2009). This political history could be evident in the preferred language of the school and, indeed, in the materiality of a particular physical setting—some children's classroom space was relatively expansive, with places for constructive and dramatic play and for playing instructional games on computers; another's "classroom" was out under a tree, as children sat with slates on their laps; still another's was in a classroom space stuffed with desks for 89 children. There were those classrooms stocked with materials, and others in which the one textbook

TABLE 1.1 Case Study Children

Child's Name	Country Resides In	Level of Schooling	Language(s)	Researcher
Gareth	England	Reception Class (first year of statutory schooling)	English	Jackie Marsh
Ta'Von	The United States (Illinois)	Preschool and Kindergarten	English (with features of African American Language)	Anne Haas Dyson
Danti	Indonesia	Early Childhood Center Class B (intended for 6- to 7-year-old children)	Indonesian, Sudanese	Sophie Dewayani
Gus	Australia	Kindergarten, Reception, First Grade, Second Grade, and Third Grade	English	Barbara Comber & Lyn Kerkham
Sheela	India	Second Grade	Hindi	Urvashi Sahni
Miguel	The United States (New York)	Pre-Kinder-garten (Head Start, 2 years), Kindergarten, First Grade, and Second Grade	Spanish, Receptive skills in Mixteco, Learning English in school	Celia Genishi
Natalia	Mexico	First Grade	Spanish, Learning náhuatl in school	Iliana Reyes
Rafiki	Kenya	First Grade	Kamba, Swahili, Learning English in school	Esther Mukewa Lisanza

was copied on the board by the teacher and then copied by the children. These may be global times, but the movement of capital across national borders is uneven between and within societal boundaries.

Further, curricular definitions of "writing" varied notably, as earlier seen. They did not necessarily entail composing or intentional children expressing and organizing meaning through marks on a page (much less on the rarely available screens). If children did compose, their symbolic efforts could be made, not just to appease adults, but to participate in a text-mediated activity with their friends. Children could at times seem to have asked some version of: When and how do I get in on this? What do I need to say or write to be viewed as a player? Our basic unit of analysis, then, was not a multimodal text but an event—an enacted social practice (Barton & Papen, 2010; Street, 2000).

And so we as a collective listened to one case and then the other, pausing periodically to compare children's stories. Differences among the sites initially grabbed our attention, since they were strongly evident in the materiality of children's everyday lives. However, when we entered the body of the stories through the words and images of the scholar/storyteller, we met intentional children, relating to teachers and to peers. In viewing schooling from a child's perspective, thematic threads became more boldly evident. Children played, sang, danced, and reached out to each other as companions for doing their "work" and for transforming work into play. In their play, children could draw on a wealth of experiences, be they local happenings, religious observances, and the media, both local (e.g., popular songs on local radio) and localized global media (e.g., an Indonesian-speaking Dora the Explorer, who was originally a little American Latina, bilingual in Spanish and English). Thus, while children's material and curricular conditions varied dramatically, all children worked out elbow room in school, sometimes visibly in official composing spaces but sometimes—and sometimes exclusively—in unofficial spaces, in which they snuck in their communicative and symbolic repertoire and their cultural resources for composing. Thus, agency, resources, and language were our thematic threads as we compared each studied case to others, although identity and power were constant thematic accompaniments.

After the storytelling, we met in small groups so that each participant could discuss how they saw their own case, or others, as relating to a major theme. Two of our members (Iliana Reyes and Urvashi Sahni) had to participate through Skype, because of personal injury and a family tragedy. So, in these discussions, Celia Genishi thought of Iliana's case in addition to her own; and Peggy Miller, who was originally solely our consultant and discussant, helped with Urvashi's case. Described here, the meetings sound rather somber affairs, but we laughed a lot. Children have a way of upending the staid. For example, while a case might bring us into the boring repetitiveness of rote schooling or the maddening ideology that labels some children as not smart, underneath that boring curriculum or deep in its corners we might find children bursting into song and even dance, having uproarious adventures on paper, or unexpectedly trying out a mother's voice in a handwritten field trip "permission" letter. While a case could be heartbreaking, there were moments of possibility and of fun.

The discussions were the formal beginning of the analytic work of comparing the cases, although that work continued and is even now, as I write these words. Those first discussions were taped and, after everyone went home, transcribed by Jenn Raskauskas, the project assistant, and given a first analysis for subthemes by me. Then the transcripts went around to the group and were used most especially by the participants in charge of drawing together our comparative work for each of the major themes. Through that comparative analysis process, the interplay of composing and enacted childhoods was probed, its dynamic enactment was better understood, the sociocultural factors that mattered took shape, and the larger sociopolitical processes the cases entailed sharpened. I hope, then, that the book is truly relevant globally for understanding the situated nature of children's written language use. In the final section below, I draw this introduction to a close and, at the same time, set the stage for the textual adventures to come.

The Textual Adventures to Come: Overview of Book's Content

> It is . . . wise to remind ourselves of the fact that the world is big . . . . Our own environments, from which we so often deduce principles of human communication, may well be (and probably are) highly peculiar environments with norms, codes, and conventions . . . .
>
> *(Blommaert, 2005, p. 50)*

An ethnographic study of a particular case—herein, situated in a childhood culture and its textual play—does not provide findings that can be generalized to some broader population. It is not a sample; it is a case. Its power, to borrow from Geertz (1973), is that it gives us concrete material with which to think about abstract phenomena, like relevance, agency, and power. How could we think about childhoods and composing without some young children constructing their childhoods in some particular circumstances?

Hence, after this introductory chapter, Chapter 2, The Situated Cases, presents concise versions of all eight case studies. Although different developmental pathways and educational issues may be foregrounded in different case studies, each case takes you, our readers, into a classroom in a particular geographic site and situates that site within the institution of schooling, itself set within a political and, when relevant, religious context. Each case provides relevant information on the official writing curriculum, and, most centrally, a narrative portraying the child's participation in official and unofficial composing curricula. These cases are the heart of the book.

Next, in Section 2: Thematic Threads of Continuity and Contrast, are the three thematic chapters, written by Barbara Comber (Chapter 3 on agency), Peggy

Miller and Urvashi Sahni (Chapter 4 on cultural resources), and Celia Genishi (Chapter 5, on the key resource of language). Key issues that arose related to those themes included:

(a) **child agency**: variation in nature of, and official curricular provision for, child social relations, play, and other forms of agency through composing

(b) **sanctioned and unsanctioned cultural resources for composing**: variation in official and unofficial use of experiential and textual material from varied sources, including popular media, religious practice, folklore, and peer social play. "Unsanctioned" resources somehow go against dominant societal ideologies (e.g., gender appropriateness, cultural "taste" in textual material, dominant linguistic values)

(c) **language**: variation in the role of vernaculars and home languages in children's composing.

Issues of power and of identity—of who children are allowed or assumed to be— work their way into all chapters.

In Section 3: On Composing Childhoods, I return to the textual spotlight and consider the project's implications for theory and research, for policy, and for pedagogy (Chapter 6). I aim to situate our basic project question in the professional concerns of diverse educators: Whatever our educational role, we must share a concern with how writing becomes "relevant" to children as children. For that to happen, we must pay respectful attention to childhood worlds of relations and intentions, of power and play. The diversity of experienced childhoods in this book counters any simplistic generalizations about how children learn to write and, pragmatically, makes possible an openness to diverse resources and pathways to literacy.

Certainly the case studies make abundantly clear that relatively affluent nations have socioeconomic supports for education that less affluent nations, struggling with substantial rural and/or urban poverty, do not; in addition societal ideologies related to gender, class, race/ethnicity have their own constraining power. Nonetheless, all children need social companions and meaningful—"relevant"— activity; and they all have resources with which to build possibilities for composing. Thus, we aim to improve education for the most vulnerable by promoting children's opportunity to build on what they know and to have some agency in taking control and making sense of new symbolic tools for participating, extending, and even transforming their worlds and their very selves.

Section 3 closes with a Concluding Commentary by Peggy J. Miller.

As You Embark . . .

. . . on the textual journey crafted for you, please prepare to focus your attention on the words and deeds of small children. All around the world, children are iceless as social beings who deserve a meaningful, satisfying childhood. Further, l around the world, the literacy education of young children viewed as "at risk" may be reduced to a bare-bones curriculum focused on "the basics," despite now longstanding views of literacy, not as a set of knowledge or skills, but as a cultural activity learned through participation and use. An understanding of written language development that takes into account children's experienced worlds does not discount the critical role of adults but it does acknowledge the importance of children's resources and perspectives. Children are not mindless receptacles or passive apprentices to the adult world on offer. In the pages ahead, the very young, in all their diversity, will allow you the opportunity to experience their worlds up close. At least for me, this was an adventure I felt the need for some 35 years ago; I hope you benefit from it as I did—with new understandings, new empathies, and reinforced respect for children and, also, for their teachers.

On we go.

References

Barton, D. & Papen, U. (Eds.) (2010). *The anthropology of writing: Understanding textually-mediated worlds*. London, England: Continuum International.

Blommaert, J. (2005). *Discourse*. Cambridge, UK: Cambridge University Press.

Collins, J., & Blot, R. (2003). *Literacy and literacies: Texts, power, and identity*. Cambridge, UK: Cambridge University Press.

Corsaro, W. (2011). *The sociology of childhood, third edition*. Thousand Oaks, CA: Pine Forge Press.

Dyson, A. Haas (1989). *Multiple worlds of child writers: Friends learning to write*. New York, NY: Teachers College Press.

Dyson, A. Haas (2003). *The brothers and sisters learn to write: Popular literacies in childhood and school cultures*. New York, NY: Teachers College Press.

Dyson, A. Haas (2013). *ReWRITING the basics: Literacy learning in children's cultures*. New York, NY: Teachers College Press.

Geertz, C. (1973). *The interpretation of cultures*. New York, NY: Basic Books.

Gillen, J. & Cameron, C. A. (Eds.) (2010). *International perspectives on early childhood research: A day in the life*. New York, NY: Palgrave Macmillan.

Joyce, W. & Ellis, C. (2014). *The Numberlys*. New York, NY: Atheneum Books for Young Readers.

Kress, G. (1997). *Before writing: Rethinking the paths to literacy*. London: Routledge.

Kress, G. R. (2010). *Multimodality: A social semiotic approach to contemporary communication*. London, England: Routledge.

Matthews, J. (1999). *The art of childhood and adolescence: The construction of meaning*. London, England: Falmer Press.

Nelson, K. (2007). *Young minds in social worlds: Experience, meaning, and memory*. Cambridge, MA: Harvard University Press.

Olwig, K. F. & Gullov, E. (Eds.) (2003). *Children's places: Cross-cultural perspectives*. New York, NY: Routledge.

Ortner, S. B. (1996). *Making gender: The politics and erotics of culture*. Boston, MA: Beacon Press.

Street, B. (1984). *Literacy in theory and practice*. Cambridge, UK: Cambridge University Press.

Street, B. (2000). Literacy events and literacy practices. In M. Martin-Jones & K. Jones (Eds.), *Multilingual literacies: Comparative perspectives on research and practice* (pp. 17–29). Amsterdam, The Netherlands: John Benjamin's.

UNICEF (2012). *Inequities in early childhood development: What the data say*. New York, NY: UNICEF.

Vygotsky, L. S. (1978). *Mind in society: The development of higher psychological process*. Cambridge, MA: Harvard University Press.

Wells, K. (2009). *Childhood in a global perspective*. Malden, MA: Polity Press.

2

THE SITUATED CASES

Child Agency, Cultural Resources, Language

Anne Haas Dyson and Case Study Authors

PROLOGUE

In this chapter, we meet the eight children whose documented lives are the heart of this book. The children are spread across six continents, so we have some textual traveling to do. We find each child in a local school. There they venture into literacy along official paths negotiated with their teachers and, also, along unofficial paths tied to their desire for peer companionship and social belonging (Corsaro, 2011; Nelson, 2007). We are most interested in their literate productions—their composing, be it with stick and dirt, pencil, crayons, and paper, tablet computer, or chalk and slate.

Each child is a unique story, and each story is told by an author with particular interests in the goings-on in school; that is, with a particular angle of vision. All the authors, though, take us into a child's educational circumstance; they give us a sense of the school's physical site and its official curricular guidelines. Most importantly, they collectively allow us a global view of children as symbol users and social participants in the official and the unofficial worlds of school. No matter where young children go to school, they are expected to learn to "write" (although writing, as the cases illustrate, does not always mean "composing").

Every case study child is in a very particular circumstance, undergirded by the sociocultural, economic, and political dynamics of the corner of the world they call home. Nonetheless, in Chapters 3, 4, and 5, these cases are compared and, in fact, common issues are found. As readers may recall, these issues center, first, on *child agency*, or variation in curricular provision for children's room to maneuver as composers. In order to maneuver, or take action through composing, children need resources; thus, the second set of issues concern *sanctioned and unsanctioned cultural resources for composing*, or variation in children's official (and unofficial) use of such resources as popular media stories, popular and religious songs, folklore, and their own social relations, real and longed for. Chief among children's resources though—indeed, the raw material for composing—is *language*; thus, the third set of issues involves variation in the role of vernaculars and home languages in children's composing.

Certain cases provide especially vivid examples of particular issues in child composing. Hence, in the current chapter, the case studies are presented not in some kind of geographic order (as in air travel), but in thematic order. That is, first we visit the two children featured in Chapter 3's discussion of child agency: *Gareth*, in a city in north England; and *Ta'Von*, in a small urban area in the upper Midwest of the US. Next we journey to meet the three children featured in Chapter 4's probing of child resources: *Danti*, near a busy street intersection in Bandung, Indonesia; *Gus*, in urban Australia; and *Sheela*, in a rural village in northern India. Finally, we travel to the sites of the three children featured in Chapter 5's discussion of language: *Miguel*, in a New York City neighborhood; *Natalia*, in a rural town in Central Mexico; and, finally, *Rafiki*, in a rural area in the Eastern province of Kenya.

Now it is time to meet these children. Gareth and his narrator Jackie Marsh are waiting for us to arrive in England. So hang on to your hats. We're off.

I CASES FEATURING CHILD AGENCY: GARETH AND TA'VON

Gareth: The Reluctant Writer

Jackie Marsh

Gareth was aged four years and seven months at the start of the study. He lived with his mother, father and three-year-old sister. The family lived in a city in the north of England, in a neighborhood that consists of publicly funded houses on a sprawling estate, built just before and immediately after the Second World War. During the Conservative Thatcher government (1979–1990) many publicly funded houses were sold to private owners, and the estate therefore now consists of private owners living alongside families who rent their home from the local council. Gareth's parents owned their own three-bedroom semi-detached house. Gareth's father was an engineer who worked in a local factory, and Gareth's mother worked part-time as a receptionist for a music school. The fact that they were both employed meant that they were relatively comfortable financially compared to many people who lived on the estate, which constitutes an area that has one of the highest indicators of socioeconomic deprivation in the city.

loved how she described SES here

The neighborhood consists largely of White British working-class families, many of whom have lived on the estate for generations. The neighborhood has a higher than average level of crime, with teenage gangs clashing intermittently, which leads to violence and, occasionally, murder. Other official statistics in relation to health and well-being suggest that the area has significantly higher than average indicators of ill-health. The area also has significantly low school attendance rates and low educational attainment compared to other areas of the city. All of this has led to the stigmatization of the neighborhood, and, as Devereaux, Haynes, and Power (2011) point out, such a process of pathologization ignores the positive elements of an area and the lived experiences of community members, and can impact on the self-image and life-chances of residents (Permentier, van Ham, & Bolt, 2009).

Gareth attended the local primary school, which included a nursery class that his sister attended. Gareth was in the first year of statutory schooling. In 2011, the government made it possible for all children in England to start school from the first September after her/his fourth birthday. At the time of the study, the school had adopted the new national curriculum, which commenced officially in September 2014. For Gareth's year group, the school followed the "Early Years Foundation Stage Profile" (Department for Education, 2014), which, in terms of the writing curriculum, states that by the time a child reaches the age of five, he or she should:

use their phonic knowledge to write words in ways which match their spoken sounds. They also write some irregular common words. They write simple sentences which can be read by themselves and others. Some words are spelt correctly and others are phonetically plausible.

(https://www.gov.uk/government/publications/early-years-foundation-stage-profile-handbook/exemplification-of-eyfs-profile-expected-descriptors)

Gareth was in one of two Reception classes that shared one large classroom base. On one side of the base, there was a role-play area, next to a carpet that was used for brick play. Gareth's class was located on the other side of the base, which contained a creative area and a water-play stand. A stand next to the creative area contained paper and writing materials. Both sides of the base had carpet areas facing an interactive whiteboard, linked to a computer. The classrooms were bright and cheerful, with displays featuring the children's work, in addition to class rules. When they were not directed to a task, children were free to wander between the two sides of the base. There was an outside area, which was set up daily to foster gross motor and imaginative play. The structure of each day remained largely the same. The children entered the base from 8.45 am and were free to choose activities until whole class sessions on the carpet were conducted for both literacy and mathematics. After lunch, there was normally a shorter whole-class session focused on another aspect of the curriculum, for example science, or a cross-curricular topic. The children were then free to choose activities for the rest of the afternoon, including outdoor play, before story time finished the day off.

This provides the context for the following case study, which draws from observations of Gareth over a period of four months, including observations of five (whole) days of school, one observation of an after-school world book day reading event attended by Gareth, his mother, and sister, and four observations in his home at the end of the school day, for a period of between one to two hours. Written observations were made and photographs taken of key events, texts, and practices. The family was given a gift voucher at the end of the study as a token of gratitude for their participation in the study. The case study highlights two key aspects of Gareth's early writing experiences. In the first section, the official curriculum framework for writing is considered and in the second section, Gareth's digital literacy practices are outlined. In reviewing these two areas, I aim to outline how Gareth's school-based literacy practices were shaped by the wider political context, in which government interventions privileged one particularly constraining approach to literacy education that ignored digital literacy, whilst his home-based literacy practices were very much rooted within the digital world.

"Read Write Inc."

My first meeting with Gareth did not go as well as I had planned. Following permission from Gareth's mother for the family to become involved in the study, I met with them both one afternoon after school to outline the project and gain ethical consent. I explained to Gareth's mother that anonymity would be guaranteed, and that I would change Gareth's name in any writings relating to the project. Gareth immediately burst into tears, blurting, "I don't want a new name!" It took some time for his mother to calm him down and for me to explain that I did not intend to steal away his name. I noted this as an important learning point for myself, and determined to find more child-appropriate ways of explaining the procedures for ensuring anonymity in future studies.

Somewhat fearful, then, of my first encounter with Gareth in the classroom a few weeks later, I found that I need not have worried, as he had either forgotten, or had decided to forgive, my indiscretion. I followed him during the first part of the morning as he engaged in mathematics activities before it was time for the whole-class literacy lesson. As the teacher, Miss Fairweather, was out of the classroom, a classroom assistant, Miss Smythe, led the session, and I sat to the side of the carpet area, writing down my observations. It is early in the fourth month of school:

> The children (some aged four, some already aged five) were all sitting on the carpet, looking expectantly at Miss Smythe, who began the session by telling the children that, "We are going to go through our speed sounds and go through our digraphs. Can anyone remember what they are?" One child suggested, "Two sounds making one sound." Miss Smythe clarified, "So it is two letters pushed together to make one sound?" She asked the children to read out digraphs printed on cards she held up in quick succession, and then following this, she chose a few digraphs to focus on and linked them to a related sentence, e.g., "'nk'—I think I stink. 'sh'—snake, horse. The snake is telling the horse to be quiet—ssshh!" Gareth did not read the phonemes out, nor did he join in chanting out the sentences, but he sat and fiddled with his shoes. Miss Smythe then brought out a book titled *In the Bin*, which she read to the class, asking them to join in with the "speed sounds." She asked, "Now children, when we are reading a book, what are our success criteria? That is what will help us to read." The children shouted out various reading strategies: "We need to point to every word," "We've got to look at the page," "You have to try and read by yourself." Gareth did not participate in the question and answer session, but instead pretended to shoot a gun in the air. The children were then asked to find their talk partners (children they pair up with for carpet-time tasks). Gareth moved to sit next to Mark. The children were given copies of the book *In the Bin* and asked to read it together. They did not work well together and appeared to be disengaged, until Gareth eventually attempted to read a sentence. At that point, Miss Smythe asked for

the books back and gave out small whiteboards and marker pens. She asked the children to "Fred talk"[1] the words "bin" and "hat" and write them on the whiteboards. Gareth made a number of attempts to form the letters of the word "hat" and eventually managed to write h and t. Miss Smythe asked the children to display their writing by holding the whiteboard up. Gareth hid his face behind the whiteboard as he held it up.

Gareth's non-conformity in response to some of Miss Smythe's requests on this occasion was not an isolated incident, I subsequently discovered. This was a pattern consistent throughout the observations I undertook of him in these carpet-based literacy lessons; he often did not join in chants and resisted participating in collective actions and group tasks on the carpet, choosing instead to play with his shoes, visit the bathroom, look around, or sometimes talk quietly to a friend. This led to teacher interventions on a number of occasions, as the teacher, student teacher, and teaching assistants sought to re-focus his attention to the tasks at hand. Miss Fairweather suggested that Gareth was a "reluctant writer," and it was certainly the case that, throughout my observations of him during the four months of the study, he chose to engage in writing very infrequently.

A superficial reading of Gareth's profile might locate him within the discourse on boys and underachievement, shaped by moral panics and policy initiatives that have been characterized by Mills (2003) as "backlash blockbusters." Whilst the underachievement of boys in languages and literacy has been traced as far back as standardized assessment will allow (Cohen, 1996), the topic became a prevalent discourse in the UK's educational sphere in the last decade of the twentieth century. It led to a number of interventions that aimed to enhance boys' literacy, seemingly ignoring the interests of girls, although evidence suggests that there are overlapping issues of access to the literacy curriculum for both genders (Peterson & Parr, 2012).

The approach to and content of this phonics lesson was similar to that undertaken by many schools in England. This was due to successive government policy initiatives in which a focus had been placed on the teaching and learning of synthetic phonics in the early years, despite a lack of evidence that synthetic phonics should be taught to the exclusion of other strategies (Wyse & Goswami, 2008). In 2012, the government introduced a "Phonics Screening Check" (test) for six-year-olds, which involves children reading out from a 40-word list, including nonsensical words, the outcomes being nationally published. This placed even more pressure upon teachers in the early years to approach the teaching of phonics in specific ways.

This emphasis on synthetic phonics, and the importance given to it in inspections carried out by OFSTED, the national school inspection body, meant that schools looked to published resources in order to help them implement the approach. In 2012 the government declared that primary schools could receive £3000 match funding for the purchasing of a phonics scheme, but the scheme had to be acquired from an approved list. The government-approved phonics schemes were produced primarily either by individuals on the board of a body set up to promote synthetic phonics, titled "Reading Reform Foundation" (RRF), or by people who were honorary members of that board.

The scheme purchased by Gareth's school, "Read Write Inc.," was produced by Ruth Miskin, an honorary member of RRF. Miskin is a former headteacher and ex-partner of Chris Woodhead, who was a high-profile head of OFSTED in the 1990s, with many connections to government ministers. Miskin, prior to the government's emphasis on synthetic phonics, had developed a program, which, whilst receiving some publicity, had not been widely adopted. Since the coalition government's accession to power in 2010, she has acted as a government adviser in the review of the curriculum, which resulted in a primary curriculum that has an emphasis on the teaching of synthetic phonics, grammar, spelling, and punctuation. Numerous scholars have noted this close link between Miskin and the government (Clark, 2014; Gunter & Mills, 2014), and concerned journalists have highlighted the potential conflict of interest, given that her phonics program is on the approved government list (Stewart, 2011; Warwick, 2012). Indeed, it seems that, since the coalition government came to power, Miskin's scheme has been widely adopted by many primary schools in England, being purchased through the match-funding scheme developed by the Department for Education. Margaret Clark, a literacy researcher in the UK, sought information through the Freedom of Information Act on how much had been spent by the government on the phonics programs on the recommended list and found that this amounted to over £24 million, with over £4 million of government money being spent on "Read Write Inc." (Clark, 2014). Clark points out that the publishers of the schemes purchased would have received double this amount, as primary schools had to match the funding.

In the "Read Write Inc." scheme, spelling is integrated with phonics, so that children's writing activities are tightly defined; children write the phonemes they are learning to recognize in reading activities, most often in a decontextualized manner. Nevertheless, despite the very regimented program, as outlined by Miskin in the training materials, Miss Fairweather adapted it at times for the children's needs and incorporated meaningful tasks, such as oral storytelling using story maps as a prompt, as the following observation, from the fifth month of school, indicates:

> Gareth sat at a table with five other boys and one girl. The children had been sent to the tables following an activity on the carpet in which they had retold the story of the "Little Red Hen" using a story map, which had been displayed on the whiteboard. (However, when asked to re-tell the story as a class during this carpet time, Gareth had chewed his fingers, again resistant to group instructions.) At the table, sitting between his friends Stephen and David, Gareth began to draw the head of a chicken, the first item on the story map, as he said, "Knock, knock, who's there? Chicken Licken!" David taunted Stephen, "Don't forget, Stephen's

a little baby." Gareth countered, "Don't forget, David's a little baby." Gareth drew the second item on the story map, a sun, and then moved on to the third item, a spade, saying, "I've drawn an arrow that's shaped like an axe. Gonna chop your head off!", pointing to Stephen. David echoed, "Gonna chop your head off!" Gareth gave Stephen instructions, "Stephen, when I say it's gonna chop your head off, go back." He thrust his head backwards, to make his meaning clear. Gareth then said, "It's gonna chop your head off!" Stephen dutifully rolled his head backwards. Miss Fairweather came over to the table and re-focused Gareth on the task, suggesting he draw the next item on the story map, the clippers. Gareth retorted, "I know how to draw this because my dad's got clippers!" When the teacher moved away, the only girl at the table, Sophia, informed one of the boys that he had not drawn a spade correctly on his story map. Gareth said firmly, "You can do it like you want to. That's a really good spade. It's gooder than Stephen's spade." There was then a few minutes' silence as all of the children concentrated on their story maps, perhaps reflecting on Gareth's point that it didn't matter whether a spade looked like a spade or not. Sophia and four of the boys finished their maps and drifted off, leaving Gareth and Terry at the table. Gareth drew the next three items on the story map—the basket, the oven and cooking bowl, and, finally, the knife, fork, and piece of bread on a plate. He did not draw the book containing the words "in The End," as on the model map, but began to draw a series of Xs. [See Figure 2.1] "I'm done before you, Terry," said Gareth, "I'm going to do an X, 'cos X marks the spot."

In this episode, Gareth and his friends play with imaginary axes drawn on their maps in ways that recall Myra Barrs' rich and extended observation of a five-year-old boy, Ben, whose writing was accompanied by talk and embedded in complex play scenarios (Barrs, 1988). Gareth uses his everyday experiences to inform his multimodal authoring as he draws clippers like those his dad owns, or draws Xs on his imagined pirates' map. This brief vignette confirms that the children brought their imagination to the everyday site of writing and, as Dyson (2008) suggests was the case in a class she observed in the US, the children "exercised agency and recontextualized official practices, giving them relevance and meaning in their ongoing lives. The unofficial world thus generated centrifugal forces that diversified children's responses to official practices" (p. 152; see also Dyson, 2013).

Following the Christmas break, Miss Fairweather introduced the theme of superheroes, and the role-play area was populated with superhero costumes. Children were encouraged to create comics and write about their superpowers, with outputs visible around the walls in bright displays. Superhero play has long been noted as important for many young children (Dyson, 1997; Marsh, 2013), and for Gareth this was no different. During much of the time I observed him outside of carpet sessions, he played superhero scenarios either individually or with friends, drawing on Superman, Ninja Turtles, and Power Rangers in these

FIGURE 2.1 Gareth's Story Map for *The Little Red Hen*

play episodes. Instead of spending time on the carpet attempting to resist teachers' instructions, for this theme he was engaged fully, as in the following vignette from the fifth month of school:

> A student teacher on placement, Miss Garber, was leading the carpet session. She asked the children to list the superheroes that they knew. Gareth shouted out a number of names. Miss Garber reminded Gareth that she would not write down the contributions that children shouted out. Gareth sat up on his knees, his right arm folded back over his head and his finger on his lips, desperate to be chosen to relay his knowledge. Miss Garber responded to this, asking Gareth to name superheroes he knew, which she listed on the sheet.

This can be seen as an example of a sensitive teacher, quick to spot that Gareth's head was fit to burst with superhero knowledge and thus demonstrating an act of "pedagogical thoughtfulness" (Van Manen, 1991). For Gareth, the superhero discourse threaded throughout his engagement with learning. On the same day, Gareth wandered over to the mark-making area and wrote on the back of a paper plate with a red pencil, then stuffed the plate into his coat pocket. I asked him what he had written, and he said that it was "A message." He ran out to play in the outdoor space:

> Gareth grabbed his friend Stephen, who was building with bricks. "I'm Superman." He ran off to a corner of the playground, which contained a tire embedded in the ground. It was a favorite place for Gareth and Stephen, and they spent much time sitting underneath it. Gareth took out his paper plate as he sat there, waiting for his friend [see Figure 2.2]. Eventually, Stephen joined him, and Gareth passed the plate to him. It was not possible to hear what they were saying to each other, but they soon emerged from underneath the tire, thrust the paper plate aside, and ran around being superheroes, jumping off logs and raised areas, a common play pattern of theirs.

The tire provided a private place for Gareth and his friends, a place where writing performed functions that were often not possible within the busy and public space of the classroom, functions relating to their imaginative play as superheroes, as I assumed was the case in this instance.

Observations of Gareth suggested that he found the public space of the official writing curriculum a difficult one at times, and he often resisted adult instructions in both covert and overt ways, unless the topic was focused on an area of interest (usually related to superheroes, or film and television characters). In the more private spaces of the base, however, the role-play area, the brick carpet, and the outdoor space, he explored his passions through play, with writing and multimodal meaning-making embedded into his richly conceived imaginative scenarios. This mirrored his play in the home, which was informed by his popular culture interests

FIGURE 2.2 Gareth Holding His Message, Written on a Paper Plate

and supported by his parents through their purchasing of toys and artifacts that reflected these interests.

Gareth's multimodal meaning-making in the home was very much centered on digital practices, and, in the next section, I move on to share observations that relate to Gareth's engagement in digital literacy practices. In using the term "digital literacies" I am referring to a set of practices in which reading, writing, and meaning-making are mediated by digital technologies. In the twenty-first century, many young children in England are increasingly engaged with screens of all kinds and communication requires competence in the use of a range of modes, including images and sounds (Kress, 2010). In this analysis, I consider the nature of the relationship between home and school literacies in the digital age.

Digital Literacy

The children in Gareth's school did not have access to computers allocated for their use in the classroom. The only computer was one placed upon the teacher's desk, which was used to support whole-class lessons. Miss Fairweather informed me that the children had not yet had their first lesson in the school's computer room, but would be doing so later in the spring term.

This lack of use of digital technologies in the classroom was in contrast to Gareth's home interests. On each of my visits to his house, Gareth would take out his parents' iPad and use it independently to play games such as *Angry Birds*, or watch videos on YouTube, as in the following field note excerpt from the seventh month of school:

> Gareth showed me his YouTube channel. He saved his favorite videos on it and scrolled up and down them to show me what he had saved on his channel. His mum told me that he loved watching "EvanTubeHD." I asked Gareth what this was, and he scrolled to a video that he then started playing. A young boy appeared on the screen, unpacking a Lego toy. Mum told me that Gareth and his three-year-old sister loved these videos and watched them repeatedly.

In this instance, Gareth was confident in curating his own digital collections (Potter, 2012) and navigating the complex interface of YouTube. His skills were highly developed in relation to the use of the iPad, and he was able to swipe, scroll, minimize, and find his way through menus and sub-menus. Gareth's competence with the iPad and its apps reflects a growing use of this technology by children of this age group in the UK. An OFCOM (Office of Communication) (2015) survey found that the tablet is the media device that has grown most in popularity amongst five- to seven-year-olds in the UK over the last year, with 69% using them in 2015 as compared to 54% in 2014.

One of Gareth's favorite activities was to watch videos featuring children talking to a perceived child audience, as the observation above indicates. Children's interest in peer-produced online material has been noted in a previous study of animated films produced in virtual worlds (Marsh, 2014; 2014b); Gareth's love of EvanTubeHD offered a further example of this phenomenon. This is a trend noted increasingly in the media, which has identified how YouTube celebrities, often children and young people, are becoming more popular than traditional celebrities (Precey, 2014; Marsh, 2015).

Gareth's online practices were also closely related to his offline interests, which focused largely on Lego play. Gareth loved to make Lego creations from sets, helped by his father, who had also loved using Lego when he was a child. This longevity in the use of Lego can be attributed to a number of factors, as discussed in Marsh and Bishop (2014), and which include the processes of participation, socialization, and mobilization. Lego fans participate in online communities through their uploading of videos produced of their play with Lego, or films made in Lego computer games using screen-capture software. They socialize through the use of YouTube comments, chat rooms and/or fan-produced wikis and blogs. Finally, mobilization is made possible through the use of Lego apps on tablets and smartphones. These factors have helped Lego to maintain a strong presence in children's lives and meant, in Gareth's case, that he and his father could share their passions for the product and engage in multimodal practices that linked online to offline in fluid ways, characteristic of contemporary popular culture (Marsh, 2014c).

Conclusion

These vignettes demonstrate that the semiotic tools Gareth drew upon to make self-generated meanings included talk, image, and sound as well as writing, and all were embedded within imaginative episodes. In this sense, as Wohlwend (2011) suggests, play was a literacy practice. Some of Gareth's meaning-making at home was digitally mediated, with screens important in the dissemination of messages and his literacy practices embedded in intergenerational family communication involving technology (Marsh, Hannon, Lewis & Ritchie, 2015). However, screens were not prominent in his school activities, and, as Dyson (2008) has commented in relation to her observations of writing in a US classroom:

> the multimodal nature of children's productions—combined with the exclusivity of the official focus on print—contributed to the lack of a dialogic relationship between official and unofficial worlds, even as it seemed to provide a space for children's fictional exploits and other child-initiated practices.
>
> (p. 153)

Further, Miss Fairweather was focused on creating an environment that fostered children's creativity, as indicated by her choice of the superhero theme and the provision of both indoor and outdoor play areas; nonetheless, the literacy curriculum was inevitably subject to the restrictions imposed by the use of a regimented synthetic phonics scheme, as offered by the "Read Write Inc." program. Yet, in the interstices that inevitably appear in any curriculum, however constrained, and in the private spaces of the outdoor play area and his home environment, Gareth was able to express himself and thus demonstrated agency in his meaning-making practices. Perhaps, in recognizing this, we might suggest that Gareth was not so much a reluctant writer as a child who was reluctant to align himself to the austerity literacy model embedded in "Read Write Inc.," a model which looks set to continue to serve the coffers of publishers and diminish the literacy lives of children in England in the years ahead.

★

Ta'Von: Negotiating Inclusion in a Stratified World

Anne Haas Dyson

It is near the end of Ta'Von and Salvia's time in preschool. Kindergarten looms ahead. Both are now four with summer birthdays. Like most children in their class, they are both also children of color from low-income backgrounds—Ta'Von, whose linguistic repertoire includes phonological and semantic features of African American Vernacular English (AAVE), is African American; Salvia, who speaks Spanish at home, is Latina and African American. Across potential borders of gender and language, they are best friends. They play with everyone but depend on each other. Soon, though, they will separate, as they are going to different schools in the fall.

On this day, the friends are engaged in a rare game that accentuates their gender—that of "being married." The play, and their relationship, is being mediated by drawing. Ta'Von has made a heart between a picture of himself and of Salvia, who, like him, is depicted as all legs and feet (see Figure 2.3). The more comfortable-with-a-crayon Salvia has produced a detailed picture, with Ta'Von wearing red, his favorite color, and their baby, a girl, like the newest member of Ta'Von's family.

When these two friends went their separate ways, I followed their transition from the play- and talk-filled preschool to their respective and much more explicitly academic kindergartens in their small urban community in the upper Midwest of the US. The two and a half hours I had spent weekly observing during their last three months as preschoolers doubled as I watched each child constructing a social and communicative life in their new school space—and apart from each other. Herein, I focus on Ta'Von and his transition to kindergarten; of the two children, he faced the more daunting relational challenges.

In anticipating his new class, Ta'Von, "bubbly and lovable," looked forward to "making new friends [including a special friend, like Salvia]," wrote his mother to his new teacher, Ms. Norton, in response to a parent information request. Still, Ta'Von was entering a new space in which, unlike in his preschool, his race and his social class, not to mention his openness to cross-gender friendships, marked him as something other than the local norm. (Salvia, in contrast, was entering a school in which low income and minority children were the majority.)

Referring back to that affection-laden sample in Figure 2.3, one might expect that Ta'Von would find daunting the composing demands of his kindergarten. He was shaky with crayon and pencil (in part because he repeatedly switched between his left and his right hand). He showed no particular grasp of the alphabetic system. Indeed, in the mandated assessments in the first week of kindergarten, he was one of the "lowest" children in the class, identifying no letter/sound connections and only eight lower case letters (but 22 upper case ones). And yet,

FIGURE 2.3 The Married Couple Ta'Von and Salvia

within four months, he became an "amazing" writer, in his teacher's view. Compared to his classmates (and to Salvia), he was more fluent, more textually elaborate, and more driven, making agential use of composing beyond the assigned writing period.

meaningful real life purpose

Ta'Von's progress was fueled by a desire for inclusion and friendship and aided by his teacher's curricular flexibility. Still, despite that amazing progress, Ta'Von did *not* become one of the officially designated "bright" children, whose designation rested on their initial assessments. Below, I provide a backdrop for Ta'Von's case, briefly discussing the theoretical notion of stratified space and describing his play-mediated preschool. Ta'Von's kindergarten story will unfold through key incidents (Emerson, Fretz, & Shaw, 2011); those events reveal both composing's role in Ta'Von's search for belonging and, at the same time, the challenges and constraints posed by institutional discourse and societal structures as reconstructed in the lives of small children.

Shifting Locales: Reconfiguring Inclusion

Ta'Von reacted to his new kindergarten place with practices honed in the familiar rhythms of home and preschool (Rogoff, 2003). The traveler, explains Jon

Blommaert (2005), brings resources from the past into a newly stratified space. Ta'Von's new space had its official relations, organized in official practices, undergirded by official values, and resting on markers of status, like test scores implicitly indexing being "bright." Within and underneath those practices, Ta'Von aimed for respectful inclusion and playful companionship.

In his efforts, aspects of Ta'Von's self reverberated differently than they had in his much-loved preschool. His bursts into song, his often playful ways of interacting, his written language know-how, indeed, his hair style—all were brought into relief. In response, Ta'Von adjusted and adapted—and caused others to do so as well. And so the story of his entry into formal schooling (i.e., state required and more heavily regulated and monitored schooling), including his entry into composing, was configured by, and configured, the stories of others.

In Ta'Von's search, composing became a way to declare himself and to forge relations with others, and these social desires, along with a willingness to take needed (but only needed) help, was interwoven with his "amazing" progress. Before examining his construction of a social life with the help of composing, I provide a brief glimpse into his first schooling experiences.

Ta'Von's Preschool: "You Can Play Inside and Out"

Ta'Von said that he "really really loved preschool." For Ta'Von, its distinguishing characteristic was the pervasiveness of play (and Salvia, of course). For example, as a kindergartener, he told me that he remembered "stomp stomp stomp[ing]" like a dinosaur out on the playground, *and* he remembered that "you can still play [dinosaur] in the [preschool] classroom": "Stomp stomp stomp!" Indeed, children could move freely among the classroom's marked-off spaces, among them, rugs for animal figure play, puppet theater, or book reading; tables for puzzle doing, clay sculpting, and Lego building; easels for painting; and housekeeping paraphernalia for family dramas (although sometimes "the house" was transformed, into, for example, a train station or a doctor's office).

That talk- and play-focused preschool was part of the local school district and had a long, long waiting list. Located in his city's downtown area, the school targeted children with special needs (e.g., autism, Down syndrome) and, mainly, children deemed "at risk" (e.g., from low-income and/or limited English homes). In Ta'Von's class there were 16 four- and five-year-olds, all included in the routines of the day by his low-key but child-focused teacher, the Spanish/ English bilingual Ms. Sheila. Her curricular emphasis was on language development. Everyone—parents, teachers, aides, and students—was encouraged to talk, especially in playful contexts most often chosen by the children themselves.

Ta'Von and Salvia had become, said Ms. Sheila, much more communicative over their two years in her class. They were socially skillful playmates. For example, Ta'Von regularly built Lego planes while Salvia was taken with Lego houses, but they narrated and elaborated stories that integrated their separate productions in a singular adventure. They seemed most joyful, though, when running fast in the gym or on the playground; they coordinated their actions as they sped away from a "Monster" teaching assistant or led a long line of other children under and over the plastic jungle gyms.

As for composing in any media, Ta'Von, like Salvia, made things for others (including Lego planes), demonstrating an understanding that self-made objects can mediate one's relationships with others. In terms of the written medium itself, at least once weekly, Ta'Von drew and dictated a message with Ms. Sheila, usually about a book she had read or a science unit happening (e.g., a butterfly leaving its cocoon or a seed sprouting roots). Still, Ta'Von, like his peers, was interested mainly in names, which were emphasized in official rituals like the daily sign-in. Accompanying the child-initiated shaping of a letter with clay or templates was talk about who needed which letter for their name. Names were thus an important playground for the arrangement of letters in precise ways for a socially recognizable end.

Accompanying most activities was much spontaneous singing, usually led by Ta'Von. He knew cartoon theme songs, popular songs sung by his older sister, and nonsense ditties he improvised. Salvia, and whoever else was around, tended to join in.

In sum, Ta'Von's preschool unfolded in a playful mode, in which Ta'Von's interests and relations drove, and were informed by, classroom activities. This approach to early schooling was about to change dramatically, as was the absence of dualistic (e.g., male/female) and hierarchical ("highest" and "lowest" students) labeling.

Ta'Von's Kindergarten: "You Have to Learn"

The first day of kindergarten, the grinning Ta'Von could barely contain his joy. Although the day did not begin with signing in and getting down to playing, the long opening rug time did contain some familiar activities. Ta'Von listened intently to the book read, eager to have his say; he quickly learned any songs Ms. Norton sang (although official songs had a curricular purpose, like "R-E-D I Can Spell Red"); and he smiled without reservation at his new peers. Kindergarten seemed to be a familiar place, despite the fact that half the physical space was now taken up with four large rectangular tables, at which he had an assigned seat.

The first week of kindergarten, Ta'Von's playful nature was on display. Early on, he and his 22 peers were to walk quietly in a line through their new school, experiencing its hallways and meeting other teachers and school staff; ostensibly, they were to ask if these others had, by any chance, seen the gingerbread men. Those gingerbread men, a promised treat, had run away, said Ms. Norton.

As he and his new class walked down the hall, most children quiet and pensive, Ta'Von stood out. His salience was only partially due to his being one of only

African American boys in a majority White classroom. The other children were walking, just as directed. Ta'Von was on his tippy toes, thrusting one foot ahead of the other, like a stealth detective; his fingers formed binoculars over his eyes. He could not suppress his delighted grin, as he looked this way and that, hunting for the escaped gingerbread men and deep in the play scenario Ms. Norton had set. Children had often done role-play when walking through the preschool's hallways.

Still, in time, Ta'Von sharply differentiated preschool and kindergarten. Ta'Von wanted to belong in the kindergarten, something he had done with ease in his beloved preschool, but which was harder in the kinder, despite his appreciative, supportive teacher. As Ta'Von told me, kindergarteners did not play. In kindergarten, he said, "you have to learn," and, to this end, he felt time was spent mainly in assigned "literacy centers and math centers." Those centers could involve alphabet puzzles, magnetic letters for word-making, and even enacting read stories—but Ta'Von did not regard them as play.

Ta'Von's view that kindergarteners did not play surprised me. A believer in children's play, Ms. Norton took some play-related liberties. Consistent with a national pattern, she seemed freer than teachers in schools serving lower SES students, like Salvia's (Bassok & Rorem, 2012; Dyson, 2013; Zacher Pandya, 2011). As long as her mandated test scores were solid, she felt that she would be fine. Moreover, since she was getting ready to retire, she felt unintimidated by the district.

Thus, resisting the district's lack of support for play, Ms. Norton had a regular morning recess and, in fact, an afternoon "choice time" when children could choose among varied activities. And yet, agency is not, as Adair (2014) noted, just about choosing activities from a set of choices; in school, it involves interest-driven choices that allow children to stretch their knowledge and know-how and, I add, to potentially negotiate a social place for themselves. For Ta'Von the classroom activity of composing did become a sometimes playful, sometimes serious means for negotiating classroom space that included him.

Composing as Negotiating Space

There was a mandated writing curriculum in Ms. Norton's district. She kept that curriculum's goals in mind (sounding out spellings, using grammatical "standard" English and appropriate punctuation, and producing varied nonfiction genres). But she did not follow strictly the dictates of the required writing program. For example, Ms. Norton did introduce the featured nonfiction genres. But for Ta'Von, as for others, a blank piece of paper in the company of peers could lend itself to drawn stories that veered away from the "true" to the imagined. Ms. Norton responded with interest to all such texts and then wrote a sentence or two with the child that used phonologically based spelling to produce a nonfiction text.

However, to allow insight into the importance that composing assumed in Ta'Von's negotiation of space and place in kindergarten, I need to begin not with writing time, but with the relational issues that arose for Ta'Von in that space-making.

Declaring Space for a Racialized, Gendered Self

Ta'Von's elementary school (K through fifth grade) was down the street from his apartment but, in the neighborhood school, children of color were a minority, as were those whose families lived below the poverty line. Ta'Von and his three African American peers (and another who was classified as mixed race) were "hot lunch" kids and "water fountain" drinkers (as opposed to lunch box bringers and water bottle users—which sort of bottle Ta'Von thought he might "borrow" from WalMart). Most notable for Ta'Von, though, was his hair.

Ta'Von had an African American braided hair style, worn by a number of Black peers (and parents) in his old school site and unfamiliar in his new site. Moreover, his hair style seemed inappropriate to his gender-conscious peers. That consciousness was loudly displayed in, for example, the absence of cross-gender playmates with no romantic meaning (a meaning indexed especially by hand holding). Even Ms. Norton had the "girls'" coat closet and the "boys'" closet and often had girls and boys respond chorally but separately to letter naming and sound/symbol manipulation activities.

So, in the first full week of school, Ta'Von was deemed having "girl hair" by peers at his assigned work table. (Ta'Von, I hasten to add, stood up for his hair style, which was akin to that of his father, a barber.) Then there was the day he wore his hair in two Afro puffs. His peer Vida voiced her concern that his hair looked like a flower, which was not appropriate for a boy. "I have two meatballs," he responded confidently, "one on the back and one on the top."

Vida: Do you sleep with this?
Ta'Von: Yes I do . . . It's my meatball. That's what I call it. I sleep with it.

Not only did Ta'Von defend his hair styles, which eventually ceased to be an issue, he himself became attentive to how he represented his racial self. After the first incident highlighting his hair, Ta'Von almost always added braids to his pictured self (even early on when that self was a circle with two appendages). Further, he always colored himself brown, usually after verbally declaring himself as "Black." Finally, he played with, and expressed himself through, aspects of his speech that constituted his identity as a social and aesthetic being. As in the preschool, Ta'Von's speech was relatively standard in its syntax, selectively AAL (African American Language) in its phonology (e.g., voiced and, for Ta'Von, even unvoiced [th] as [d], deletion of [r] after a vowel, both illustrated by "*brother*" [brudah] [Smitherman, 1986]). However, Ta'Von began to use words he "liked to say," words distinctive from most classmates, like "dude." And this dude wanted friends.

Constructing Shared Space

Ta'Von was on occasion pushed from shared space by his peers. The "bright" kids sometimes assumed he needed help (which he took only if he needed it). One of his initial tablemates, Brittany, was especially critical of his early efforts. She was often critical of others, including herself, but her tablemate Ta'Von seemed to merit particular attention.

"How come he's in kindergarten? He can't spell his name," Brittany said to her teacher as Ms. Norton helped Ta'Von grasp a pencil with his left hand. Ms. Norton pointed out that he *could* spell his name; he was simply learning the kindergarten way of spelling his name, just like she was. And Ms. Norton promptly moved over to help Brittany with her unruly '*a*'s.

Ta'Von's only evident response was a determined, unsmiling demeanor. Indeed, like his old teacher in the preschool, he concentrated on his progress, saying "I did it!" when he felt he had improved upon an initial effort. Ms. Norton too proved over time to focus on his progress.

Ta'Von's typically upbeat nature *was* evident from the very beginning of school. He was socially alert, asking others what they were doing or drawing the attention of his five tablemates to his efforts. Not all children were responsive (and, as seen, Brittany could be quite negative). But Vida, the child so curious about his hair style, was socially reliable. She was, I thought, becoming a friend.

A Little Support from a Friend

A recent immigrant from Iran, Vida seemed to find Ta'Von an appealing fellow and, early on, borrowed ideas from him. During Week 4, a composing task was to draw themselves helping their family in some way, followed by writing words and, even better, a sentence. Ta'Von was initially going to make his family looking at magazines, as the baby played with a toy in the bed. But his drawn chair, with its long legs, reminded him of a water slide—so he made his mom and his dad slide down the slide, a huge water bubble forming ahead of them.

"Guess what, guys?" he said to the children at his table (*guys* seemingly appropriated from Ms. Sheila's reference to the children). "My mom and dad are going down the slide. I figured that out all by myself."

Ta'Von was quite pleased with his drawing, but Brittany (still a table mate) was not. "How does that help out?" she said.

From down at the other end of their work table, Vida piped up: "They're working together to go down the slide." Indeed, she herself started to make a water slide.

"They're going down backwards," laughed Ta'Von about his picture.

"And where are you?" persisted Brittany.

"Oh," said Ta'Von. "I forgot to make me. And I'm gonna make my sister, because I'm going to be changing my baby's diaper."

"Euu," said the others, giggling, and stories of "stinky" things (e.g., feet, socks) began. Ta'Von had influenced the entire table's conversation.

Ta'Von went on to write "baby," copying the letters of *baby* and, also, of *the* from the chalkboard, which, all together, he read "ba" [*baby*] "by" [*the*]. Ta'Von's handwriting was readable, and he clearly had some sense of breaking words into sounds (syllables, to be accurate). Moreover, when his table mate Josh was going to write "making," Ta'Von picked up on the "ing," mimicking Ms. Norton who said that I-N-G sounds like a telephone ringing. He sang a ringing "ing" to the table and began writing *ing* on his own paper (and thus made his first clear link between sound and letters).

Thus, with initial support from Vida, Ta'Von's composing play was responded to, allowing him a role as a fun classmate (if a not quite up-to-par one, according to Brittany). Vida, though, treated him as a clever classmate (and, in fact, in about two months, he on occasion helped her spell when she asked for assistance). Ta'Von seemed to appreciate Vida—she even joined in on his singing, especially if it was an invented ditty or an official song. A few weeks on from the "slide" event, Ta'Von orchestrated his budding knowledge and know-how to reach out to Vida. He interwove his story with hers, marking their relationship and the intertwined trajectories of their classroom lives.

Composing a Bid for Affection

Ta'Von understood composing practices that reached out to particular others. In preschool he had made Lego planes and drawn pictures for Salvia and, collectively, his class had made presents and cards for varied occasions. On the day in question, he transformed his daily composing into an affirmation of friendship and a bid for affection from the socially responsive Vida. Perhaps her physical likeness to Salvia (e.g., thick long dark hair, a penchant for purple and pink clothes) influenced his decision. Moreover, as good fortune would have it, she was recently assigned a seat right by him, and Brittany had been moved to another table.

The official task on this day, the designated "Hat Day," was to draw and describe the special hat one had worn to school. Ta'Von drew himself, his brown crayon obliterating his pencil-drawn braids, and then made his SpongeBob hat. Next he drew Vida and her jester hat (with a few pointers from her on drawing the hat's shape). Ta'Von talked himself through coloring Vida's image, representing her as "Black" verbally and brown visually. (Vida *was* darker in hue than the European American girls.) Next Ta'Von drew her long, wavy hair, remarking, "Your hair's long . . . There goes hair." Finally he directed himself to "make dark eyes." And there she was, standing next to him on his paper!

Now Ta'Von was to "sound out his words" (the bench-marked skill) and write a complete sentence describing his hat. Ta'Von, however, was bent on describing his relationship to Vida. He used every possible symbolic resource— talk, drawing, names and numbers, and his beginning understanding of sounds, along with a reading voice to elaborate on written symbols. He also sought help from his hoped-for special friend, from his teacher, and, at my suggestion, from an earlier page of his journal. Ta'Von was energized by the desire to mark his affiliation with Vida, whom he regarded as Black like him and Salvia. Perhaps because she was so conscious of gender lines (as was her family, Ms. Norton told me), she did not respond as he hoped, but she did not reject him either.

Below Ta'Von's written text is in **bold and italics** (see also Figure 2.4); his read text is in *quotes and italics*:

FIGURE 2.4 Ta'Von's Written Bid for Affection From Vida

Ta'Von begins by writing the first line on the bottom of his paper (I have added spaces between written words to make it easier to match what was written and what was read):

6

I My to S V   V   **lik to like**
*"I like to see Vida. Vida is 6 years old. She *likes to see*

Ta'Von   5 and.
"me, Ta'Von. I am 5." I made a 5! *"Vida is 6 years old.* (pointing to the earlier written 6, above the second V) *And."*

(*Ms. Norton had helped Ta'Von spell *"like"* the previous day and thus abandon spelling it *My*. Today, at my suggestion, he looked back at that spelling but did not maintain it, reverting back soon to *My*.)

Having finished his first line of writing, Ta'Von turns to Vida:

Ta'Von: Vida, look what I writed. "I like to see Vida. Vida likes to see me."
Vida: I don't like to see you *always*. I like to see my sister always.
Ta'Von: Oh. But not me. I didn't know that. (seriously)
Vida: I like to see *every*body.
Ta'Von: Oh! I'll write that. (begins writing)

> **I My to**
> *"I like to see Vi—"*

Ta'Von: How do you spell your name?

          Vida spells her name.

Ta'Von: Thanks for telling me how to spell your name. Thanks for helping me.

Ta'Von continues, writing Vida's name and an *s* for "see." He then listens for the first sounds he hears in "everybody" (*uw*[e], *v*[v]). Time is up! Ms. Norton's timer has gone off. Ta'Von quickly adds a few more letters.

(Event first reported in Dyson, 2015)

Ta'Von was not singled out as special by Vida, but he was included in the "everybody" of the class. As the year progressed, so did Ta'Von's composing and his evident sense of agency as a composer. His writing became an important part of his communicative repertoire beyond the writing period. Indeed, it was a new means for managing inclusion in the "everybody" and in old and new relationships.

Managing Inclusion

Seemingly socially energized, Ta'Von reached out and made use of literacy practices that were not in the curriculum but were ones he had learned about in school and out. And he used those practices to solve problems related to inclusion in relationships. He made birthday cards, including for children who paid him little attention. He wrote a letter to Salvia's new teacher, telling him to let Salvia come to his school for a visit. He wrote amusing stories to entertain others (and himself). Most dramatic, in my view, was a school genre he composed at home in early November, a couple of weeks after the "hat" event. Ta'Von took it upon himself to write his own permission letter for a class field trip to a roller skating rink;

he was worried that his mom would forget to sign the official form. Below, his written letter is in **bold and italics**; his read text is in *quotation marks and italics*:

"*Dear Ms. Norton*" *(with no accompanying text)*

Visock togo
"*It's OK to go to*
Rat
"*skating [roller skating]*"
My Ta'Von go
"*My Ta'Von is going.*"

As he is reading, Ta'Von interrupts himself: "I haven't write Ms. Norton!" And he adds his name and Ms. Norton's name [**M No.ru**] to the end of the text.

Ms. Norton praised his letter and taped it to her file cabinet; she was impressed with his use of writing to solve a problem. (He would, though, need to have his mother or father sign the permission letter she had sent home. And he did.)

More broadly, by the end of the fall semester, Ms. Norton thought Ta'Von's progress was "amazing." She said she did not care if his preschool had not emphasized letter sounds. She thought Ta'Von's progress had to do with his imagination, his fluent speech, and, quite literally, the fact that he was a player. Ms. Norton noted that he wrote more than the "bright" kids . . . which suggests that Ta'Von himself was not "bright."

Institutional Exclusion from the Discourse of Being "Bright"

On my last day observing Ta'Von at the end of the first five months of school, we went out into the hall-way, where I gave him some colorful markers and a book of blank pages. This, he said, was "a good thing to do for me." His next act was to write "a thank you note" to me, his "friend from my old school," as he described me to others. With his writing to me, he enacted my basic sense of Ta'Von—an other-directed, friendly child who found writing a useful tool for social action of varied sorts. He was, thought Ms. Norton, a more fluent writer than the small group of middle-class children deemed "bright."

The "bright" children, though, came to school already on the top rung of the kindergarten literacy assessments. They could name the letters and associate them with sounds; and they had begun reading conventionally. That is, they already "knew" (or could display) literacy and mathematical skills that used to be learned during the primary grades (Brown, 2013; Genishi & Dyson, 2009; Graue, 2006). Since children are judged by what they can do on their own, not, as Vygotsky (1978) argued, by how they stretch their capacities in interactive activities, Ta'Von was behind before school even began. His social agency, along with his imagination and flexibility in chosen genres (i.e., breadth of initiated written repertoire), cannot be reduced to quantifiable test scores; hence, in the end, they do not count.

This official view may have unofficial ramifications in certain interactional spaces. Ta'Von's early efforts at forming letters and "sounding out" spellings yielded a sense among some children, mainly "bright" ones, that Ta'Von needed help. He most certainly regarded himself as needing help given certain tasks, but he explicitly did not like help when he did not feel a need (and, of course, he called attention to his productions when he felt he had done well "all by myself"). Toward the end of the observations, Ta'Von had begun to help others when they requested it; he emphasized process just like his teacher did (e.g., helping a child listen to the "sounds" of a word she wanted to write), and he expressed exuberant joy when "you did it!", just as he did about his own progress. The "bright" children, though, did not accept Ta'Von's literacy knowledge and paid no attention to his burgeoning know-how.

Ms. Norton did praise all class members at times for their academic insights or productions. Clearly, though, it would take more than her praise to help Ta'Von in his ongoing journey to be, and to be seen as, a bright, playful, and attentive learner, player, and friend. A sharing time, when teachers and children have the opportunity to appreciate publically child productions, is one potentially helpful classroom practice (Dyson, 1993b, 2013).

In sum, in his representations of self and in his search for classroom companionship, Ta'Von illustrates that writing is not just a subject; it is a potential tool for composing a classroom space in which one matters. Thus, we as educators have a responsibility both to know our children and to offer curricular room to maneuver; that is, to keep classroom spaces "always under construction" (Massey, 2005, p. 6). Moreover, we must work toward the respectful inclusion of our children as learners, players, singers, peers, friends, fans, and on and on. Our very language (e.g., our choices of "boys and girls" or "friends" to address children) and our images (e.g., of variably racialized, classed children) close classroom space or keep it in motion. Finally, children's classroom identities and resources have traveled along trails that lead back to lives beyond the school. We must open classroom spaces to the breadth of children's experiences and, in this way, enrich the talk, images, and texts of budding composers, like little "dude" Ta'Von.

In such ways, we help ensure writing's—and, more importantly, children's— potential for constructing an included self ready to take social action in a complex and ever widening world.

Epilogue

Ta'Von did negotiate friendships in the class, including with a quiet "bright" girl named Ella, who had long brown hair and big brown eyes. Ella, as it happened, loved to spend recess running on a pretend road with sharp turns. Perfect (even if, at times, she insisted on holding hands).

★

II CASES FEATURING CULTURAL RESOURCES: DANTI, GUS, AND SHEELA

Danti: Glocalizing Dora the Explorer in Indonesia

Sophie Dewayani

Two young street musicians, each holding a guitar that seemed as big as their body, were teasing one another one hot afternoon in a busy intersection in Bandung, Indonesia. Surrounding them were parked intercity buses with their loud noise and black smoke, waiting for passengers. "Hey, watch this!" said the boy musician to his companion, a little girl musician. The boy started to play the guitar he was holding. He played a popular love song I often heard on a local radio station, a song originally sung by a famous Indonesian pop band. Amazed by the flawless performance of the six-year-old, I commented, "Wow, you play really good!", to which he replied, "I know. It's been a long time." "Did somebody teach you to play?" I went on asking. The boy shook his head. "I learned by ear." (All dialogues were conducted in Indonesian language and have been translated into English.)

The sight of children spending time with friends while playing, working, or sometimes studying in street intersections of big cities in Indonesia is common. Children help families earn additional income by playing music, dusting the stopping cars when the traffic light turns red, or selling knick-knacks. Responsible for their own safety, for providing lunch for themselves, for managing their own income for personal expenses and for families, and sometimes for developing diverse skills to increase earnings, these children assume the role of capable adults when they are four or five years old. However, in an Early Childhood Center located just a hundred meters from the intersection, children are assigned a different role. They are to wear uniforms and to listen and obey their teachers and caregivers. They are given school assignments to help them improve their understanding of letters and numbers. They sing nursery rhymes, children's songs, and memorize Quranic verses. Children are cared for by responsible adults and are protected from what the caregivers perceive as the negative influence of the street life. Danti, the focal child in this case study, was one among children who were struggling in meeting the school's curricular expectations, yet, like the aforementioned young musician, was able to demonstrate capabilities the curriculum could not measure, deemed the "unofficial" school activities (Dyson, 2003).

This case presents Danti, who, like other children across the globe, had "cultural resources" (Dyson, 1994; Paley, 1997) commonly not acknowledged by the restricted school curriculum. Since waking up in the morning, watching television while having breakfast, attending the Early Childhood Center from 10.30 to noon, and then spending time in the street after lunch, sometimes until late at night, Danti's routine daily activities were surrounded by Indonesian popular songs. When singing in the street using her handclap as a musical instrument, Danti, like other street singers and musicians at her age, presented popular love songs as a means of communicating with friends and attracting an audience (public minivan or private vehicle passengers). Meanwhile, in the classroom, Danti picked up school-appropriate songs taught by her teacher while drawing or doing other school assignments. In so doing, Danti demonstrated awareness of school's learning expectations and the type of songs appropriate in such a context. The wide range of songs available for Danti enabled her to move from one context to another, or sometimes appropriate a song in a certain way and use it as a resource for her drawing.

Despite spending most of the time in the street and having limited access to educational facilities, Indonesian street children like Danti embrace the penetration of popular media in many aspects of their lives. Local popular love songs and also television shows and video games are among the significant topics of conversation among friends. *Dora the Explorer*, the children's show broadcasted internationally, has one of children's favorite characters. In this case, I will present how the bilingual English and Spanish speaker Dora was interpreted in an Early Childhood Center participated in by children who worked in the street. The creation of a kind of "third space" (Bhabha, 2004) or "glocalization" is enabled by the school flexibility in assuring that learning should be attractive for these street children. In presenting Danti, a Dora fan, I will first present how the Indonesian street children are viewed within the government's education policy, and then I will discuss how popular culture was situated within the context of the Center and the Pasundan neighborhood where Danti lived. Next, I will analyze Danti and her drawing activities, which were her major means of graphic composing. All the data collected for this case is part of the larger data analyzed in the ethnographic study of Indonesian "street children" (Dewayani, 2011).

Indonesian Street Children within the "Education for All" Policy

Mr. B, a high-rank official in the Social Department in Bandung, spoke in front of nine- to fifteen-year-old children, some of whom were Danti's neighbors, working in the streets in a training event to promote the Education for All policy, in which the children were paid some amount of money for attending the training, given school supplies, and free lunch:

> Please do remember that knowledge is useful not only for the present but also for your future. Because you can't stay young forever; you will grow old. It is impossible that, for instance, a person is appointed as a president, or a businessman . . . in an instant. It's all through a process. The process is to pursue education or learning. . . . So, for those of you who are still [enrolled] in school, finish that and do not quit. Because that's the only

way you can achieve your dreams ... I know that some people are successful without [formal] schooling but when they're asked about the [graduation] certificate, they cannot show it. So it just doesn't work that way. Companies, the government, can hire you only with your [graduation] certificate.

Mr. B's speech represents the government's concern with the school dropout rate of the street children. The Ministry of Education reported in 2009 that as many as 60% of children who work in the street were still enrolled in school, with off and on attendance. Meanwhile, the rest of that population had dropped out of school. Children's activities in the street for income-generating purposes have thus far been blamed for contributing to these children's absence from formal schools. Therefore, to reduce the number of children in the street, one policy implemented is aimed at enabling their access to formal schooling.

The Child Social Welfare Program is one of the policies that attempt to reduce children's activities in the street, through educational grants provided to the parents of these street children. During the four months of the grant installment, the children are not allowed to work in the street. While this grant was proven to be able to diminish the sight of children in the street, many parents complained that their income had been reduced and that this had affected children's schooling activities. "Kids need snack money; they wouldn't go to school without the snack money. Also, sometimes schools charge additional fees for things like field trips, supplies, and many others. How could my kids pay [those] without working [in the street]?"

With the prevailing corruptions and the issues of unequal educational facilities among urban schools, the government's approach to ensuring children's access to school attendance through providing monthly installments of grant funds to street children simply reduces the complexity of the education issue as it relates to urban poverty. At the same time, it reflects the government's failure to support facilities and supplies for classroom learning. In many public schools in Bandung, including those in which the observed street children studied, schools have to fund many of their own activities, especially the complementary ones such as field trips and extra-curricular activities, because the government's funds cover only classroom-based activities. In addition, snacks and lunch are not provided in school, when buying snacks and sharing them with friends are activities that constitute the school culture.

Other than simply perceiving that a monthly allowance is what street children need for staying longer in school, the government assumes that the children's income-generating competence will distract them from learning. This perception is embedded in the government's perspectives, as evident in Mr. B's speech as follows:

To be responsible is to think about how to live better. For instance, if your father is not successful [in earning a good income], then you must be more successful [earning more money than him or making a better life]. Don't be like, your father works as a garbage collector, and then you become one too. No! That means no progress. Do you understand? . . . Street is not a place for your future. . . . So tell this to your mom. . . . Tell her that you need to reduce your activity in the street. Tell her that she shouldn't ask you to earn a certain amount of money each day. We, the government, have given you opportunities, your rights to get education. Now, your obligation is to take those opportunities, to study hard! . . . Don't be like this, spending all your life in the street. There's no such thing as living in freedom.

An assumption persists that financial need does not serve as the only reason for children to work in the street. Certain qualities such as irresponsibility and laziness are assumed to have led children to work in the street and thus to not take school seriously. Parents are also believed to have forced children to participate in families' income-earning activities, not only to have approved of such action. The assumption that poor families do not demonstrate interest in schooling, and choose the work in the street instead, represents attitudes associated with the "culture of poverty" addressed recently by Ruby Paine (Bomer, Dworin, May, & Semingson, 2008). The Education for All policy thus is believed to improve financial capacity and break the poverty cycle, by introducing qualities such as being responsible, hardworking, and living in an orderly manner (as opposed to "living in freedom").

The Early Childhood Center, in which Danti studied, was established to serve such purposes. Bu Sri, the founder and a local resident of Pasundan, revealed her struggle in the establishment of the Center as follows:

It's easier to teach the young ones rather than the older ones. That's why I founded this Center. . . . I hope to influence these little ones by letting them experience that learning is fun and useful for them. Still, I was struggling at the beginning [when the Center was just founded]. The people here did not realize the importance of early childhood education. They [the parents] would rather take their children with them to the street [sometimes vehicle passengers are more generous to the little street musicians or beggars while refusing to give their money to the adults/parents]. You know, at the beginning, I had to buy these children. I paid their parents eight thousand [rupiah, equals around 0.75 USD, which is the average amount they would earn in two hours working in the street] for the two hours that their children spend in the Center. Now I don't do that anymore because parents are willing to send their children here.

With a mission to introduce fun learning, Bu Sri hoped to make the Center a "home," in which the children could stay, listen to stories, learn, and play, without worrying about earning money. The parents eventually could see their children's excitement in attending the center and regarded it as beneficial for the children's future. With her efforts in making children's learning attractive, Bu Sri rearticulated the government's educational campaign that formal schooling should serve as a way out to transform the children's—as well as their parents'—behaviors, from working in the street to pursuing education like the majority of Indonesian children. To make the children's learning sustainable, Bu Sri worked hard to maintain their readiness for elementary school by teaching basic literacy skills, which include reading, writing, and counting. Realizing that enrolment in elementary school is sometimes distressing because some schools require children to master basic literacy skills before school entry, Bu Sri ensured that every single student could proceed and that no one would be left behind and go back to the street. In doing that, Bu Sri attempted to make classroom learning attractive and engaging for children. One of the ways was by incorporating television shows and children's favorite characters in a way that she considered appropriate.

Popular Culture in the Lives of Pasundan Families

Susis oh oh oh
Suami takut istri [The union of husbands afraid of wives]

Two boys were singing a popular song and chuckling while waiting for their turns reciting reading. Bu Sri caught that noise and told them while smiling teasingly, "Hey, that is not an appropriate song to sing. When you are in school, sing only the good songs." The boys stopped singing and giggling.

Bu Sri did not seriously prohibit children from singing "inappropriate" adult love songs. There were many other moments in which she pretended not to hear when the children were singing such songs. Concerning television shows, Bu Sri shared her judgments:

> This [singing songs that are not intended for children] I could tolerate. Before, the only words Rio said were the inappropriate and dirty ones [and then she went on mentioning examples of curse words]. From where can he get it if not from the older boys in the street? And maybe [he got the words from] this television show. You don't know what these kids watch at home.

Bu Sri herself had a television set at home and liked to watch Indonesian soap operas with her family members. Living in the same neighborhood as the children, she knew the popular shows and soap operas being watched by her neighbors and their children. In Pasundan, families who worked in the street rented a room of around 3 x 3 meters. Danti lived with her parents, two older sisters, and two younger sisters in a room that accommodated the entire household's activities including sleeping, cooking, watching television, and receiving guests. The room, along with those of neighbors, lined a narrow alley, which was often alive with television noises.

As a focal source of entertainment, television shows served as a conversation topic among mothers and among children. In the Center, children talked about popular television characters, either cartoon or adult characters, as they drew, copied writing, or worked on a math worksheet while sitting or lying down on the classroom's floor. Bu Sri and other teachers sometimes joined a conversation too and used the children's knowledge of popular characters (especially the ones considered child-appropriate like Dora the Explorer and SpongeBob) to develop ideas in their drawings.

The children's rich conversations during classroom activities, the involvement of children's popular culture as their cultural resources, as well as the interactions among children and teachers, characterized the "permeability" of classroom learning, which was maintained, as Bu Sri mentioned earlier, to make the learning attractive to children (Dyson, 1993b). With the small classroom size (a room around 3 x 5 meters, which held about 15 children) and the lack of facilities and supplies (there were no tables, desks, chairs, nor illustrated picture books in the classroom), teachers' caring and understanding of students' interests and needs as well as their efforts to keep the learning organization flexible were intended to make children stay longer in school.

My Friend Dora

Dora the Explorer represents a globalized popular culture delivered to children all around the world by television. In Indonesia, children can watch an Indonesian-dubbed Dora series in the free, local based, non-cable television channels, or the original bilingual English and Spanish speaking Dora, along with Indonesian subtitles, in a paid, cable television channel. Indonesian Dora fans such as those in Pasundan neighborhood, therefore, enjoyed the Dora speaking only Indonesian. Children watched *Dora the Explorer* prior to leaving home for school, from seven to eight o'clock every morning. Some girls also owned locally produced Dora merchandise, such as backpacks, hairpins, plastic accessories, and outfits. Danti was known to be so obsessed with Dora that she even had a Dora hair style.

"Teacher, I got a new hair style," Danti told me one day.
"Oh yes. You look beautiful!" I replied.
"It's Dora!" She exclaimed so excitedly.

Dora was incorporated by Danti in a drawing activity led by Bu Sri. Like other thematic composing events in the Center, Bu Sri structured the instruction first by introducing the topic, and then modeling some drawings on the board. At this particular drawing time, Bu Sri told the class that it had been raining hard the day before, and that a rainbow had appeared after the rain. Bu Sri drew pictures of cloud, rain, and rainbow on the whiteboard while telling the story, along with a picture of a student holding an umbrella in the rain. She then asked the children to draw the same thing: the cloud, the rain, the rainbow, and then they could add any objects to the picture. "After drawing a cloud, rain, and rainbow, you can add anything—people, parks, anything." Danti added Dora, as explained below.

At first, Danti seemed reluctant to draw (a typical response other children also demonstrated in drawing activities as most children did not consider themselves a good drawer):

Danti:	I want to draw a rainbow!
Bu Sri:	Yes, draw a rainbow.
Danti:	But I can't!
Bu Sri:	Yes, you can! Look at the board. I've given you an example.
Danti	*(to Bu Sri)*: Like this? (pointing to her cloud drawing)
Bu Sri:	Yes.
Danti:	Then what else?
Bu Sri:	Then the rain, rainbow, and you can draw yourself.
Danti:	Yes, I can do it! I can do it! (an exclamation that may have been appropriated from the Dora show)
Bu Sri:	Yes, you can do it!

Children were free to talk while drawing. On the thin carpet, some children were sitting down and drawing on the floor while some others were lying down on the carpet while drawing. Lying down, Danti incorporated some songs relevant to the objects that she drew (Figure 2.5).

Danti:	Teacher, is this how you make the cloud?
Bu Sri:	Yes, that's good.
Danti:	The rain. (singing the popular nursery rhyme, the Rain Song, to herself)
Danti:	What else, teacher? What else? Rainbow? (drawing a rainbow) My rainbow, my rainbow, you're so beautiful. (singing another popular nursery rhyme, the Rainbow Song, to self)
Danti:	What else, teacher? What else?
Bu Sri:	Draw people or anything.
Danti:	I'll draw Dora!
Bu Sri:	Yes, you can add Dora.
	Danti draws Dora.
Danti:	Dora! (inaudible) Give her bangs (with a singing tune).
Danti:	That's Dora's house. (drawing)
Danti:	And this is the pillow. It has sheet. I wanna sleep, I wanna sleep. (singing tune) And a blanket! And this is the body pillow. Done!

FIGURE 2.5 Danti's Dora

Danti :	Dora Clap. (nods the head two times) Funny face. Has bangs. Carrying a backpack. Carrying a map. (singing to self)
Me:	What was that again?
Danti:	Dora Clap.
Me:	Who taught you that?
Danti:	Me! Me! (singing the Dora Clap all over again)

Danti demonstrates that literacy connects the global and local phenomenon through a popular notion of "glocalization" (Sarroub, 2008), which is adapted from Robertson's (1995) study of modernity in locality discourse. The glocalization in this case refers to a sphere between globalized phenomenon and local interpretation, in which globalized commercial merchandise is adopted in locally social practices. This case demonstrates that children's popular culture serves as a significant means of glocalization in which children, like Danti, play as active agents.

Danti's play with Dora Clap (a commonly performed children's clap play) confirms children's agency as cultural "producers," not as passive cultural "consumers" (Dyson, 1997; Marsh, 2003). However, this third space created in the production process is adapted through several degrees of contextualization. The first contextualization relates to the presentation of the original Dora show to the larger Indonesian audience, with Dora as an Indonesian speaker. The bilingual English-Spanish Dora is only available for the "middle class" families, consisting of those who can afford to subscribe to the television cable. The Indonesian-dubbed version thus represents the "popular Dora"—one that is watched by the majority of child viewers—in which Dora is "textualized" (Briggs & Bauman, 1992) from its original context, and then is given a new meaning which Briggs and Bauman would deem "recontextualization." With the new given meaning, the Indonesian-speaking Dora attracts young viewers with her cuteness, songs, and engaging adventures.

Dora's fans, such as Danti, proved themselves to be an active audience of the "popular Dora." In trying to "imitate" Dora—for example, through appropriating Dora's hair style—Danti framed Dora in a cultural practice similar to her own. In so doing Danti situated Dora in a house and snuggled her in a blanket, along with a pillow. The Pasundan Dora even had a body pillow like most Indonesian young children, who tend to be given a mini body pillow from the day they are born.

Adding to that third space was the school or religious text being taught in a format of play. On Fridays, children were taught how to perform ablution (a wash-up ritual before Islamic prayer) through the Ablution Clap. Both the Ablution Clap and the Dora Clap that Danti had performed while drawing had similar rhythm, pattern, and could be performed alone, collectively, or collaboratively. Collectively, a group of children would perform the Ablution Clap by clapping their hands to the rhythm while singing together. Collaboratively, children would form a circle and clap their hands with those of friends next to them while singing together. Each lyric of both the Ablution Clap and the Dora Clap represented significant features of a theme. Intended to introduce children to the order of acts in the ablution ritual, the Ablution Clap featured the ablution's steps in order. In contrast, the Dora Clap, invented by the children, presented the physical features children could associate with Dora, including her distinctive look and the things she carries with her (see Table 2.1).

Another distinction was that the Ablution Clap tended to be teacher-led and performed in the "official" classroom activities, while the Dora Clap was played among circles of friends in "unofficial" events. This distinction, however, was not clean cut. Bu Sri knew the Dora Clap and helped me write it down. I also witnessed Bu Sri perform the Dora Clap with Danti as she helped Danti expand her drawing.

Regarding the origin of the Ablution Clap, Bu Sri acknowledged that it was taught in a government-sponsored teachers' workshop she had participated in a while ago. "We have a lot of claps like that. You can make anything you want to teach children into a clap like that. That way, children will be interested more."

ution Clap	Dora Clap
Say *Bismillah*★, wash your arms,	Funny face,
[Clap three times]	[Clap three times]
Rinse your mouth, clean your nose,	Has bangs,
and rinse your face,	[Clap three times]
[Clap three times]	Carrying a backpack,
Arm to elbow, head and ears, feet is	[Clap three times]
the last one, and then say a prayer.	Carrying a map,
Amen!	[Clap three times]
[Clap three times]	We did it! We did it! Yes! ★★

★ In the name of God. ★★ Yes! was spoken in English with pumping the fist down.

The didactic content "disguised" in a form of play and popular characters from television shows have provided resources that children interweave in their play events. Thus, the third space is not a single space inserted between the globalized and the local culture, but rather an intricate and layered space interwoven with meanings, as children bring cultural practices from home, school, or other forms of cultural resources into their reinterpretation process.

Bu Sri's Use of Children's Resources in Scaffolding

Due to her petite figure as compared to other classmates, I was not aware that Danti had turned seven years old, the age at which Indonesian children are normally enrolled in elementary school, until Bu Sri told me. "I decided to retain her last year. With the demands of first grade, I think she'd better learn with me here." While being the oldest among the children at the Center, Danti often mixed up the numbers 2 and 5, and the numbers 6 and 9. She knew alphabet letters but was still struggling with decoding syllables. Being an active talker in unofficial events, Danti was relatively quiet in copying writing and math activities. She stopped a lot while working on her individual assignments and stared outside of the door, as if she was daydreaming.

During the drawing event described above, Danti and her peers were distracted by the sight and sound of the musical pedicab passing in front of the Center. (A pedicab, equipped with loud music, can transport children around the neighborhood for a fare of around a thousand Rupiah.) Bu Sri seemed to understand the children's interest and curiosity toward the pedicab's activity and let them run back and forth to the door to the sound of the pedicab. Bu Sri, however, tried to engage Danti more in her drawing by sitting next to her and scaffolding Danti's adding of details. In so doing, she made use of Danti's interest in Dora:

Bu Sri:	This is Dora? How would you make it nicer? Give it a color. What color is Dora? What does Dora have? Backpack, right?
Danti:	And the map too!
Danti:	Dora clap. Funny face. Carry a backpack. (singing tune)
SD:	Dora clap?
Danti and Bu Sri sing Dora Clap:	Dora clap. Funny face. Carry a backpack. We did it. We did it!

Danti sings the Dora Clap all over again.

Bu Sri:	*Danti*, what is this? (pointing to the picture of a cloud)
Danti:	A cloud!
Bu Sri:	A cloud. And then rain's coming. And this?
Danti:	Dora's house.
Bu Sri:	Dora's house. And this?
Danti:	That's Dora. (pointing at Dora figure)
Bu Sri:	Where's the bangs, then?
Danti:	Here!
Bu Sri:	Oh OK. What color is Dora's cloth?
Danti:	Yellow!
Bu Sri:	OK. What does she bring?
Danti:	Backpack!
Bu Sri:	Backpack. What else?
Danti:	A map!
Bu Sri:	So where's the map here? So draw the map. Dora carries a map, right? Draw the map first. (but Danti ignores that directive and keeps coloring Dora's bed green)

Cazden (2001) points out that the individual scaffolding strategy involves dyadic interactions in which an adult and a child engage in power sharing. This event is usually marked by adults' attempts to extend children's zone of competence, which Vygotsky (1978) deems the "zone of proximal development"; that is, the distance between children's actual competence as evidenced by individual problem solving and their potential development evidenced when children are guided by adults or more capable peers.

Dora, along with other media characters, constitutes children's popular resources allowed to be incorporated in school's official activities. Some other resources, however, such as adults' love songs and jokes children brought in from home or from the street, encountered teachers' disapproval. Danti, like other children, was aware of this boundary and able to interweave approved and disapproved resources in creative ways to obtain her teacher's approval. Danti's teacher even joined children's play, as she permitted flexibility in the school's learning method. All of the permeability was provided to make learning attractive, and to make children stay longer in school. Unfortunately, as evidenced in the larger study, as children moved along to elementary school, where street children comprised a minority percentage of the student population, playing with popular culture was no longer allowed. Children had to adapt to a stricter, standardized test-oriented school curriculum. Danti's case serves as one example in which literacy learning can be extended by accommodating children's cultural knowledge derived from their experience with popular culture. This case also suggests that culturally relevant curricula should be made available in formal schools, especially those participated in by children working in the street, along with other policies to help eradicate street families' poverty.

★

Gus: "I Can't Write Anything"

Barbara Comber and Lyn Kerkham

In our earlier studies of children's literacy development, we were able to follow children closely for extended periods of time, sometimes as they made transitions into, within, and beyond formal schooling (Comber, 2015; Comber et al., 2002); we undertook a considered analysis of what made a difference to their learning for better and for worse (Comber, 2014; Kerkham & Hutchison, 2005). In particular, we could see how a "permeable curriculum" (Dyson, 1993a) allowed children to use home, peer, and school resources as they assembled repertoires of literate practices. In undertaking that work we were inspired by literacy scholars who take the perspectives of children (Dutro & Selland, 2012; Dutro, Selland, & Bien, 2013; Dyson, 1993b, 2013; Genishi & Dyson, 2009; Miller, 1979) and/or children's families (McNaughton, 2011) and communities (Moll, Amanti, Neff, & Gonzalez, 1992), because these researchers make us think differently about the resources diverse young people bring to the task of learning at school.

We brought that standpoint to the present case study of Gus. When his grade 2 teacher invited us to observe Gus, and other children whose literacy she was concerned about, we noted that he participated actively in discussions of literature and in brainstorming ideas. His hand was often up. The social aspects of classroom life appeared to be his forte. However, when asked to write he often yawned loudly and repeatedly, looked around the room to check what others were doing, spent time getting out his books and so on. Gus's default response to writing tasks, even when they included drawing, was avoidance, and sometimes he claimed, "I cannot."

In writing about Gus, we are very aware of our partial understandings. The gaps in our knowledge are due to the design and limits of the present study as well as to Gus's interrupted schooling. In this case, we piece together Gus's journey toward school literacy, but recognize that we do not know enough about what his family might say and that we have witnessed elements of his recent schooling only during grades 2 and 3. We have attempted to trace his experiences of starting school by speaking with his kindergarten and Reception teacher (when Gus was four and then five years old).

One reason that our understanding of Gus's development as a writer is incomplete is that his schooling so far has been quite disrupted. Since his Reception year, Gus has been excluded frequently from the classroom, as we discuss below.

Policy and Curriculum Context

Our study of Gus and his peers is part of a broader ongoing project entitled, "Educational Leadership and Turn-around Literacy Pedagogies."[2] The study is investigating how leadership teams, in schools located in high poverty areas, are attempting to change school cultures in order to improve pedagogy and students' literacy learning. Currently we are conducting ethnographies of four such schools, which are showing small but definite signs of improvement, in order to understand how:

- school improvement plans can be used to bring about reforms in schools
- the common sense definition of literacy that often prevails in schools can be interrupted
- student learning data can be skillfully used to improve literacy pedagogy
- high expectations for student learning can be sustained.

When we began researching at the school, the principal described it as a "work in progress." He had been appointed to lift students' literacy performance and change the culture from low expectations and an emphasis on students' poor behavior to a focus on learning. In other words he had been charged with contesting the deficit discourses (Comber & Kamler, 2004) that pervaded the ways in which staff spoke about students and their families and which he understood had negatively affected the curriculum and pedagogy.

Children who attended Sandford Primary School, where Gus was a student, were growing up in one of the poorest urban areas in Australia. Intergenerational unemployment and complex issues around health, housing, and possible futures persisted. Their education was framed by the contemporary international policy milieu of high stakes accountability, where teachers' freedom to imagine and enact a high expectations and engaging curriculum was dwindling. In 2008, the Australian Federal Government introduced NAPLAN, the national assessment of literacy and numeracy, an annual standardized test. All children in grades 3, 5, 7, and 9 are tested on reading, writing, and language conventions (spelling, grammar, and punctuation). Currently the test is a pencil and paper exercise conducted at exactly the same time across the nation during three days in May, with the results returned to schools in September or October. (The Australian school year runs from end of January to mid-December.) The test results for year level cohorts are also published and publically available on the MySchool website. The website indicates how each school compares with others with similar levels of educational disadvantage and with national standards. In 2013, Australia commenced implementing a national curriculum in the subjects of English, mathematics, and science, with literacy as a cross-curriculum capability. This period has seen significant standardization of curriculum and assessment, including moves to ensure standardized reporting using A–E grades. When Gus started school as a five-year-old boy in 2011, he entered an early-childhood educational milieu quite different from anything that had preceded it. The emphasis on literacy standards had already filtered into kindergarten and the early years of school, competing strongly with progressive traditions of play and inquiry.

What Happened When Gus Started School?

Gus attended the on-campus kindergarten as a four-year-old and then transitioned into Reception after he turned five. To enhance his transition to school, Gus was placed in a class with his former kindergarten teacher. She recalled Gus as an anxious child, not knowing how to engage in play or learning activities, and retching when invited to eat fruit or participate in cooking activities. He generally avoided tasks that required drawing or writing.

In his Reception year she noted that he needed explicit step-by-step instructions and typically waited for one-on-one assistance, or wandered around the classroom. By the end of that year he understood 11 of 23 concepts of print, although he couldn't yet show the "part that you would read next" when reading a text; he could recognize almost all lower case letters but no capital letters, and he knew two sight words: *a* and *look*. As far as writing was concerned, left-handed Gus had difficulty with fine motor skills and would often sit with his book in front of him and "do nothing." In response to our invitation to talk about Gus's early literacy development, his teacher described what he could not do: He couldn't use a ruler to guide his pencil to draw a straight line on the left-hand side of his page (a common layout expectation, along with writing the date at the top of the page); he could not write his name; he could not write numbers as far as he could count orally; he couldn't write the alphabet or draw a picture of himself. Writing and drawing seemed to be overwhelming challenges. It is clear that Gus was assessed by a pre-existing grid of standardized expectations.

Gus Learns to Read, But Where Is His Writing?

When Gus was seven and in grade 2 our ethnographic study was getting underway. Several early-career teachers were recommended to us as having achieved outstanding results in terms of children's reading performance. Heather, Gus's grade 1 and 2 teacher, was one of this group. The principal had recruited her to the school because she had expertise in teaching English literacy to students learning English as another language. We were curious about what she was doing to enable students to make significant progress with reading. In line with the school's mandated literacy agreement, she used a range of programs in her literacy block, including leveled texts (Fountas & Pinnell, 2006), Choosing to Read (Kindig, 2012), Jolly Phonics (Lloyd & Wernham, 1992), and genre writing (Derewianka, 1990). This eclectic mix of approaches sought to find a balance between explicit instruction of skills, enjoyment of literature, and children's development as academic writers.

Heather put enormous energy into differentiating the curriculum so that tasks were suitable for the very wide range of learners in the class. She designed guided reading lessons to ensure that she had as much instructional time as possible with small groups of students. Gus was one of the students in her "less independent" reading and spelling groups. Heather worried that she didn't find enough time to work closely with her small groups; nevertheless, we witnessed a number of very productive interactions around texts in which Gus was an active participant. As Heather said in an interview, she recognized that:

> He's very good orally, like during shared sessions he's got all the answers a lot of the time. He's very good with his vocab, it's just trying to get that onto paper now, and knowing how to do it, how to segment words.

Heather also expressed concern that "When he's forming letters, like they're in separate actions," recognizing that handwriting was an ongoing challenge for Gus and that letter formation was not yet an automatic process. Her over-riding goal was to hold high expectations for all her students, and she worked hard to communicate this on a daily basis. She also worked intensively in small groups with students to enhance their understanding of what they were reading. In the transcript below we see the kind of approach she took with Gus, Charlie, and Jill. While most of the students were at tables working on their writing tasks, Heather reread *Who's in the Shed?* (Parkes, 1997), which they had just read as a class big book, paying close attention to details of words, picture cues, and rhyming words.

Heather:	In the beginning of this story, what happened? At the start of the book, what happened, what day was it?
Charlie:	Sunday night?
Heather:	Sunday night, was it?
Charlie:	Yes.
Heather:	It was night.
Charlie:	(reads) "One Sunday night . . ."
Heather:	Is that "Sunday"?
Gus:	Saturday.
Heather:	Saturday. Saturday night. So it was "One Saturday night . . ."
Charlie:	"They saw a . . ."
Gus:	"They saw a . . ."
Heather:	Where were they?
Gus:	Umm, they were in the forest but . . .
Heather:	In the forest? So you think they were in a forest. Where do these animals—a horse, and a cow, and a pig, and a sheep, and a hen—where do they normally live?
Gus:	Umm, they live . . . they usually live in a umm farm.
Heather:	In a farm. Is there a word there that says "farm"? Are you using your sounds—"ar," "ar-m." (pointing toward the words on the page) Over here.

Gus: Farm.

Heather: Yes, so where did it happen? Did it happen in the forest?

Gus: No, it happened in the farm.

Heather directs the students to draw on their knowledge of phonics ("ar") and word knowledge ("Saturday") to crack the code. She encourages them to use picture cues and their knowledge of the (textual) world of "the farm" to interpret the setting. As we see in the next few exchanges, she also provides feedback on specific reading strategies.

Heather: So, at the farm there were lots of animals and they were woken up with a terrible . . . ?

Jill: Bang.

Heather and students: Fright.

Heather: A terrible fright. And they were wondering what that was. And then it [the text] goes on: "There was howling and growling—"

Gus: (talking over Heather as she reads) Oh, I think it was a tiger and a um wolf.

Heather: ". . . and roaring and clawing." You're predicting that there was a tiger, or a wolf?

Heather acknowledges Gus's enthusiasm and his prediction. She explicitly names the strategy, making it a potential resource for his development toward independence as a reader.

Despite Gus making good progress in his reading, where he showed concentration and motivation, he was less confident with writing. In order to start or complete assigned tasks involving any form of writing, Gus needed considerable encouragement and step-by-step prompting. By the end of grade 2, we realized that we had observed very few occasions when he had actually produced written texts or images. Notes from our fieldnotes frequently read:

> Gus is yawning a lot and lies on the carpet. Heather asks him to sit up.

> Gus wanders around and watches what others are doing.

> Gus asks for help and waits.

Heather's pedagogical focus had very much been on helping Gus to crack the code. Where was Gus's writing? Heather admitted that she had concentrated more on reading, the focus of the school's improvement plan, but stated that in the future she would like to provide more opportunities for children to write. Heather took maternity leave at the end of the year, and Gus was placed with a new teacher for grade 3.

We decided not to observe in term 1 of the following year whilst Gus's new teacher, Lara, established herself in the school and formed relationships with her students. To our surprise when we arrived to continue our case study work in term 2, Gus was not there.

Grade 3: A New Teacher

At the beginning of the year, Lara worked at "all the relationship stuff" to establish a respectful culture of inclusion in the classroom. Valuing children's skills and interests and nurturing positive dispositions to learning and "having a go," collectively and individually, she believed were crucial to children's success socially and academically. She introduced the students to problem solving resources, to meditation, and to strategies from positive psychology that would benefit their negotiation of relationships in and out of the classroom as well as their longer-term learning. In terms of teaching English, Lara's passion for literature and her intentional inclusion of popular culture enabled the students to make connections with texts, ideas, and topics that stretched their learning, their imaginations, and their reading and writing. While she described herself as "having a lot of structure in the room," she was not so prescriptive that she couldn't respond to students' interests in "what happened on the weekend, or something they heard on the news" that could be the focus of "fantastic discussions."

Literacy Lessons

The daily literacy block in Lara's class included independent reading, a variety of activities to learn spelling words, including iPad applications, and "5 minute writing" on a topic Lara chose. Sometimes a more extended piece of writing on a theme or topic was discussed with the whole class. Brainstorming interesting words related to the topic, or talking about sentence beginnings, adjectives, or persuasive writing techniques and so on, supported the students' writing. In addition, Lara often focused on a science theme and experiments during the literacy block, providing opportunities for hands-on learning and the development of concepts and language that the students could draw on as resources for writing.

Given her interest in literature, film, and popular culture, we were not surprised to hear about Lara's exploration of the writing of her favourite author, Roald Dahl. Taking a whole-class approach, she incorporated comprehension and reading strategies such as prediction or making connections to enable the students to build an in-depth understanding of the texts they were reading or viewing. She included critical analysis, and in this process she made a point of analysing Dahl's "wonderful language." She introduced "sophisticated words" such as "procrastinate" and "serendipity" into the language of the classroom, expanding the students' linguistic resources for classroom talk and for writing.

From what we knew of Gus and his active participation in guided reading and related oral activities in Heather's class, it seemed a classroom environment in which Gus might thrive. But Gus was not there.

Where Was Gus?

We were unaware that Gus had a history of internal suspensions and being sent home for inappropriate behavior. We had neither observed such behaviors, nor heard his teachers talk about them. Later we discovered that Heather had done her utmost to keep Gus in the classroom to minimize disruption to his learning, despite his frequent low-level annoying behaviors, such as not following instructions, and his occasional lying and aggressiveness toward peers. Lara reported that Gus had persisted and escalated these behaviors in his first term of grade 3 to the extent that he was suspended from school five times. In term 2 Gus was excluded altogether, and placed for ten weeks at a nearby school.

The teacher in the placement classroom spoke about Gus not making friends with peers in class and his worry about failing. His lack of "emotional resilience" and unwillingness to persist with tasks that challenged him stood out for her. Her approach was to "put things in perspective" when he was angry or upset over something he could not do. For instance, he could in fact do something about his cutting skills, as she explained in an interview in mid-November:

> People having nowhere to live and things like that, that's something to get upset and angry about, whereas, "Yes, you're having trouble cutting, but take some scissors home, here's some sheets of paper, practice cutting for homework," and I told him that, and I think mum did that with him, and eventually that emotional resilience got better.

Once Gus had settled into the class, "he was willing to please and wanting to try." For ten weeks, there were no disruptive behaviors in class and only one instance of time out for inappropriate yard behavior. Overall, the teacher felt that he "thrived" and even recalled "a few times where [mum] had tears from happiness from some of the things that he was doing in class." This suggests that Gus responded to his new school environment in positive ways. It also suggests Gus's mother was anxious and concerned about her son. These observations offer a perspective on Gus and his mother's involvement that was not as visible at Sandford. Lara, at Sandford, often commented that something may be happening at home to elicit Gus's negative behaviors, but that she did not see his mother so she did not really know what might be going on. Several Sandford teachers, including his Reception teacher and Lara, implied that Gus's mother had problems that prevented her from supporting Gus's learning at school. Yet his mother's presence at the placement school reminds us of the dangers of unquestioned assumptions and misunderstandings about students and their families that circulate in schools. Both Gus and his mother exhibited different behaviors in this new school context.

Emotional work (anxiety, worry about failure, frustration), physical work (fine motor skills), intellectual work, and identity work are just some pieces of the puzzle we were beginning to put together to understand what was involved for Gus as he negotiated how to be a school student.

A New Start in Grade 3?

When Gus returned to Lara's class she reported that "we really looked at it as a clean slate, 'This is the new Gus, a new start for you,' and I think he really took that on board."

However, Lara expressed concern about Gus's lack of confidence and independence as a reader and writer. She assessed his comprehension and inferential skills as lacking and didn't think that he had "the intellectual capacity to delve into a text at such a deep level." This was counter to our observations of Gus in grade 2 where his interpretive skills were often visible as he made connections between texts during guided and shared book reading events. Lara believed that the "big thing" for Gus was that he sometimes felt "self-defeated, and thought, 'Oh why bother?'"

Lara's assessment of Gus's progress since his return from exclusion was framed in terms of his personal qualities:

> So he's been lovely . . . He would have never put up his hand before, and he's putting his hand up, bless his little heart, it's nearly always wrong, and then he says, "It doesn't matter if we get things wrong in this room." I said, "That's exactly right," because that's something that's really important in my room, and the kids are fantastic, no one has ever commented, so that's been a real positive for him, the fact that he's just willing to give it a shot. That's significant for him.

While most of the children might accept Lara's mantra that "it doesn't matter if we get things wrong" as long as we are "willing to give it a shot," Gus was still missing the mark as a reader and writer.

Lyn spoke with him about his experience with writing.

Lyn: So when you have to do writing, is there something that helps you do that so you can do a really good job?

Gus: Yeah.

Lyn: What helps?

Gus: People helping me.

Lyn: People help you?

Gus: Yep!

Lyn: What do they do?

Gus: Well, they tell me what to do and then, and then I don't listen because
           I'm too sleepy, and then, and then I say, "Can you repeat like a little
           bit louder?" So then that time I hear and then, yeah, I go, I get, I go
           and get it right.

Lyn: What happens if you want to write a word but you're not sure how
           to spell it?

Gus: Then just find a friend what sits next to you and ask them, if they're
           smarter than other people.

Although Gus had a social solution for writing the words he did not know, he
had few resources for independent writing. In his response to the task to "Design
a poster" for a real or imagined ride at The Show,[3] Gus's difficulties were clearly
evident in his talk of himself as a student who could not write. Lyn's observation
notes give the following account:

> Gus was very settled, interested, and focused on the task. He completed a drawing
> on a double page in his writing book [see Figure 2.6]. The drawing depicts what
> appear to be two vehicles surrounded by a range of scary characters, including
> people flattened on The Fly Train (just one part of the Death Ride) perhaps by
> the shock of the horror of the ride and one main highly animated character,
> whose hair is buffed up, eyes red, and arms stretched out in terror. I asked him
> about his drawing, and he willingly talked about what he had included.

Lyn: So, what are you calling your ride?

Gus: "The Death."

Lyn: "The Death"—with a big deep voice? Yeah? And what are some of
           the words you're going to write around it?

Gus: I don't know, 'cos I can't write anything.

Lyn: OK, well, what are your ideas, then? What are you thinking about?

Gus: I've been thinking for some since last night, and it hasn't been working
           yet.

Lyn: Oh, it hasn't been working yet?

> "The Death" ride is reminiscent of similar rides at the show, such as the Ghost
> Train, where ghouls jump out of the dark shouting "boo" or making horror noises
> to scare the participants on the ride.

Tania, sitting next to Gus, tells me her poster is about a Haunted Hotel.

Lyn: Oh, and you've got words like "scream."

           Gus points to a word on her page and asks what it is.

Tania: Freak, freaky.

Lyn: (to Gus) So would your words be a bit like that—you'd want words that make you feel a bit scared?

Gus: I've already done "evil."

Lyn: Yeah. I can see "evil" there.

> Gus starts to sound out and write "kill." He gets as far as "c-i-l," and asks for help. I tell him it starts with a "king k" and that it needs another "l." He corrects what he's written. He wants the word "killed" so adds a "d." I don't see what he writes after that, but I did hear Lara's feedback to him when he took it to her desk. Lara tells him that the words "I killed a man" written in red letters is "a bit too scary, too harsh" for her. He accepts her suggestion of replacing it with "I scared a man." She wants to see more words that will make people want to come on the ride. She scribes "It is fun," suggests "scary," and sounds it out as she writes it on his page while he watches. She encourages him to add more words:

Lara: "What else could you say—something about your hair? It makes your hair stand on end? How would you say it?"

Gus: My hair will go up. (she reads aloud as she scribes "Your hair will go up!")

Lara: I feel better about that. When you go back to your desk just write a couple more words because you've got all the basics here.

Gus's comment that he doesn't know what words to write around his poster "'cos I can't write anything" and that he'd "been thinking for some [words] since last night" suggests that, for Gus, writing was hard work. It was hard work to remember how to spell, or to activate phonetic knowledge. It was difficult to choose the language and ideas acceptable in his grade 3 classroom, as he discovered in the teacher-sanctioned space of the one-on-one conference. In this space the teacher was responsive to a point ("You've got all the basics here"), but could not accept the violence implied in his "Death Ride."

Gus did not fit comfortably in the official world of the classroom. This was yet another opportunity lost to "interactive trouble" (Freebody, 2003), where Gus missed the mark and failed to read the unspoken rules of what counts as appropriate writing in grade 3. He was unable to count as an asset his knowledge of popular culture. Understandably teachers get nervous around depictions of violence in children's texts, but sometimes they misinterpret the students' intentions, to the students' detriment (Simon, 2012).

The moral judgment concerning the Death Train is quite paradoxical given the actual existence of ghost train rides at the show. Moreover, several weeks later we observed a writing lesson for Halloween in which the children were invited to write about vampires, ghosts, and blood-sucking bats. It is not immediately obvious what kinds of "scary things" are OK for classroom writing and which are not.

FIGURE 2.6 Gus's Train

As observers we witnessed Gus's lack of fit in the academic and social worlds of the classroom, despite his best efforts and clear intellectual potential as exhibited in reading lessons in grade 2. The social isolation of silent writing meant that he could make little use of peer resources and only problematic use of his cultural know-how. It is not surprising that he came to view himself as one who didn't know and who couldn't write.

Conclusion: Questions Gus Raises

In the case study of Gus we did notice hopeful moments as he engaged with peers in guided and shared reading, and in his seeking ideas and support from them as a writer. But our observations also give cause for concern for him as a literacy learner, now and in the future. The "interactive trouble" (Freebody, 2003) we became aware of, and the intransigence of deficit discourse unwittingly spoken by the teachers as they named what Gus lacked and could not do, continue to shape his difficult journey into the academic world of the classroom. While we have learnt much about Gus's learning trajectory, we are left with many questions.

While teachers recognized Gus did have difficulties as a reader and writer, his needs were not recognized as serious enough for additional support or for a different approach to teaching. In part this can be explained in terms of the pressure teachers face to meet relentless literacy improvement targets and to focus on a narrow literacy measured by standardized tests. In these circumstances whole-class teaching tends to take priority. It is difficult to "turn around" (Comber & Kamler, 2005) to students and engage pedagogically with the resources students already have, especially when they may involve ethical dilemmas, such as implied violence.

Although Gus did sometimes act in aggressive ways, suspensions and exclusions did not address what we have come to understand as his frustrations and anxieties. The "new start" for Gus had already begun to unravel toward the end of term 3, when his off-task behaviors, swearing, and disruptions in class had resulted in internal suspensions and a one-day exclusion. Our concern is that school exclusion and suspension (Kupchik & Catlaw, 2015) present significant risks of school alienation, drop-out, and later a lack of community participation. Of course, children's progress in literacy is likely to be hampered by absence, whether that absence is a result of anxiety, illness, bullying, or misbehavior (Campano, Ghiso, Yee, & Pantoja, 2013; Fisher, Albers, & Frederick, 2014).

Like the teachers, we do not know very much about Gus outside school, but as researchers we are in a position to consider what difference such knowledge might have made for a young boy who struggled with peer relationships, and a place in the unofficial world and official world of the classroom.

★

Sheela: Finding Her Voice

Urvashi Sahni

The case study of Sheela emerges from a 30-week-long action research project that attempted to understand literacy as it was practiced in a second grade classroom of a government rural primary school, in the state of Uttar Pradesh, India; my intent was to understand the social, cultural, and political dynamics of literacy practices. The study included a brief observation phase, during which I tried to understand the official curricular definition and practice of literacy, along with the children's role in it, and a longer participation phase, in which I took on the role of a teacher-researcher and invited the children to negotiate the curriculum with me. I observed how they developed as writers and persons in the process of this transaction, asking the questions: What did they do with their writing? What did they use it for? What purposes and needs did they reveal? How did they develop as writers and persons? What social and symbolic resources did they draw on? I initiated literacy events, taught the children, observed them, audio taped their conversations, and took field notes.

As teacher, I saw my role as one of helping the children appropriate literacy as a social and personal tool with which they could realize their own culturally embedded purposes and needs. As a researcher, my role was to understand how the children did this. The two roles overlapped, because of my vision of literacy, culture, and knowledge as a mutually constructed practice. I visualize the classroom as a site of cultural and ideological production, an intersubjective space in which culture, literacy, and ideology are constructed as they are practiced.

Further, I carried with me a developmental view of written language (held by scholars like Dyson and Britton), believing that it develops when it is embedded in the lived experiences and worlds of the learners, when they find they can do something with it, and when it is contextualized in their social lives, their intentions and experiences; this is counter to a view of literacy as a set of discrete decontextualized skills—"an unimaginative copying of lifeless letter forms, connected to and signifying nothing" (Dyson, 1991, p. 112). The latter was the official view in Sheela's rural primary school.

Sheela's School

Sheela's primary school had an enrollment of 236 boys and girls from grades 1–5. The children all came from a very low socioeconomic background. According to the village headman, 80–85% of the families were below the poverty line and only 22% of the population had ever had any education. The school had two rooms, but grades 1–3 were conducted out in the open under trees. Sheela's class had 48 children and was housed under a Gulmohur tree, where children sat on six jute mats laid out in neat rows. The class was very close to the road and a row of shops, where men hung out regularly talking and laughing loudly. There was a mud path leading out to the fields and a mango grove. It was frequented by pedestrians, motorcyclists, cows, buffaloes, goats, and dogs.

The children were a cheerful lot. They did not wear uniforms and carried their slates and text books in a cloth bag, which they used also to serve as a small table. They often placed it across their knees and rested their slates on it as they wrote. They removed their shoes and slippers before seating themselves.

Every morning boys carried outside a portable 3' x 4' wooden blackboard, the stand on which it sat, and a large wooden chair for the teacher. This was the sum total of the class equipment. Writing materials consisted of a wooden slate, chalk paste, and a handmade reed quill. The class with its equipment had to be shifted frequently, depending on the position of the sun or contingencies of heavy rain.

The Literacy Curriculum

I observed both official and unofficial literacy events (Dyson, 1993b) in the school. The official events included writing and reading events in Hindi (all texts presented herein are translated into English).

As for writing events, every day the children were assigned a writing task, which consisted of copying as many lines as could fit on their slates from the lesson they were currently reading in their school text book. The children would be instructed to call out what they were writing and to write beautifully. The children rarely called out what they wrote, but they did indeed copy very carefully, forming beautiful letters. They wrote quickly and mechanically, keeping one finger on the words in the book and looking at each word in the text as they copied. The children did not discuss their writing at all, putting their wooden slates aside as soon they had finished the available space on them. There were no official *composing* events. The teacher did not write any messages either. She wrote isolated words and short sentences like "Raju go home. Mira go fetch water." These were always meant for spelling drill. The only other writing she did was in her attendance register.

As for reading events, they took the form of recitation reading. The teacher read from the text once or twice a week. She read a word at a time, the children reciting after her, pointing out the words in their readers. Often I observed them simply reciting along, without even looking at the text. At times, they had their fingers on both the wrong word and the wrong page. The teacher conducted a brief spelling and word-recognition drill every day.

The only reading material available was the basal reader. I never saw the teacher bring any extra-textual reading material into the class, nor did she bring out the books from the meager school library (a few books in a box). She said she was afraid the children would damage the books, since they weren't used to handling them. There was very little variation on the curricular stage. The children read and wrote the same four to five lines of one lesson for two weeks!

Apart from the official literacy events described above, there were several unofficial events constructed by the children themselves. I did not observe many unofficial writing events, which is not surprising considering the extremely constraining writing materials used by the children, the nature of the writing instruction, and the fact that there was very little presence, consumption, or production of written language at home. I saw a child write his name on a scrap of paper once. On another occasion I saw a girl write a sentence she had memorized in class on the dirt floor using a twig. And twice I saw Sheela and her friend copying poems from scraps of newspapers.

As for unofficial reading events, even though the teacher only read from the first paragraph of each lesson with the children, some of the children worked together to decode the entire lesson. They read whenever they had the chance. As soon as they had finished their writing assignment, they pulled out their readers and started reading. They did this individually, but also in pairs or threes. Their concentration was centered on decoding. That seemed to be a challenge for them. They helped each other decode, pitching in when the other seemed stuck.

The text book was a much respected and much used object. In most cases it was the only text available to them in school and at home. The children exploited it more exhaustively than the teacher did. Even though the teacher never called attention to the pictures, the children spent much time looking at them, discussing them, and making up stories about them. The children did not draw any pictures themselves, as there were no drawing materials or requirements to draw; they used the pictures in the book to symbolize their own imagined meanings and to play with each other. Touching the pictures, making believe they were real, and manipulating the book physically were all ways to enact their make-believe play.

Sheela: A Person Addressed and Addressing

This case study of Sheela attempts to understand how she appropriated literacy, the various purposes that aided appropriation, the purposes that drove her development as a writer, and how she enacted her purposes in this context and grew as a person. The term "appropriation" is used in this context to mean "making one's own"; that is, acquiring written language as a conceptual and symbolic tool with which to enact one's purposes, goals, wishes, and desires and, therefore, one with which to act in the social world.

Sheela at Home

Sheela was an eight-year-old, tall but slightly built little girl. She had large expressive eyes set in a round face and a wide disarming, charming smile. She lived with her family in Sannasibagh, a village near the city of Lucknow. Her house, a few minutes' walk from the school, was a mud hut with a raised platform in front, a courtyard inside and a couple of rooms around it, one serving as a kitchen and storage area and the other as a bedroom. The family did all their living in the courtyard. Since there was no electricity, they lit oil lamps in the evening and went to bed early to save on fuel costs. Sheela was the youngest of four children. Her older sister, Bimla, was enrolled in the sixth grade in the same school. Her oldest brother, Vijay, was an eighth-grade drop out. His wife and infant son lived in the same house as Sheela. He ran a cycle repair shop in the village and was the chief provider for the entire family. Sheela had another brother, enrolled in high school in Sehlamau, another neighboring village. He had been trying to graduate from high school for the last two years but had been unable to because of bad grades. He was a source of great concern to his family. Both Sheela's parents were illiterate.

When interviewed, Sheela's mother stressed that the family lived in a village, which meant, "I'm going to marry them off as soon as they pass eighth grade. What will they do with more education?" Thus, though she had enrolled both her girls in school, Sheela's mother expressed skeptical doubts about its value for girls.

Moreover, Sheela's mother complained that her daughters did very little housework, since "all they do is go to school and loaf." She had very little to offer by way of comment about the effectiveness of the school, saying that she really couldn't judge it, given that she was illiterate. Clearly she saw no economic value of an education for her daughters:

> School would be good, if it didn't cost us anything and if it paid some economic dividends at the end.

Nonetheless, she was very concerned that her son graduate from high school; she discussed his lack of proficiency in school at length, although she had no response to my comments about Sheela's progress in school. She saw nothing wrong with corporal punishment to help her children learn:

> Of course you have to hit them. If you don't hit them how will they learn?

Our conversation took place in front of Sheela, her sister Bimla, and many of Sheela's friends, who had accompanied us. Sheela sat with her nephew in her lap and said nothing throughout the interview. She and her friends listened attentively, giggling at comments like the above.

There was a sign on their entrance door that said "WELCOME" in English and "Vijay" in Hindi. This is unusual for the village, and I expected to find more literacy materials at home. This turned out not to be the case, however, the only print available to Sheela being her own school books and those of her siblings.

Sheela's home environment is not an unusual one in the village, especially in its gender stance. Girls are supposed to be silent little creatures, who should try to make themselves useful around the house as soon as they possibly can. Since the only end in mind for their daughters is marriage as soon as they attain puberty, Sheela's parents took very little interest in their daughters' education.

Sheela at School

Though very shy and diffident in her relationship with her teacher and me, Sheela participated actively in her friendship group, laughing and chatting with her friends Geeta, Saroj, Mira, and Shakun as she worked and played. Sheela allowed them to copy from her, shared her things with them, and as they read together, they traded texts and competencies. I saw Sheela and her friends, more than any other children, bring texts in from home—especially poems on scraps of newspaper or from their siblings' text books. They would all copy these onto their notebooks, trying to increase their stock of textual materials. Sheela liked to sit at the back, far away from the teacher's gaze, and tried not to attract too much attention. A very careful child, she was afraid of making mistakes and worked cautiously and painstakingly at her writing. Not a risk taker, Sheela was happy to follow her friend Shakun's lead, copying from her book.

Literacy Conceptions and Competencies in the Observation Phase

Sheela was very interested in writing and reading, working busily at all the official and unofficial literacy tasks in the classroom. Like other children, she conceived of literacy as "copying" print. She had not yet understood that speech could be written down, and was unable to generate any sentences of her own. Sheela drew flowers and saree borders for fun. She told me she had learnt these from her sister, who got this from her fifth grade art class. Sheela used written language like an object to be transferred from page to page and handed to others, like the poems she copied and shared with her friends. It was still an external "thing," a sometimes "fun" thing to be played with, a valued thing to be stored and saved, one that lent prestige. Sheela had not yet discovered the potency of written language as a subjective and inter-subjective transactional medium, nor its constitutive, constructive, and creative potential as a symbolic tool with which to represent, create, and construct personal and interpersonal meanings.

Finding Literacy Personally and Interpersonally Relevant in the Participation Phase

Early in the participation phase of the study, Sheela wrote, "I greet mamiji with folded hands" ("mamiji" means aunt, and it was the children's term of address for me). She brought her writing to show me. It was her first sentence generated without any help from me. It was her way of making a connection with me, adopting me as addressee and forming her circle of mutual address and response. She had found a dialogic context in which to embed her writing.

Sheela began to find other contextual supports for her writing. She wrote "your ball is pink" responsively to Shakun, after Shakun wrote "My ball is pink." The sentence emerged from—and was embedded in—the social context that was physically present in the social moment. It was in her mind, and her writing was embedded in her purpose to communicate with her friend, writing speech instead of speaking it.

Sheela began to discover drawing as a symbolic support. She copied a poem about a parrot from her friend and brought it to me, asking me to draw a parrot for her. As I was drawing, she told me she had a real parrot at home. Expressing interest, I told her she could write about her parrot. She gave me a very tentative look, willing to try this out to see what she would find, surprised, too, that I should be asking her to write and draw about herself. She then took the drawing, colored it and generated these sentences:

> My parrot speaks and he calls out "Bimla" [her sister] and calls out to me, calling out "Sheela."

FIGURE 2.7 Sheela's Parrot

Sheela built on the dialogic support she got from me to compose these sentences, as I prompted with questions like, "What does your parrot like to talk about?" Most importantly, she had found a real, live personal context to write about. In response to her, I wrote "What is your parrot's name, Sheela? Do you like him a lot?", hoping to firm up the circle of mutuality that she had begun to build. Interested in my interest in her, and responding cautiously, Sheela began to write and draw her worlds, adopting me as her addressee. The few minutes I spent with each child negotiating topics, providing verbal scaffolding or drawing supportive contexts, were moments of individual addressal for them and extremely important for Sheela. Her writing developed as she discovered its transactional potential, that with it she could build and maintain relationships with others.

Building Relationships: Her Guiding Purpose

The main purpose that seemed to drive Sheela's writing was maintaining and building responsive relationships, which she characterized as "love." In the beginning of my participation phase, the following were the only sentences Sheela composed; she always addressed me in the third person:

> Mamiji loves us a lot. She teaches well and Bahenji (their teacher) also teaches us well.

In another message she borrowed her friend Ravi's idea to write about my car and wrote:

> **CAR**
>
> Mamiji's car is brown. She comes to our school. And she teaches us poetry and loves us a lot.

Being "loved" featured increasingly in Sheela's writing. In a more extended composition later in the study she wrote:

> If I was a parrot I would eat guavas, jamun [a berry-like fruit] and apples and oranges and I would sit on trees. Would eat many nice things. Would fly with my green wings. A parrot is the best bird. The parrot calls out, "Mithu, Mithu." If you catch the parrot and keep it at home then it will run around in the cage. A parrot has a red beak. If the parrot was in Sheela's house then it would love me a lot. I would feed it bananas.

The subject shifted constantly as Sheela alternated between writing about herself, her parrot, and love. She alternated between a sense of "a subjective self" who describes objects and labels and "a narrated self" who weaves into a story elements of other senses of the self (e.g., agency, intentions, causes, goals) (Stern, 1985, p. 174). In writing, Sheela seemed to have found a self-referential and a self-objectifying tool.

Expressing Personal Worlds

Early in the participation phase, I encouraged the children to draw their ideas, and I also led them in writing known poems and rhymes, which they copied. Sheela stayed close to teacher-led written texts and, despite my encouragement, would not experiment with drawing, unless she found a context which gave her an opportunity to express her personal world. She first began to use drawing as a symbolic support when she wrote about Holi (an Indian festival of colors). She drew a picture (see Figure 2.8), writing all around it to express her meaning. She drew a plate with the food on it, labeled it with "there are gujiyas and papad on the plate and everyone is eating it. Today is Holi." She did not draw people around the plate, using writing to refer to them instead. The words stand for people eating from the plate. She used drawing to organize her writing and then used both symbolic media to express her meaning. She wrote this narrative to go with it:

> We played with colors on Holi and had great fun. We throw colors on each other. Saroj threw color on me and it felt cold. When I had a bath it felt very cold.

Her composition is supported by the social and personal context of her world and by the symbolic support provided by the drawing. She first tried to represent the narrative with her drawing, labeled it, and then wrote out the narrative.

Though she participated interestedly in all the literacy activities in the class, Sheela once declared in a heading for a composition, "I liked this dictation very much." It was not a dictation, but she had no other label for the stories she composed, so she called it "dictation." She wrote in this composition:

> Sunita [her friend] was coming to school. On the way she saw a golden stick. She picked it up. Sunita made the stick dance [waved it around] and it gave off shining stars and the stars began to say—Sunita we will give you whatever you ask for. Sunita said—Clothes, laddoos [Indian candy] to eat. A plate full of laddoos came. You should not eat it she thought. She took this to the police then the police said that you did very well. Then the police loved Sunita a lot.

Bruner (1990) mentions that "stories define the range of canonical characters, the settings in which they operate, [and] the actions that are permissible and comprehensible" (p. 91). Sheela's storyline is well in consonance with the stories

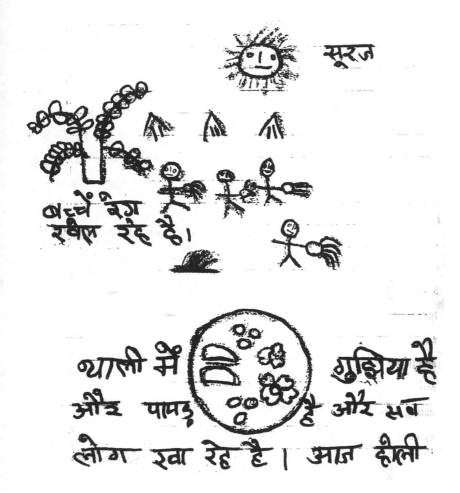

FIGURE 2.8 Sheela's picture of Holi

in her text book, taking the same moral stance. In the stories in the text book, children are portrayed as "good" little altruistic children denying themselves little pleasures in obedience to moral principles of honesty, being rewarded then with adult approval. Here she seemed to be negotiating the tensions between her experienced self and the permissible self as officially given to her by the stories in her school text book. It seemed to give her the opportunity to objectify herself, to step back and take a self-reflexive look, or adopt the "spectator role" as Britton (1970) calls it, important in the construction of a self.

Writing as Social Presentation of "Self"

Sheela realized that writing was a way of committing herself socially or presenting herself socially and was careful about her self-presentation. In trying to help her compose some sentences about herself, I asked her what her father did for a living.

Sheela: (after a brief pause) Nothing.
Urvashi: Oh, then who supports the family?
Sheela: My brother supports us all.

She brought her composition to me, in which she had written:

> My mother, father and brother live in my house. My brother pays the household expenses. Mother and Father are there.

She had erased the last two lines, however. When I asked her why she had erased them, she just took the book back, shaking her head, and said, "No, no." Viewing this in the context of our conversation prior to the writing, it seems as though Sheela did not want to admit that her father was unemployed. Her writing had acquired real meaning. She saw it not simply as descriptive but as a presentation of her personal world, and she wanted to be careful about how she presented it.

In a later composing event, the children were writing about their personal histories in school. Sheela wrote:

I AM MY STORY

> I am studying from class one to class three. My mother came to enroll me. My mother understood very well that is why my mother wanted to educate me—that if I educate my daughter it will be very beneficial to me. Mother says—I like educating my daughter. My mother liked sending me to school so she sent me to school. [If] I will educate my daughter then it will be good for me.

My interview with Sheela's mother had revealed her mother's apathy toward her daughters' education. Sheela was using writing to reconstruct her reality according to her own needs and desires. It was a "wished-for-representation" (Stern, 1985) and presentation of her life. She had discovered the constructive possibilities of writing—its "constitutiveness," as Bruner (1990) calls it—"the capacity of language to create and stipulate realities of its own" (p. 89) and was using it to reinterpret her own lived reality, to "distort it and transcend it" (Stern, 1985, p. 182).

Declaring Her "Self": Negotiating Difference and Distance

In the composition about "my story," Sheela also wrote:

> Mamiji is my friend. Friend means she is Sheela's friend. Why do I like to study—because my teacher teaches then I like it. I like Bahenji's way of speaking. Bahenji and Mamiji are very good friends and I am very good friends with Bahenji and Mamiji.

She brought this to me, beaming brightly, as though she had made an important discovery. Mrs. S, her teacher, was standing close to me and read it over my shoulder. Not very pleased at the declaration of friendship, she frowned gently. "What's this about friends? How can you be friends?" she asked Sheela.

Sheela was undaunted. She stood her ground without saying anything and kept smiling at us. I find this very significant considering the traditional norms of distance between adult and child, teacher and student, upper and lower caste and class, specifically in the very hierarchical structure of her school, the village, and generally in the Indian context. Sheela seemed to transcend all these boundaries with this declaration of friendship. Friendship is a relation of equality, and she was declaring herself an equal person, staking her claim to an equal relationship. In using writing as a personally expressive and exploratory tool, Sheela had found its empowerment potential, that with it she could position herself in the power structure and alter the structure for herself as she did so (Bakhtin, 1986; Dyson, 1994). She had appropriated literacy as a symbolic tool to define herself in relation to others in a way that was compatible with her vision of herself. After this, she continued to write narratives peopled with "friends." She even extended her claims to friendship to Mrs. S's daughter Ekta as well, writing "Ekta is my friend."

Sheela's relationship with her peer and friend Shakun had changed over the course of the study. She stopped following Shakun's lead, as she had been doing, and their relationship seemed to have assumed a more equal transactional nature. In one event, Shakun appropriated Sheela's statement of friendship and wrote in her composition on my next visit, "Mamiji and Raakhi are my friends and Kanchan is my friend." In the course of negotiating her relationship with me, Sheela had negotiated her relationship with her teacher and with her peers too.

Like her friends, Sheela used literacy to take symbolic action in the world, though they all did so in different ways. Sheela dissolved power differences and distances by redefining herself and her relationship with the distant powerful others in the school context, an important one in her life. She declared the differences dissolved with her redefinition of our relationship in terms of friendship. Retaining the third person form of address and the suffix of deference, "ji," she acknowledged the difference of age and the deference traditionally due it in the Indian cultural context. Yet, with her declaration of friendship she denied the power differences

.eted the symbolic circle of mutuality, the construction of which had
.r development as a writer.

g Distance to Negotiate Distance

The way in which Sheela used writing illustrates that written language mediates
relationships, especially differential power relationships, in ways sometimes not
possible in speech. Sheela could not have *spoken* any of the things she wrote. She
could not have declared her status as my "friend" in speech, given the culturally
defined power differences between us. Ricoeur (1981) posits distanciation as being
constitutive of writing. The distanciation offered by writing lent itself to a
reduction of power distance and provided a safe distance from the powerful other,
thus supporting Sheela as she made a statement that involved risk.

Writing may lend itself to the construction and expression of "voice," aided
by its distancing potential. During the participation phase of this project, the writing
event could become a bounded context insulated from the real world, providing
a private space for the construction of a possible self in opposition to an externally
imposed negative social identity. Over the course of the study, I saw Sheela grow
not only as a writer but more importantly as a person, as she accessed literacy in
a personally empowering way. As illustrated in this case, she learnt to use writing
in a variety of ways to serve purposes of her own.

Sheela depended on varied resources for her writing. Among them,

- her peers, who provided social energy and collective negotiations
- interactive, or dialogic, support, from me as teacher and from her peers, all
  of whom were potential addressees and audience members
- her own experiences
- symbolic tools, among them dramatic play and drawing
- structural support provided by an enacted curriculum structured to nurture
  her growth as a writer and enable and allow her freedom to negotiate her
  purposes and needs.

As Sheela learned to use literacy to pursue her own purposes and to negotiate
her composing practice, she also learned to view herself as an autonomous,
purposive agent, as a person having negotiating rights. In this case, Sheela has
been seen, for example, making decisions about topic and genre, interpreting
official assignments to suit her own purposes, and claiming her place in the world.
From being a passive copier of other people's words, she became a composer of
her own texts, a writer of her own worlds. In feeling addressed, responded to
and heard, she found her own voice.

III CASES FEATURING LANGUAGE: MIGUEL, NATALIA, AND RAFIKI

Miguel the *Artista*: A Case of Mismatch and Misguided "Reform"

Celia Genishi

Miguel was born in New York City of parents who emigrated from southwestern Mexico. He was part of multiple dynamic communities: global or transnational some of the time (United States–Mexico); local in his family's Latino neighborhood in New York City; and local in the educational context, that is, in classrooms that had changed every year since he was three years old and enrolled in a Head Start center.

Miguel's experiences in his Head Start center and in school provide a clear case of phenomena that are increasingly common in US public schools: mismatches between large numbers of children and narrowing curricula, especially in the language arts, and an overall derailing of "reform." Instead of reform based on rethinking approaches to education for children of widely varying abilities and sociocultural backgrounds, there is a misguided concept of standards that has been made concrete in the standardization of curriculum, assessment, and, hence, of children (Genishi & Dyson, 2009). Education for many young children is on the wrong track!

Methods of the Longitudinal Study

To build the case of mismatch, I use the boundaries of time and space. Miguel was a participant in a longitudinal study from 2005 to 2010,[4] and I was fortunate to collaborate with Ariela Zycherman for the first two years when our six focal children were in prekindergarten (preK). The six were selected because their families spoke Mixteco, an indigenous language of southern and southwestern Mexico. We viewed the children as potentially multilingual although we almost never heard Mixteco spoken in the center or school. Thus, in school contexts the children were or became emergent bilinguals in Spanish and English. (We used the term *emergent bilingual* [Garcia, Kleifgen, & Falchi, 2008] to emphasize the positive aspects of bilingualism and the process of developing languages over time.)

Once the six children started public elementary school in 2007, Lorraine (Lori) Falchi and Ysaaca Axelrod took charge of data collection until 2010. Because the majority of children at the sites were bilingual or emergent bilinguals in Spanish and English, we focused on language use, including the use of the printed word, in both languages. We, the data collectors, are bilingual and biliterate in English and Spanish to differing degrees. Ysaaca is the only native speaker, having grown up in Puerto Rico, which she considers to be home.

The primary source of data was field notes. During the first year when the children were enrolled in the three-year-olds' (3s) room at Head Start, there was relatively little talk as many children were in the process of learning Spanish and/or English. The next year (4s) at the same center there was much more spoken language, but it was possible to focus on individual children like Miguel or on particular areas of the classroom. Audiorecording was difficult because of the combination of talk in most areas of the classroom and a high level of ambient noise.

Children's verbatim utterances were occasionally inserted into the field notes and analyzed within social and educational contexts such as block play, dramatic play, or planning time. The first questions of the study were related to foundations of language use: Who was speaking to whom? In what situations? What was the children's focus or topic? What were the signs of language growth in Spanish and/or English? In the elementary years questions were shaped by the mandated and highly structured curriculum, which centered on literacy learning. In the primary grades (K to grade 2) the content of field notes and interactive episodes within the notes became less child driven and play based and more teacher directed and lesson bound. As the examples below show, the story of Miguel's composing began in a broad arena with symbol weaving (Dyson, 1990), as Anne has called the child-controlled interplay of different symbol systems, but by the second grade ended in a constrained space where particular written words and genres were of greatest value.

Miguel the Quiet Builder and Symbol Weaver in PreK

Fortunately for Miguel and his peers, the Head Start center that they attended was known locally for a curriculum that was play based and not standardized or structured around academic goals. The staff encouraged the use of multiple languages both at the center and at home, where at the time of data collection families spoke African American Vernacular English, English, Mixteco, náhuatl, Spanish, or Wolof, although the majority of children lived in Spanish-speaking homes. The classrooms at the center were not officially designated "bilingual," but a visitor would probably use that term to describe many of them.

Head Start centers are regulated by the federal government in the United States, and they are required to use the High/Scope curriculum (Hohmann, Banet, & Weikart, 1979), organized around the components of "plan, do, review." As enacted at Miguel's Head Start, the curriculum was play based and open ended. Children planned by choosing among a variety of activities, including art, block play, the family center/housekeeping, and table-top manipulatives. In the 4s' room, there were also a computer and library centers. At the end of each day, children talked about what they did; in High/Scope terms, they reviewed the "doing."

In the Head Start 3s' room, teachers Fran and Lana viewed Miguel as quiet, at times a loner (Genishi & Dyson, 2009, chapter 3). Establishing relationships with either peers or adults was not his preference, and the activities of solitary block play or play with trucks were clear favorites. He spoke when asked to speak, so, for example, during planning time he would respond briefly with "*área de bloques*" ("block area") when asked what he chose to do. Miguel, along with some other boys, demonstrated abilities to focus on his favorite objects; that is, trucks and blocks. His most prominent utterances were sound effects that mimicked truck sounds or the sounds of vehicles in motion. The symbols he drew upon, then, were not only words, at this time in Spanish, but also gestures, sounds, and facial expressions. In short Miguel coordinated a network of symbols across modes. His use of language was best described as language-and-action (Lindfors, 1999), as he appeared to bring meaning to his play by combining spoken language and dramatic vocalizations with a variety of actions.

During the 4s year at Head Start, Miguel continued his language-and-action ways of participating. For weeks at a time, our observational notes showed that he chose the block area where he made block constructions of roads and bridges for his favored trucks, whose movements were accompanied by loud and hard-to-imitate sound effects. Miguel also began to use longer utterances that reflected a more elaborate vision of play; for example, our field notes indicate that at the beginning of the year he said "*área de bloques*" (block area), whereas later in the year he elaborated and said "*área de bloques, con los dinosauros*" ("block area, with the dinosaurs") and then, "*con la casa, a pintar*" ("with [in?] the house, to paint"). Although teachers Pat and Dominga reminded children to use complete sentences, Miguel seldom did, responding concisely to the planning question, "What are you going to do?"

In the middle of the 4s year, whilst Miguel still preferred acting on objects to talking, he showed a growing interest in his peers. On some days he chose to follow Sam wherever he went. When Sam went to the block area, so did Miguel; they were joined by Rebeca, who occasionally took Miguel by the arm and led him to join other children in particular areas, such as the computer center. Along with this budding interest in friendships, Miguel demonstrated greater knowledge of English, for example, when he said loudly, "Thank you, Pat!" after she gave him a cup for brushing his teeth. Indeed the beginning of a new calendar year marked a higher level of social interaction for almost all the 4s in the room (of whom there were 16). As the year progressed, Miguel had longer conversations in Spanish and English, and he was observed to have conversations and disagreements in both languages. The following is an example from February of 2007 (first reported in Genishi & Dyson, 2009, p. 45):

Miguel: Look, Anthony, I am going to show you.

(Anthony takes a plastic figure.)

Anthony: I took one.
Miguel: *Damelo*. [Give it to me.]
Anthony: No.

Miguel: Give it me.
Anthony: No.
Miguel: I am going to hurt you. I am going to get you. Hurry, get in my car.

> (Miguel gives a pretend ride to Anthony instead of hurting him, and their play continues.)

The significant preK years offered Miguel a flexible space within an individually paced timeline in which to lay a foundation for symbol weaving. He became more comfortable and competent with spoken words and dialogues in Spanish and English, and he consistently manipulated favorite toy trucks, blocks, and animals on the stage of the block area as his play became more social. Thus his social and linguistic abilities grew and became more differentiated across languages while he maintained his skills at creating dramas and inimitable sound effects for inanimate and animate playthings. As Miguel left the Head Start center and entered the primary grades, he was able to move across symbol systems that he appeared to coordinate playfully and imaginatively.

Bridging PreK and the Primary Grades: The Common Core State Standards?

Data of the longitudinal study were collected beginning in 2005, well before the Common Core State Standards (CCSS) were adopted by most states in the United States after 2011. Interestingly, the Head Start curriculum met some of the preK standards (New York State Education Department, CCSS P-12), especially those related to the most general umbrella domain, *Domain 1: Approaches to Learning*, for example: Interacts with a variety of materials through play; Engages in pretend and imaginative play—testing theories, acting out imagination.

Other aspects of this domain include "Curiosity and Initiative" and "Persistence." Question-asking and problem-solving are named as evidence of these aspects, and curricular boundaries are not fixed. Although he may not have articulated his questions about the movements of vehicles and blocks for building, Miguel met all these standards as he played with blocks, trucks, and peers, across symbol systems. He tested theories about road or bridge building as he imagined vivid, noise-making vehicles in rapid motion. In an informal narrative assessment of Miguel's preK development for his teachers and parents, Ariela (field notes, 7-07) captured his growing symbol-weaving, social, and linguistic abilities:

> Miguel has become an excellent code switcher, switching between English and Spanish and becoming the true communicator and go-between while playing with Anthony and Sam. Miguel is a regular in the block area and spends time playing with the other boys with blocks and trucks. However, Miguel loves the dinosaurs and often finds ways to incorporate them into his play. You can often hear him making dinosaur sounds when he plays.

Contrast this description of Miguel as an accomplished player with another preK CCSS domain, *Domain 4: Communication, Language, and Literacy*. It includes much more prescriptive guidelines than Domain 1, such as: Viewing—Asks questions related to visual text and observations; Representing—Writes and draws spontaneously to communicate with peers and adults during play.

Consider alongside these standards children like Miguel who are emergent bilinguals and whose play is spontaneous but does not incorporate drawing or writing. One wonders how teachers can allow for the open-endedness of play and the social agendas of preK children at the same time as they ensure "spontaneous" written symbols. Teachers are also expected to prepare preK children to show "increasing awareness" of concepts of print (e.g., written texts in English go from left to right) and phonological awareness (e.g., words are made up of sounds). These few examples are but a tiny slice of the preK standards, which are in general more academic than the above examples and pertain to math, social studies, science, and the arts as well. Teachers in a half-day (morning or afternoon) preK would be hard pressed to "cover" the large array of CCSS. In other words, despite the goals and parameters of typical classrooms for young children, in the environment of CCSS the ground is clearly being prepared in the preK for more academically oriented and defined behavioral evidence in kindergarten (K) through grade 2.

In the following sections, teachers worked in a pre-CCSS environment, but they still faced assessment standards in the form of curricular "benchmarks."

Kindergarten (K): Another Bridge to the Primary Grades

Simply put, the time and space for children to explore and solve problems through play shrank; and time and space for academic learning, specifically, literacy learning, expanded in the public school K that most of the children from Miguel's Head Start attended in the fall of 2007 (see Falchi, Axelrod, & Genishi, 2014 for contextual details).[5] The school had a dual language (Spanish-English) program in which children had a team of bilingual teachers, one of whom taught in Spanish and the other in English. At this school, there were Spanish days and English days; and regardless of cultural or linguistic heritage, all children shared the goal of becoming or remaining bilingual. The opportunity to be emergent bilinguals who could also become biliterate was valued by the parents of the children we were observing and who were making a transition from Head Start to the primary grades.

A less desirable aspect of the transition was that important social relationships were disrupted because children were placed in two different K classrooms; so, for example, Miguel found himself in a different room from friends Sam and Rebeca. As importantly, the curriculum shifted and was dominated by a "balanced literacy" program (Calkins, 2003; Fountas & Pinnell, 1996) adopted by many New York City elementary schools.

Visits to Miguel's classroom revealed that reading and writing had taken center-stage. Not surprisingly, Miguel took some time to adjust to the new curricular structures, and we inferred that he looked forward to choice time at the end of the day when children chose a playful activity. If they did not finish their work, however, they had to attend to their work tasks before they could play. This delay of gratification was unfortunately a familiar situation for Miguel since he chose what to attend to and when. For example, the teacher routinely gave children sentences containing new words for word-study. Miguel wrote the words on his paper, looked at them or at the word wall, and repeated them to himself. He neither sounded them out, a strategy often suggested by the teacher, nor asked peers for help even while they socialized with each other. He wrote the words carefully and read his sentences once they were written. Occasionally he took the opportunity to write creatively, something that was rarely encouraged (Genishi & Dyson, 2009). Despite this evident attention to writing, Miguel ended the year below grade level since he knew fewer letters, sounds, and sight words than he should have, according to curricular benchmarks.

According to Ysaaca's field notes (5-12-08), Miguel was still an eager player who extended his list of favored animals beyond dinosaurs to other toy animals. Ysaaca noted that he chose to play with a tiger and a Lego pinwheel, which he had constructed, making exploding noises the whole time, apparently the sounds the tiger made while climbing on the pinwheel's spokes. Thus although the K curriculum was heavily tipped toward literacy instruction, Miguel tried his best to balance instruction with play, weaving together varied symbol systems.

Work Rules: Miguel in First and Second Grade

Our take on Miguel and his work and play shifted according to which "standard" we considered. If the standard was similar to that of the staff at his Head Start center, then his progress was acceptable. He drew on his knowledge of both Spanish and English as he became a reader and a writer in the primary grades, although he was progressing more slowly than the teacher and prescribed curriculum expected. At the same time, his writing appeared to us to be more creative (more distinctive and imaginative) than the balanced literacy program allowed; and this tendency toward creativity continued to develop in the first grade. According to the curricular standard of grade-level benchmarks, though, Miguel was at such a low level of achievement that he was "at risk" of failure and retention in grade. Perhaps for Miguel and a number of his peers the mismatch between the children's abilities and the demands of the literacy curriculum started early, since there was no flexibility in the benchmarks for children who were emergent bilinguals or approached learning in nonlinear ways.

Miguel the "Artista" in First Grade

In first grade Miguel and his peers were expected to advance within the framework of balanced literacy, so, for example, children were introduced to different genres such as "personal narratives." As authors they wrote about the events of their lives, and the events became the substance of their writing. Miguel wrote a four-page narrative in Spanish about doing dishes entitled *"Yo limpio los platos"* ("I wash the dishes"). On the first page below his drawing, he wrote with some invented spellings:

> *Primero mi papa me dijo—Miguel lavs los platos—Yo puse los platos en el fegadero.*

> (First my dad told me—Miguel, wash the dishes—I put the plates in the dishwasher.)

On the fourth and last page he wrote, again with invented spellings:

> *finalmente yo mi dormi y todavia estavo a labato los patos.*

> (Finally I went to sleep and I was still washing the dishes [in his dreams?].)

Miguel's drawings were straightforward and appeared to be done quickly. Contrast this assignment with Ysaaca's field notes (first reported in Falchi et al., 2014, p. 353), describing his ways of drawing when he was engaged in representing his favorite subjects, animals:

> Miguel's head is on the table and he is carefully and slowly coloring the background for his story. He colors over some of the areas, over and over again. Occasionally closes eyes and stops coloring. He opens his eyes colors more rigorously and then goes back to coloring slowly. He sometimes moves his lips as if he is talking, but doesn't interact with the boys sitting next to him.

The process of creating the drawing at his own pace was Miguel's focus here. In short he was still symbol weaving; his illustrations were as meaningful as his printed words. Further, when he wrote most productively he was in motion. He drew, moved around his work/product, put his head down on the desk sometimes, did not talk most of the time, but did sometimes subvocalize, as if there was an ongoing narrative in his head.

Children's narratives or "books" include an author's page, About the Author, or *Conozca al autor/la autora*. Miguel wrote the following (first reported in Falchi et al., 2014, p. 354):

> *Hola. Soy Miguel. Mi amigo es James. Mi faborita comida es carne con aroz y chile. A me me gusta jugar afuera Mi faborito juego es tag Mi faborito animal es oso y rinoseronte.*

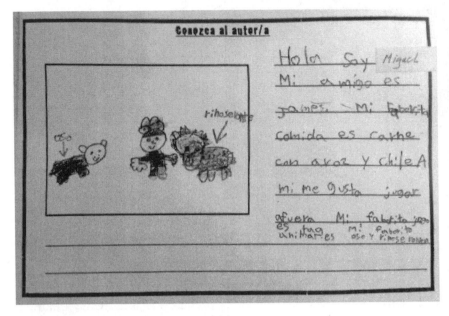

FIGURE 2.9 *Conozca al autor* (About the Author)

(Hi. I'm Miguel. My friend is James. My favorite meal is meat with rice and chile. I like to play outside. My favorite game is tag. My favorite animal is the bear and rhinoceros.)

Miguel was clearly following a template about personal favorites that scaffolded his author profile, but what captured an important aspect of his first grade literacy learning was the distinctive drawing that incorporated his favorite things: his hat that resembled bear ears (they are not mouse ears) and animals. Illustrations like these led Ms. M, his teacher, to say, "*Miguel es un artista!*" ("Miguel is an artist!") Not a reader or writer, but an artist, an identity that was much less in evidence after first grade ended, a year when his teacher bent the curriculum so that it was flexible enough to allow time and space for child artistry to emerge, alongside beginning literacy.

Rules of Work: Miguel in Second Grade

As children advanced to the next grade, the curriculum of course became more complex and, in this school, more constraining. The balanced literacy requirements included different genres that put more distance between the child and her or his work. Favorite things were less likely to appear in students' products when the genre was realistic fiction, for example. The balance between work and play or official v. unofficial tasks shifted heavily toward work. Indeed these rules were posted in Miguel's classroom:

1   Don't get out of your seat.
2   Do all of your work.
3   *Trabajar en silencio* (Work in silence).

The observed classrooms were hardly ever silent, but silence was aspired to because it was assumed to reflect a deep focus on work. Thus by the second grade the mismatch between children's ways of being and the curriculum was growing. The sounds of playful talk and sometimes boisterous actions that marked the Head Start classrooms, particularly in the 4s year, were altogether missing. Moreover the flexibility allowed by the first grade teacher was absent, except for the continued use of both Spanish and English in the school's dual language program. Although the curriculum is not duplicated in the two languages, children have opportunities to hear translations of tasks.

Miguel moved up to second grade along with his peers, but he still worked more slowly than most as his attention might wander from the task at hand. Since he said very little, it remained a mystery what his focus was; but it was not always the specific features of the genre of the day, realistic fiction. Children were told that fictional narratives start with the posing of a problem, and by the end of the narrative or story, the problem should be solved. In spite of the seeming abstractness of the task, Miguel was able to create a problem by drawing a "character map" of fictional Robin (Figure 2.10). This was a prewriting exercise in which the problem was that Robin did not like a list of things: frogs, octopus, pigs, running, and so on. The "resolution" showed that Robin now liked most of those things, plus dogs, books, animals, instruments, and apples. Whatever happened in between was not revealed, nor was there an explanation of who or what the character in the drawing, Frans, was (possibly Robin's pet).

I include this character map as an illustration of several kinds of mismatch. Early-childhood educators may question the appropriateness of teaching second graders the genre of realistic fiction. (In fact as of spring 2014 this genre was included in the fourth grade balanced literacy curriculum, rather than that of the second grade.) The child writer was expected to write in the third person about events that were fictional, but that were realistic (i.e., they could happen). Given the complexity of the assignment, Miguel worked impressively well to create a narrative in which his character Robin appeared to mediate a transition from not liking to liking. One wonders if there was a mismatch, then, between the assessment of Miguel as "low" or "at risk" in reading and writing and his abilities as demonstrated in what he actually wrote.

Recall that the character map represented the "prewriting" phase. A later phase was his "story mountain," which was literally the arc of the same story. It had

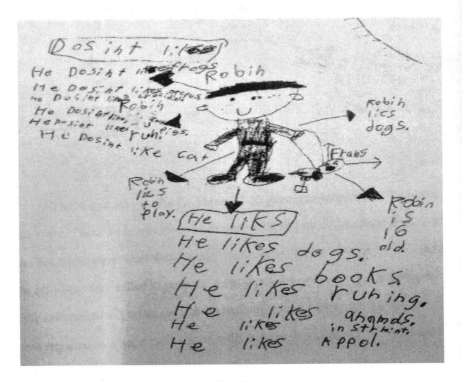

FIGURE 2.10 Miguel's Character Map of Robin

four points along a mountain-shaped arc, each with a small cartoon-like drawing that read from left to right:

> he is not hape [happy] he wont [wants] his dog bac [back]. He asc [asks] if he can hav [have] his dog bac. and he did.

The story mountain, along with other preparatory steps, was considered still to be a draft, but severely reduced the details of the character map. The final "published" version of the story was an elaborated version of the story mountain, lacking the details and sense of fun reflected in the character map.

Miguel, Mismatch, and the Standards of "Reform"

The phenomenon of mismatch between child learners and curricular requirements is not new, although recent requirements for literacy learning have placed more advanced demands on children and their teachers. What this case study has offered is details of Miguel's unique responses to the open-ended curriculum of his Head Start center and the constraining tasks of balanced literacy in the primary grades. As researchers, Ariela, Lori, Ysaaca, and I observed a boy who played, spoke, moved, vocalized, and eventually read and wrote in his way on his own timeline. We could see that his literacy performance did not meet established standards or benchmarks of the literacy curriculum, but we also saw that assigned tasks—for example, writing realistic fiction—were generally problematic. As the curriculum developers later realized, this genre was too advanced for second graders. Moreover, how much did students learn from sequenced writing activities that relied on a particular kind of "revision"? It was a kind that erased details of earlier drafts in which child composers may have been deeply invested.

The public has been told that the overall goal of CCSS is to prepare students to be ready for college and subsequent careers (New York State Education Department CCSS). This is the essence of the latest standards-based "reform." Like many of the tasks of balanced literacy, this concept of reform is problematic since its originators have reduced schooling and its goals to one size that theoretically fits all. The cases included in this chapter illustrate how individual child learners and composers around the globe resist this reductionism. Our sociocultural orientation is reflected in the following comment related to Miguel and the standards of reform of preK–12 education:

> Despite the children's home situations and literacy practices, in this classroom, they were expected to write independently with little interaction with peers and to "maintain" focus and stamina. They wrote in the third person, and they imagined themselves as an author of an original character, who resembled but was not a real person. All of these dispositions, and these specific genres, stratified the classroom based on the type of dispositions, embodied actions, and narratives students produced, and how close they were to the implicit norms.
>
> (Falchi, 2011, p. 114)

Lori's insights capture the difficulty for primary grade children of comprehending the characteristics of each genre as well as the political outcomes of a literacy curriculum with norms that are both explicit (the character map, story mountain, and so on) and implicit (behavioral norms set by high-performing students). What we authors hope for in the face of current reforms is radically different political outcomes, including one that allows for blurred stratifications and thus makes time and space for an "*artista*" like Miguel.

★

Natalia: "I Want to Speak Tata's Language!": Learning and Awakening the Local Language

Iliana Reyes

Natalia was a six-year-old girl attending first grade at an elementary school in a small rural town in Central Mexico. She attended a public school with a commitment to support bilingualism in Spanish and náhuatl, the local indigenous language. With the support of the principal and the interest of the children's parents, the school teachers were proposing activities to develop a bilingual curriculum model that supported both Spanish and náhuatl for the young children in the community. The dialogue around this topic, children becoming bilingual, had been going on for several years, and the teachers had based the program activities on an *additive* view of bilingualism, in which bilingualism is viewed as an asset and as a resource (Ruiz, 1988).

Natalia was born in Nealculiacán to a working family who considered náhuatl their heritage language. Nealculiacán is a small agricultural town in the state of Puebla, a state in Central Mexico. Mom had been part of a larger school project initiative, Community Literacy Canastas. In this project, over 40 families from the school had participated in monthly family–parent meetings to share and document stories about local traditions, including music from Nealculiacán, the local river, and its stories. This effort had been led primarily by the first grade teacher, Natalia's teacher, with the support of local teachers, parents, and myself as a collaborator.

The Potential for Emergent Bilingualism and Biliteracy

One of the complex but positive features of this community linguistic context was that Natalia, like many of the children in this community, was growing up with the potential of bilingualism. The children were currently emergent bilinguals, because the potential and support to learn the two languages within the school and home contexts existed but they were latent (Reyes, 2012). In addition, biliteracy at school might have been possible because the current conditions were beginning to foster children's writing in both languages. The term biliteracy has been used in our field to describe children's competencies in two written languages, developed to varying degrees, either simultaneously or successively (Dworin, 2003; Reyes, 2012). In previous case studies presented in the literature, we have learned how in addition to the family, the teacher plays a mediator role in supporting a child's development of biliteracy. The findings from Martínez-Roldan & Sayer (2006) and others support the role of the teacher in fostering "additive" conditions for children to develop biliteracy in the classroom. More specifically, it has been recommended that for a positive environment and outcome in both languages, these should be used and encouraged with a comparable status in the classroom (Dworin, 2003).

In the case of Natalia, she had heard Spanish predominantly at home when growing up, and she had also heard náhuatl from her grandfather (her mom's father). However, Mom herself grew up as a passive bilingual in náhuatl; that is, she clearly comprehended the indigenous language but only spoke or responded in Spanish, the dominant language, just as many of the children in the community did, including Natalia. The school was officially bilingual—half of the staff, including teachers and the principal, were native náhuatl speakers. Natalia's teacher, Mariana, was a native speaker and a strong promoter of the bilingual program in the indigenous language. Recently with the encouragement and support of parents and families, teacher Mariana had taken initiative along with local teachers to revitalize the language or as she described it: "We are working on *awakening* the language" (personal communication, December 2014).

Methodology

In this study, which is part of a larger longitudinal project working with families from the same school, a case study design was used to describe in-depth a child's literacy practices and experiences in the first grade classroom. Through classroom observations and documentation in field notes I describe how various interactions and social factors influence the development of Natalia's literacy in Spanish and in their family language, náhuatl. Using ethnographic tools I document the different literacy events in which Natalia participated at school, and how these shaped her understandings about print in her early writing experiences. As part of the classroom observation I observed how Natalia negotiated between two worlds using her linguistic resources to make sense of print and to comprehend local stories that parents were sharing in the classroom.

Background Educational System

In Mexico's public schools, students expand and systematically come in contact with diverse types of texts in the school text books that are provided by the SEP (Secretary of Public Education) and that each child is entitled to have. The general objective, according to the principal and Natalia's teacher, is for every child to become knowledgeable and learn appropriate functions and characteristics of the writing system, integrating literacy (reading and writing) as well as oral language development (speaking and listening). Overall, early literacy in public schools is important but often follows a more phonetic learning strategy, although efforts to include a more holistic and sociocultural approach have emerged in this recent government.

In the academic year of 2008–2009, preschool education in Mexico was made mandatory, beginning at three years old, making it a priority to focus on young children. However, the lack of funding and resources from the government to provide these early educational services has not allowed for all children to receive universal preschool. State-run primary education has been free, obligatory, and non-religious since 1867. Children from low-SES homes often attend public schools in which resources are scare. Natalia, the case study I present here, had attended a year of preschool at a public institution and was attending a public elementary school at the time of data collection. The school was supported by the SEP and also the Indigenous Secretary of Education. Therefore, the collaborating teacher and the principal in this project were strong supporters of Bilingual Indigenous Education.

School Language Context in Mexico

In general the school system in Mexico imposes the Spanish language and ways of learning on indigenous children. For these children, academic success often comes at the expense of their own linguistic and cultural resources (Azuara, 2009). Even though Mexico recognizes all Mexican Indigenous languages officially in its Constitution, there are prevalent subtractive practices at schools and in society. Therefore, indigenous children, in general, grow up negotiating between their two cultures and languages. In the case of Natalia, she had the opportunity to learn her family's indigenous language, specifically her grandfather's, *Tata's*, language (she called him *Tata* as a nickname) because of a strong support and school commitment to revitalize the language. From a sociocultural and language socialization perspective this case study contributes to the field by presenting

FIGURE 2.11 Bilingual Spanish–náhuatl School Sign in Spanish Only

a young girl's journey to learning language and developing literacy within a classroom community where the teacher and children value both Spanish and náhuatl.

The context for language use in this particular school was mixed. For one part the language arts curriculum was based on additive bilingualism where the teachers try to balance Spanish and náhuatl as children learn to read and write. However, there were contradictory messages of language power within the larger school context, and there was a clear struggle to keep it "equally balanced." A picture of the front of the school, with its name and title, proudly announced that it was a bilingual indigenous school, but an analysis of the text showed that all of the title was in Spanish (see Figure 2.11).

And as mentioned before, the teacher was making efforts to integrate some of the cultural and linguistic resources from the community for children to develop emergent bilingualism and biliteracy. Together with families she was trying to accomplish this goal as part of the bilingual program, and her motivation was powered by the fact that she was a náhuatl native speaker, and had seen how language had shifted in the various communities where she had grown up and worked as a teacher in the state of Puebla.

Classroom Literacy Practices

Natalia engaged in frequent literacy events, which served various functions in her day-to-day activities in the classroom context. At school the teacher invited the children to participate in literacy events related to reading and gaining information through text books in Spanish and náhuatl (although these were limited), and newspapers and magazines in Spanish. All children had access to different writing contexts in which the teacher provided specific guiding activities and at other times in which she provided the children with the opportunity to decide on what to write and in what language to write. Although most texts were in Spanish, there was a small resource collection in náhuatl that belonged to the teacher and some books provided by the Office of Indigenous Language Education. This small collection was used as a resource for teaching children the written indigenous language.

An important influence in Natalia's writing practices was her classroom participation in listening to stories from the mothers who participated in the Community Literacy Canasta project with the teacher and researcher, in which they shared local and traditional stories in náhuatl. The teacher invited them several times to come to her classroom to share some of the local stories about music, wedding traditions, and the origins of the náhuatl language in this community. Natalia's mother participated in this project, and for her group activity had interviewed her dad to learn about the first local band and music in the town. The father—Natalia's *Tata*—was the only surviving member of the original band. Natalia and her classmates paid close attention when her mom started sharing the story. The mom shared that 15 local Nealculiacán men, one of them Natalia's grandfather, made up the original band. Their themes and stories were told among members of the band in náhuatl while enjoying the music. However, when writing the songs' lyrics they translated the texts from náhuatl into Spanish so they could share with a wider audience. An additional reason for the use of Spanish was that they themselves did not learn how to write the indigenous language back then in the sixties. During that time, according to the grandfather, the band would gather important themes and terms that they would relate to the story told in a song. The vignette below shows how Natalia's mom shares with the group of children about this and how Natalia makes a connection to learning náhuatl (original Spanish text in italics; English translation of original text below):

Mom:	*Mi papá fue parte de la primera banda local aquí en Nealculiacán.*
	My dad was part of the first local band here in Nealculiacán. But before it became a Mariachi band as we know it today they played more traditional music.
Student:	*¿Tocaban con guitarras?*
	They played with guitars?
Mom:	*Antes no pero ahora sí.*
	Not back then, but now they do.
Student:	*¿Entonces con cuál?*
	Then, with which ones?
Mom:	*Tocaban con instrumentos antigüos de aire—como este.*
	They played with ancient wind instruments—like this one.
	(Mom shares a picture of couple of small wind instruments)

Then she explained to them how over the weekends the members of the band used to get together to write the lyrics of the song. Most important, the grandfather shared that they would tell their stories in náhuatl but translate to Spanish when composing the lyrics. The heritage language was used among peers for conversation, that was important for them, but Spanish was used as the "formal" language to communicate their stories and music to others.

Mom:	*¿Quién entiende aquí náhuatl?*
	Who understands náhuatl here?
	(she asks the children this question; only a couple of children raise their hands; then Natalia raises her hand too)
Natalia:	*Yo quiero hablar como mi* Tata, *su lengua.*
	I want to speak *Tata*'s language!

Here Natalia expressed enthusiastically during group time that she would like to speak her grandfather's language. The sharing of the story by her mom and questions by the children continued for another ten minutes. After this interaction the classroom teacher asked the children to write their version of what they had heard and illustrate how they imagined the band looked together when performing in the old days. The teacher encouraged children to write down the version of the story in Spanish and náhuatl. As I observed, children wrote mostly in Spanish and used some of the vocabulary they had learned as they listened to this mother and other presenters during the semester. Specifically, Natalia wrote a short story about the theme related to music. Her text was written with Spanish as the base language and included some words in náhuatl related to nature that were included as part of one of the songs written by the band: *tepetl* (mountain), *tlaltikpaktli* (world), *metstli* (moon), and *iluikaltl* (sky).

As I observed classroom activities during language arts there was a strong emphasis on encouraging kids to write and connect to some of the stories that they had heard and also to read directly from their text books. Significant to notice is the lack of children's literature books or material in either language available in the classroom; this is unfortunately not an exception, but the rule across most classrooms in public schools in this country. On one particular day the children were engaged in making a connection and description about their community. The teacher encouraged the kids to write the different "layers" of community connections and to use different symbols and drawings to represent that connection. (See Figure 2.12 for Natalia's community wheel.)

In her wheel, Natalia writes in Spanish but connects some of the knowledge she has discussed in class to family traditions. She includes religious events (e.g., Christmas celebration), community festivities (e.g., local music and the mariachi band), and community landmarks (e.g., the well-known volcano and mountain Popocatépetl). She also describes local services available in the community and the family networks.

Natalia and her classmates were engaged in writing activities focusing on náhuatl. What is interesting is that despite kids' strong motivation to write in náhuatl and the support they received in the classroom to learn it, the students wrote what they had learned about the local knowledge in Spanish. Through the exercise (see Figure 2.12), the teacher had a goal for the children to write a paragraph after making as many connections as they could to what they had learned from texts and the mothers' stories about their community.

Later during the same week, on another classroom exchange, children were required to write a short paragraph about connecting some festivity from home to some of the key vocabulary they had been learning that week in náhuatl. Since the key vocabulary the children needed to integrate was in náhuatl, the text written was guided by the teacher's instruction and vocabulary indicated on the board. The key vocabulary in Natalia's story was in náhuatl and it referred to Natalia's dad making some typical bread *(pantsin)* for a party *(iluitl),* which they make and eat together while also telling a story *(auilyejyeko)*. Natalia wrote her text and highlighted the words in náhuatl in red (this instructed by the teacher). (See Figure 2.13 below.)

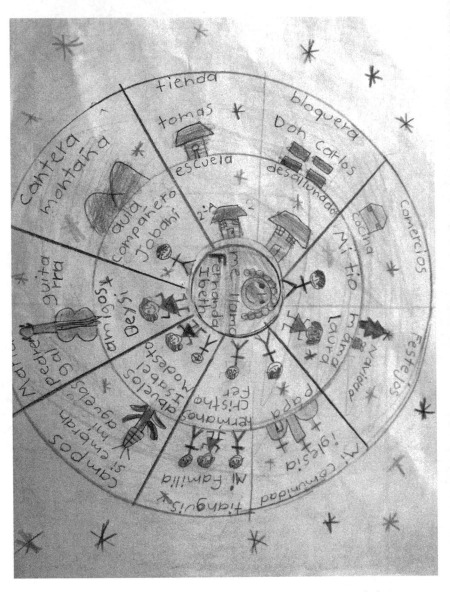

FIGURE 2.12 Natalia's Composing of Cultural and Community Knowledge as a Writing Exercise

Natalia writes about her dad Nicolás writing stories while also making this typical bread for the town festivities (text in Figure 2.13). Natalia pays close attention to writing conventions and follows instructions to highlight the words in náhuatl. A close analysis of the text shows that the base language is in Spanish while integrating náhuatl. The teacher emphasizes and plans for the key words

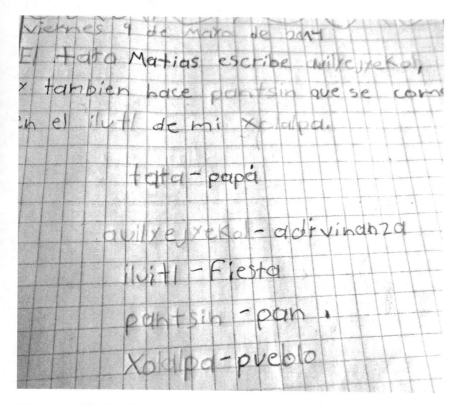

FIGURE 2.13 Natalia's Written Text in náhuatl and Spanish

in náhuatl as the words that make up the meaning of the text and story. This type of text integrates *interlanguage* as a strategy to support the biliteracy development of the child (Gort, 2012). Research from a sociolinguistic perspective indicates that interlanguage (or sometimes called code-switching) is also seen as a *practice*— a form of social action that emerges within particular local contexts (Blommaert, 2010; Martínez, 2010; Pennycook, 2010). The teacher embraces the use and mix of the two languages. This practice supports the development of biliteracy by particularly using Spanish as a linguistic base for the text, while supporting the learning and use of náhuatl as a heritage language.

Families' Language Perspectives and Bringing Local Knowledge into the Classroom

Through school gatherings and conversations during the Community Literacy Canasta project I was able to learn about the families' and parents' views about their beliefs, preferences, and motivations for maintaining the indigenous language, along with continuing developing bilingualism and multilingualism.[6] Parents who

chool meetings and the *Canasta talleres* generally are second- and third-
on *Mexicanos*—náhuatl native speakers. The grandparents overall are the
generation or the ones who continue to speak the indigenous language, and
parents are the generation who understand náhuatl but do not speak it as fluently
as the grandparents—these are the parents of the children attending the school.
Consequently, the new generation of young children (in preschool and
elementary) predominantly speaks Spanish and does not speak or understand any
more the indigenous native language of the grandparents and local community.
This situation motivated parents and teachers to plan and prepare a bilingual
curriculum infused with learning not only the indigenous language but also the
cultural knowledge and traditions of the community.

Parents valued and were concerned about the teaching standards of the school,
they expressed that teaching was good overall, and they engaged in conversations
with staff to learn if their children were in good academic standing. As for teaching
náhuatl at school, parents expressed and believed teachers must have specialized
knowledge and training, and when possible be native speakers of the náhuatl
language. A point of conflict here is that even when there was a strong commitment to support learning of the indigenous language, the parents did not
necessarily consider themselves bilinguals or as possessing the linguistic resources
to support their children's bilingualism at home. Therefore, they were strong
supporters of the school's curriculum and its initiative to bring náhuatl to the
classroom space. They shared that their children should not miss the stories of
their ancestors, because they wanted them to understand their roots, which, in
turn, could help shape the children's identity. Natalia's mom in particular argued
that if the school encourages its use it would open a space to share common
values—and also to reaffirm and greatly contribute to revitalize the náhuatl language
and culture locally.

Natalia's mom also shared that at home they supported bilingualism. They
had access to Spanish texts and reading materials, but the family's access to literacy
materials and tools in náhuatl was limited to short poems or narratives from the
text books sent by the school and provided by the Secretary of Indigenous
Education. The grandfather was the main source of oral náhuatl for Natalia;
however, geographical distance also limited the opportunities for Natalia to spend
time with her *Tata*. Both Natalia's mom and dad attended what in the US would
be the equivalent to junior high school, so that is another important factor that
shaped the literacy practices in their household by providing Natalia with support
in writing and reading when needed. Studies labeled "syncretic" demonstrate
how children actively learn within "simultaneous worlds" and that hybrid
transformations are translated and "negotiated re-creation(s) of cultural practices"
within activities (Reyes & Esteban-Guitart, 2013, p. 3). In this sense, Natalia's
experiences both at home and school shaped her knowledge and beliefs about
early writing experiences.

As part of this case study, I observed how Natalia negotiated between two worlds using "informal" knowledge of náhuatl, and the more "formal" linguistic sources of Spanish to construct meaning from written language. I observed that náhuatl, and Spanish, the former colonial language, coexisted in various spaces in the classroom. This was the case when Natalia used Spanish for writing as part of the classroom activity but switched to náhuatl for key words and for the theme of the story in the indigenous language. As in other communities where revitalization efforts are happening, there is a complex dynamic for the use of the languages. In this case study, Natalia was immersed in Spanish for most of their instruction; however, an ongoing positive shift toward the use of the oral and written náhuatl as part of her linguistic resources for learning is underway. The teacher in this school made a planned effort for linguistic and cultural knowledge in the indigenous language to be integrated in the classroom space, and parents, through their families' stories in Spanish and náhuatl, helped diffuse the cultural and space borders between home, school, and community to embrace a way of bilingualism and biliteracy for their young children.

★

Rafiki: A Teacher-Pupil

Esther Mukewa Lisanza

The case of Rafiki is drawn from a larger ethnographic study of language learning in a first grade classroom in Kenya, filled with 89 children from five to seven years old (Lisanza, 2011). The classroom was very crowded with desks, and only a single aisle for free movement. There were two female teachers; however, they were never in the classroom at the same time. They taught different subjects at different times. The chalkboard was their main teaching aid, as there was a significant shortage of literacy materials. The children stayed in this classroom throughout the day, although their teachers moved in and out of the room. This physical context greatly influenced classroom interactions and practices.

To help me tell the story of the studied classroom and, especially, its unappreciated language resources, I invite readers to meet Rafiki, one of the focal children in this study. Rafiki was a six-year-old boy and the only child in his family. His mother was an accountant at the community's coffee factory. His father was a high school teacher in one of the local schools. Rafiki liked playing with his friends in the playground. Not only was Rafiki social, but he was also very active in class. He was always among the very first children to complete his classwork. Moreover, he was also what was locally referred to as a "teacher-pupil." A teacher-pupil was a student who assisted his or her peers with schoolwork; in other words, he was a "more capable peer" (Vygotsky, 1978, p. 86). At home he had a few text books, storybooks, and wall charts. Thus, he practiced math problems and read the few books he had. Rafiki spoke Kamba and Swahili. At the time I met him, he was learning English at school as an additional language.

Rafiki's Institutional Context: The Language Policy

Rafiki attended a rural primary school in the Eastern province of Kenya. His school was a full primary school with grades 1–8. At the end of eight years, grade 8 candidates sat for a national examination known as Kenya Certificate of Primary Education (KCPE). The language of instruction in this school from grade 1–8 was English, except in Swahili classes where the language of instruction was Swahili. This school did not practice the national language policy, which stated that the language of the "catchment area" (i.e., the surrounding community) had to be used as a language of instruction in grades 1–3 (Ministry of Education, 2012). The language of the surrounding community where the children and their teachers came from was Kamba. Hence, according to the national language policy, the language of instruction in grades 1–3 would have been Kamba. However, this was not the case, and as a matter of fact, Kamba was banned in the school. Rafiki's school seemed to be in sync with many additional language programs, which believe that "language minority children must be exposed to great amounts of English to become proficient in that language. Moreover, instruction in the native language is considered a hindrance for the acquisition of English" (Soltero, 2004, p. 50). However, as second language learning research shows (Hudelson, 1987; Rymes & Anderson, 2004; Samway, 2006; Wu, 2008), a learner can apply the knowledge acquired in the mother tongue to learning the new language.

Rafiki's school bordered a shopping center and an African Inland Church. It is important to note that there were other churches within the community too. Rafiki, his schoolmates, and their teachers belonged to one of these churches. The children attended Sunday school every week. The children also attended devotion on Thursday afternoon at the African Inland Church. The reason why the children attended Thursday devotion at the African Inland Church and not any other church was because their school had a long history with the church. First and foremost, the African Inland Mission started this school in 1930. The school remained under the ownership and sponsorship of the African Inland Mission until independence from Britain in 1963 when the government took ownership. However, the African Inland Mission, now the African Inland Church, has remained its spiritual sponsor. Besides going to church on Sunday and Thursday for spiritual nourishment, the children had also spiritual nourishment every Monday and Friday morning, when there was an assembly for the entire school. During the assembly, there was singing of gospel songs, reading of the Bible, and praying. These activities were conducted in English or Swahili. Thus, it is not surprising that themes related to church resurfaced quite often during unofficial play and writing time. At the Sunday schools, the children used Kamba and a little bit of Swahili. In the African Inland Church, the devotion was conducted in Swahili only.

In their homes and the market, the children spoke Kamba and sometimes Swahili. I did not hear any child speak English at the market or in the homes I visited. Nonetheless, Rafiki and his classmates were forced by the school administration to speak in either Swahili or English at school. However, on July 2nd, 2010, the school introduced a school policy that banned Swahili in grades 4–8 beyond the Swahili classes. This school policy was passed while the current project was going on at Rafiki's school. Kamba had already been banned at this school many years back, before Rafiki started attending school.

In Rafiki's English language and content classes, the language of instruction and that of the text book was English. This English-only language policy, just like the classroom's physical context, had a big influence on how instruction and learning were done in Rafiki's English classroom.

Furthermore, Rafiki's primary school was an examination-driven school, like all schools in Kenya. The students at Rafiki's school took commercially prepared examinations in English at the end of the month and at the end of every term (i.e., semester). This school seemed to support behavioristic approaches in the way they reinforced good performance or punished poor performance on examinations. The teacher with the best mean score in his or her teaching subject was rewarded with money. Also, the class whose overall mean score was the highest in the school was rewarded with candy. In addition, the three top students in their classes were also rewarded with candy. These rewards were seen as a motivation for working hard and doing well. Therefore, on one hand the teachers in this school worked very hard to ensure that their students did well on the examinations, and on the other hand the students worked tirelessly to perform well on the examinations. In fact, the students who performed below the pass mark (which was 265 out of 400) were punished through smacking their bottoms or hitting their hands with a cane. These students were punished in the hope that it would force them to work harder and do well on the exams.

Consequently, because Rafiki's English teacher knew that her performance and that of her students was assessed through exams, drilling dominated classroom interactions and practices. The teacher drilled the students in an effort to make sure that when the same elements appeared on the examinations, the students would be able to recall them. This kind of exam drilling promoted rote learning. Oral skills were not tested in exams and, therefore, the teacher did not put much emphasis on speaking but on reading and structured writing, which would help the students in answering exam questions.

Thus, in addition to the influence the English-only language policy and the physical context had on teaching and learning, examinations had an important effect on instruction and learning as well. Teaching and learning practices were guided by what the exams tested. In fact, sometimes the teacher reviewed past examination papers in preparation for the end of the month and end of term examinations. Since examination questions required remembering the correct answers and generally did not require understanding basic principles, these examinations seemed not to provide the teacher with an adequate incentive for teaching the students the understanding of what they were learning. In addition, grammar examination questions may have further reduced the likelihood that instruction would include detailed explanations of important concepts. With this background, I now turn to the official and unofficial writing curriculum in Rafiki's classroom.

The Official Writing Curriculum

According to the National Syllabus (Kenya Institute of Education, 2006), "By the end of the first three years, the learner should have acquired a sufficient command of vocabulary and the language patterns, to be able to use English as a medium of instruction in upper primary" (p. 4). Thus, the national expectation of using English as a medium of instruction in upper primary forces some schools like Rafiki's to start teaching English from grade 1. This is because of the belief that mother tongue is a hindrance to English learning. Concerning writing skills, the National Syllabus states, "Specifically, the learner should acquire writing skills to be able to express own feelings and ideas meaningfully and legibly in correct English structure" (p. 4). Some of the specific writing objectives for grade one from the National Syllabus include:

- writing letters of the alphabet clearly and correctly
- writing patterns clearly and correctly
- writing names of objects
- drawing patterns and items
- writing simple sentences about things
- writing simple sentences to describe things
- using grammatical elements correctly
- writing legibly and neatly.

Therefore, writing evaluation criterion in this grade 1 classroom was supposed to be based on the above expectations. However, there was also another expectation for this grade 1 classroom, which is captured by the quote below from my interview with the school principal:

> By third term we expect pupils to read by themselves.
>
> (The Principal, Kalimani Primary School)

The above school expectation seemed to overshadow the national writing curriculum. Every effort was geared toward knowing how to read. Also, given that English tests were grammar based, writing practices in the classroom were controlled by this factor too. In addition, due to the shortage of literacy materials and the English-only policy, the daily official writing practices in Rafiki's classroom were instantiated by copying words and sentences off the chalkboard and filling in blanks; there was no text content created by children during official times. Thus, the values and beliefs that undergirded these writing practices, and what it meant to learn written language in Rafiki's classroom, did not value child-invented content. Rafiki and his peers were to use writing to practice reading and grammar and thereby pass tests and cover the national syllabus.

As already stated, the emphasis on exams in the Kenyan system of education played a major role in determining how writing was done in this classroom. As a matter of fact, everything done in the classroom was geared toward performing well on the examination. If knowledge was not to be tested in an exam, then it was not worthy of being taught and learnt in class. This is why non-examinable subjects (e.g., creative arts and mother tongue) were not taught in Rafiki's classroom. Furthermore, as mentioned already, a shortage of text books and other literacy materials played a major role in determining what was done in Rafiki's classroom. The children had to copy the teacher's written words and sentences from the board and into their notebooks/exercise books because of the shortage of text books. Also, the children were only supposed to speak and write in English (except during their daily Swahili class). This was a challenge, because their English was limited and there was no space for them to speak in Kamba or Swahili. The fact that the children's linguistic repertoires were not nourished in the English classroom led to very minimal use of language in the classroom. Their Kamba and Swahili voices were silenced during English lessons; this silencing of their multilingualism as a resource influenced classroom writing practices. Hence, copying and filling in blanks from the blackboard marked the children's English writing. This kind of transmission of knowledge did not encourage creativity. As Freire (1970) states, "The student records, memorizes and repeats these phrases without perceiving what these statements mean" (p. 71). For instance, sometimes students copied words from the text or chalkboard without understanding what they meant. Needless to say, there was a necessity to encourage creativity in writing, beyond recording and memorizing. However, with constrained physical conditions (i.e., a lack of literacy materials and an overcrowded classroom), a language policy that emphasized use of English only, and a context that emphasized passing of exams and covering of the national syllabus, these practices were unavoidable in Rafiki's classroom.

Therefore, looking at the official writing curriculum, it seems that the enacted curriculum did not provide insights into children's personal experiences, identities, and imagination. Neither were children's voices heard in this official writing. Even though Rafiki's English teacher, Mrs. Simba, did not encourage classroom talk during her class time, this did not stop the children from talking to each other when they copied or answered questions off board. In the following extract, Rafiki plays his role as a teacher-pupil when his two peers, Mbula and Kasuku, ask for his help. This talk took place when Mrs. Simba was at her desk grading children's work. This excerpt illustrates how talk supported official writing activities in this classroom even without the teacher's knowledge. The children were doing the following filling-in-the blank exercise which had been copied on the board by Mrs. Simba from the text book under the theme "around us." The exercise was to test the children's understanding of things around them.

1. Drinking water makes us _____ (healthy, sick)
2. We wash fruits to make them _____ (clean, dirty)
3. We smell with our _____ (mouth, nose)
4. We have _____ senses
5. We sweep with a _____

The following was the talk that ensued as the children did the above exercise. Rafiki and his friends were speaking in Swahili only, although the language of the text was in English.

Mbula: *Rafiki hii tunafanya nini?* [Rafiki, what are we doing here?] (she points at the first blank: Drinking water makes us _____)

Rafiki: *Unaandika sentensi na* answer [You write down the sentence and the answer].

Mbula: (to Kasuku in a singing tone) *Nimeelezewa na Rafiki* [I was explained to by Rafiki].

Kasuku [asks Rafiki]: Number four *tunafanyaje?* [What are we doing in number four?]

Rafiki: *Unahesabu* [You count]. (he points to his eye, ear, tongue, hand, nose as he counts in English) One, two, three, four, five. *Ni tano* [It's five].

Kasuku: *Nitahesabu* [I will count]. (she points to her eye, ear, tongue, hand, nose as she counts in English) One, two, three, four, five.

Rafiki [to Kasuku]: *Number two umeandika nini?* [What's your answer to number two?]

Kasuku: Clean.

Rafiki: *Ndio* [Yes].

Mbula: *Niko* [I'm on] number three.

Rafiki: *Hata mimi* [Me too].

Kasuku: *Niko* number five. *Nikungojee?* [I'm on number five. May I wait for you?]

Rafiki: *Ndio* [Yes].

Kasuku: *Nikungojee sana?* [Should I wait for you longer?]

Rafiki: *Hapana. Mimi niko* number five *sasa* [No. I'm on number five now].

Mbula: *Rafiki mimi niko* number *hii* [Rafiki, I'm on this number]. (she points to number five)

Rafiki and Kasuku: (read number five together) We sweep with, *ni* [it's] broom, *ni* [it's] broom.

(Rafiki takes his work for grading, and so do the other children)

The above interaction illustrates that print and talk cannot be separated when studying children's written language development. As Dyson (1993b) observed, "Children's writing cannot be studied separately from their talk" (p. 78). Thus, although the children were filling in the blanks, "they could not resist talking to each other, and in the process they built their relationships as [English] learners" (Lisanza, 2014, p. 132). Additionally, the children manipulated words (Dyson, 2003). However, this manipulation of words could not have been possible for Kasuku and Mbula if they had not received help from Rafiki through talk. Thus, through a capable peer's assistance, official writing was successful. Join me in the next subsection as I delve deeper into the unofficial world of Rafiki and his friends and show how these children were able to incorporate play and multilingualism in their school lives, despite constraining conditions.

The Unofficial Writing Curriculum

> It is lunchtime. Some children are eating their lunch under the shade of the big fig tree beside the classroom, while others are eating inside the classroom. Rafiki is one of the children eating inside the classroom. Rafiki pours his rice on a saucer and begins singing, "Happy birthday to you." Chiriku who is seated next to him joins in the singing. Both children sing, "Happy birthday to you, happy birthday to you. How old are you now?" The singing stops suddenly and the two children start eating. After a while their friend, Kasuku, enters the classroom and Rafiki sings to Kasuku, "Happy birthday to you Kasuku." Mutua and Chiriku join in the singing, "Happy birthday to you Kasuku." Kasuku smiles and the play continues with each child who enters the classroom being sung to.

Any school program that values childhood and schooling must pay attention to what children are saying and doing. It was from such moments as the one captured in the above vignette that I realized children are not just consumers of knowledge but also creators of knowledge. I therefore invite readers to join me as I venture into the unofficial world of these Kenyan children and see what they were able to do with the resources at their disposal during their free time. These resources included their multilingualism, their talking, their singing and dancing, and their drawing, among other things. Although Rafiki and his peers spent a good chunk of writing time copying words and sentences off board, as they wrote I could hear them singing church songs quietly in Kamba or Swahili, pop songs in Swahili, or reciting English rhymes. Also, during school breaks, I could see Rafiki and the other children drawing, printing text, and singing. For instance in the following extract, Rafiki had just completed copying sentences from the chalkboard, and he began speaking quietly with his friends, who had also completed copying. In the process of their talking, there was drawing and singing going on quietly. This excerpt illustrates Rafiki's agency with his peers in their learning. When the following episode took place, the teacher was at her table assessing students' work:

Rafiki: (sees a dove by the door and says so tenderly in a low voice in Kamba)
    Kavuli, kavuli [A little dove, a little dove].
Amani: (she is seated next to Rafiki and sings in a low voice in Kamba)
    Kavuli tii tii ti,
    Kavuli tii tii ti.
Titu: (he is also seated close to Rafiki and sings in a low voice to Rafiki in English)
    Winner, winner
    Jesus you're a winner
    Battle you've won forever

(Rafiki smiles. He sees some space in his exercise book and begins drawing quietly when all of a sudden Amani begins singing the following Swahili pop song and Titu and Rafiki join in as well, although Rafiki keeps on drawing)

Mtoto ni mtoto [A child is a child]
Mawe ni mawe [stones are stones]
Tuliona wengi [we have seen many]
Mtoto ni mtoto [a child is a child]
Shikamoo, Marahaba ("Shikamoo, Marahaba" is a greeting which shows respect; the child greets an elder "Shikamoo," and the elder responds "Marahaba")

(Kambua, a very soft-spoken girl who is seated next to the three children, stands up and shakes her body vigorously, enjoying the song as she takes her book for grading)
(Mhariri also stands up and shakes her body as well)

Children: (some children laugh and say in Swahili)
Anajifunza dansi [She is learning how to dance].

During the above interaction, Rafiki did the drawing in Figure 2.14:

FIGURE 2.14 Rafiki's Monster Drawing

The following was the story behind the drawing. Rafiki narrated this story in Swahili:

> The vehicle [points] is going to Mombasa. It is carrying people. And the monster [points] wants to get in and bite them.

In the above extract, Rafiki drew, talked, and sang with his peers, while Kambua and Mhariri had an opportunity to dance. Through the children's talk, different identities resurfaced. These included that of Kamba speakers; for example, Rafiki called a dove "*Kavuli*" in Kamba language and Amani sang a Kamba song, "*Kavuli tii tii ti.*" The identities of the children as churchgoers and as English learners were revealed through the song "Jesus You Are a Winner." This song, which Titu sang, was a very popular song in the churches in this community. In addition, Rafiki and his friends sang a Swahili song, "*Mtoto ni mtoto,*" which was a popular Swahili song on the radio at their homes. Hence, their identities as Swahili speakers and learners and radio listeners were exposed.

This excerpt thus illustrates the agency of these children in their language learning. They were able to make use of many resources that were at their disposal. These resources were talking, singing, drawing, dancing, and their multilingualism. These resources supported their language learning. As a matter of fact, these familiar resources made the children's language-learning experience sensible. Also, the singing, talking, drawing, and dancing nourished the children's relationships with each other. They laughed with each other, smiled, and talked to each other.

Hence, for these children, meaning was built by drawing, singing, dancing, and talking; they used these media to construct mental and social models of their experiences, to make the world they lived in sensible (Gallas, 1994; Genishi & Fassler, 1999). For instance, Rafiki's drawn story was a construction of his imagination as a child in this particular classroom. This extract also illustrates that the children learned language through listening and interacting with people in their community, for instance, through songs in the church and on the radio. Children's words were thus "borrowed" from the people around them (Bakhtin, 1986, p. 92). Finally, children's relationships were important as they learned language (Dyson, 2003) in the classroom. They needed each other's support in their learning. It is also important to note that although Rafiki's school had banned Kamba use in the school, the children were able to smuggle Kamba in through music. Thus, though the adult world may ban children's resources, like their first languages, children will always have a way to reclaim what is truly theirs.

Rafiki and his peers not only drew and sang, but also composed stories in writing. Often these stories were written in Swahili. Rafiki wrote the story below after missing school for four days because he was sick. When he wrote this story, he was seated next to Chiriku. He did not say a word till he was done writing.

Mimi ni li kuwa mungonjwa
ni li enda shuleni siku monja
Leo ni me letwe shuleni na gari
na ni lala kitanda ya juu na
mtoto wetu aka kunja aka ni ita
tuka kula chakula nani ka ku
nywa dawa nili tapika.

Here is the English translation, with punctuation for easy reading:

I was sick. I attended school for one day. Today I was brought to school by a car. I slept on the upper bed. Our child came to call me. We ate food. And I took medicine, and I vomited.

Rafiki composed the story, which was based on his experience of being sick. Through Rafiki's writing, as readers, we get to know more about his family; for example, that he was the only child. In fact, when he read this story aloud, I asked him who was this other child in the story and he told me it was his cousin. It is interesting that he did not use the term cousin in his writing, but he called him "our child." This was his young cousin and, therefore, their child. So, through Rafiki's writing we also learn something about family relations in his community. Further, Rafiki informed his readers that he had a bunk bed. Besides writing in Swahili, Rafiki also wrote in English. For example, he wrote down the following English poem that he had recited in nursery school the previous year:

AAd one ngi mbailust micholling my bed
I Avali to bed gasi fomi mam's
To bick foriti dad's to bick foriti
dursi I yavali to bed dursi
Pusi gasi fomi
Pap's gasi fomi
Is gasi fomi thegiu

The above poem is provided below with conventional spelling and punctuation:

Class one thousand and one G, by Lucy Misieni

MY BED

I have a little bed, just for me, just for me
Mummy is too big for it, Daddy is too big for it
Do you see? I have a little bed, do you see?
Pussy is too small for it, puppy is too small for it
Do you see? Just for me. Thank you.

This example illustrates one of Rafiki's experiences in preschool. Therefore, his experience as a preschooler was used as a resource in his writing. Rafiki also made use of his Swahili spelling knowledge as a resource in writing down this English poem. For example, "for me" he wrote as *fomi*, "for it" as *foriti*, "pussy" as *pusi*, and "thank you" as *thegiu*.

Therefore, looking at the unofficial writing practices in Rafiki's classroom, it turns out these are important practices that can be explored to support official writing. Children's talk, singing, and even dancing are all symbolic tools that can support children's writing. Free writing itself must be encouraged because it helps nourish the imagination of children and also serves as a record of their daily experiences at home, school, and in the community. Finally, capable peers like Rafiki are themselves a resource for language classes.

Conclusion

As I have shown in my discussion of official writing instruction, conventional English language writing practices predominantly involved copying off the chalkboard and filling in blanks. These practices did not provide insights into the children's personal experiences, identities, and imagination as did the unofficial practices. Also, the unofficial practices provided an opening into the children's "spontaneous concept development" (Vygotsky, 1962, p. 84) in a way that the English classroom's conventional practices did not. In addition, through the unofficial curriculum, Rafiki and his classmates had agency in their language and literacy development.

So, despite the existence of 89 children in an overcrowded classroom with few literacy materials, a curriculum that emphasized passing tests and speaking English only, the potential existed in the children's unofficial writing for multilingual play, talk, and singing, all of which were potential resources for children's official writing.

★

Toward Knitting Together Tangled Cases

Anne Haas Dyson

As we begin to unpack notes from our journey, our heads may be spinning; the details of each case may be tangled haphazardly, like loose cords from assorted devices at the bottom of a bag. Some members of the research team felt like this before we began to untangle the cases and knit them together thematically.

The power of case studies, after all, is to provide material with which abstract phenomena can be made concrete so that they can be not only talked about but used to better understand some aspect of the human experience (Geertz, 1973). Herein, the goal is to situate relevant abstractions—agency and cultural resources, along with identity and power—in the particular actions of children responding to the possibilities and constraints of their educational sites. Thus articulated, we as educators should gain insight into the social, cultural, and institutional factors that differentially allow children to build on what they know and, thereby, to make sense—and use—of a potentially powerful communicative tool, written language.

So we now move on to our official detanglers, the chapter authors who draw on our collective efforts to knit thematic quilts from the case studies of the children we have come to know.

Notes

1   In the reading scheme being used in Gareth's case, "Fred talk" means "sound out."
2   Educational Leadership and Turnaround Literacy Pedagogies is an Australian Research Council (ARC) Linkage Project (No. LP120100714) between the University of South Australia and the South Australian Department for Education and Child Development (DECD). The Project was undertaken between 2012 and 2014. The chief investigators are Robert Hattam (University of South Australia), Barbara Comber (Queensland University of Technology), and Deb Hayes (University of Sydney). The research associate is Lyn Kerkham (University of South Australia). In the course of this study both Barbara Comber and Lyn Kerkham have observed Gus and spoken with his teachers.
3   The Royal Adelaide Show is an annual event that attracts large crowds of city people. As well as displays of an agricultural and horticultural nature, there are sideshow rides and amusements.
4   Celia Genishi is most grateful for the collaboration while they were at Teachers College, Columbia University, of Ariela Zycherman, University of Illinois at Chicago; Lorraine Falchi, La Escuelita, New York, NY; and Ysaaca Axelrod, the University of Massachusetts, Amherst; for the generosity of the administration and staff of the Head Start program and public school where data were collected; and for the valued support of the Teachers College Dean's Grant for Tenured Faculty.
5   The case of Miguel draws on sections of Falchi, L. T., Axelrod, Y., & Genishi, C. (2014). "*Miguel es un artista*"—and Luisa is an excellent student: Seeking time and space for children's multimodal practices. *Journal of Early Childhood Literacy* 14(3), 345–366.

Toward the end of the academic year there was discussion for a multilingual program initiative to support English development as well for children of returning immigrants from the US; however, the emphasis at the time of writing Natalia's case continues to be Spanish and náhuatl.

References

Adair, J. (2014). Agency and expanding capabilities in early grade classrooms: What it could mean for young children. *Harvard Educational Review, 84*, 217–242.

Azuara, P. (2009). *Literacy practices in a changing cultural context: The literacy development of two emergent Mayan-Spanish bilingual children* (unpublished doctoral dissertation). University of Arizona, Tucson, AZ.

Bakhtin, M. (1986). *Speech genres and other late essays*. Austin, TX: University of Texas Press.

Barrs, M. (1988). Maps of play. In M. Meek and C. Mills (Eds.), *Language and literacy in the primary school* (pp. 101–112). London: Falmer Press.

Bassok, D., & Rorem, A. (2012). *Is kindergarten the new first grade? The changing nature of kindergarten in the age of accountability*. Working paper. University of Virginia-Charlottesville (cited with permission).

Bhabha, H. (2004). *The location of culture*. New York, NY: Routledge.

Blommaert, J. (2005). *Discourse: A critical introduction*. New York, NY: Cambridge University Press.

Blommaert, J. (2010). *The sociolinguistics of globalization*. Cambridge, MA: Cambridge University Press.

Bomer, R., Dworin, J. E., May, L., & Semingson, P. (2008). Miseducating teachers about the poor: A critical analysis of Ruby Payne's claim about poverty. *Teachers College Record, 110*, 2497–2531.

Briggs, C. L., & Bauman, R. (1992). Genre, intertextuality, and social power. *Journal of Linguistic Anthropology, 2*, 131–172.

Brown, C. (2013). Reforming preschool to ready children for academic achievement: A case study of the impact of pre-K reform on the issue of school readiness. *Early Education and Development, 24*, 554–573.

Bruner, J. S. (1990). *Acts of meaning*. Cambridge, MA: Harvard University Press.

Calkins, L. (2003). *Units of study for primary writing: A yearlong curriculum*. Portsmouth, NH: FirstHand.

Campano, G., Ghiso, M., Yee, M., & Pantoja, A. (2013). Toward community research and coalitional literacy practices for educational justice. *Language Arts, 90*, 314–326.

Cazden, C. B. (2001). *Classroom discourse: The language of teaching and learning*. Portsmouth, NH: Heinemann.

Clark, M. M. (2014). *Learning to be literate: Insights from research for policy and practice*. Birmingham, England: Glendale Education.

Clay, M. (2000). *Running records for classroom teachers*. Auckland, New Zealand: Heinemann.

Cohen, M. (1996). *Fashioning masculinity: National identity and language in the eighteenth century*. London, England: Routledge.

Comber, B. (2014). School literate repertoires: That was then, this is now. *Learning and Literacy, 11*, 16–31.

Comber, B. (2015). School literate repertoires: That was then, this is now. In J. Rowsell & J. Sefton-Green (Eds.), *Revisiting learning lives—longitudinal perspectives on researching learning and literacy* (pp. 16–31). New York, NY: Routledge.

Comber, B., Badger, L., Barnett, J., Nixon, H., & Pitt, J. (2002). Literacy after the early years: A longitudinal study. *Australian Journal of Language and Literacy, 25,* 9–23.

Comber, B., & Kamler, B. (2004). Getting out of deficit: Pedagogies of reconnection. *Teaching Education, 15,* 293–310.

Comber, B., & Kamler, B. (2005). *Turn-around pedagogies: Literacy interventions for at-risk students.* Newtown, Australia: Primary English Teaching Association.

Corsaro, W. (2011). *The sociology of childhood, third edition.* Thousand Oaks, CA: Pine Forge Press.

Department for Education (2014). *Early years foundation stage profile.* Retrieved from: https://www.gov.uk/government/uploads/system/uploads/attachment_data/file/30125 6/2014_EYFS_handbook.pdf.

Derewianka, B. (1990). *Exploring how texts work.* Sydney, Australia: Primary English Teaching Association.

Devereux, E., Haynes, A., & Power, M. J. (2011). Tarring everyone with the same shorthand? Journalists, stigmatization and social exclusion. *Journalism: Theory, Practice and Criticism, 13*(4), 500–517.

Dewayani, S. (2011). *Stories of the intersection: Indonesian "street children" negotiating narratives at the intersection of society, childhood, and work* (unpublished doctoral dissertation). University of Illinois, Urbana-Champaign, IL.

Dutro, E., & Selland, M. (2012). "I like to read, but I know I'm not good at it": Children's perspectives on high-stakes testing in a high poverty school. *Curriculum Inquiry, 4,* 340–367.

Dutro, E., Selland, M., & Bien, A. (2013). Revealing writing, concealing writers: High-stakes assessment in an urban elementary classroom. *Journal of Literacy Research, 45,* 99–141.

Dworin, J. (2003). Examining children's biliteracy in the classroom. In A. I. Willis, G. E. Garcia, R. Barrera, & V. J. Harris (Eds.), *Multicultural issues in literacy research and practice* (pp. 29–48). Mahwah, NJ: Lawrence Erlbaum.

Dyson, A. Haas (1990). Symbol makers, symbol weavers: How children link play, pictures, and print. *Young Children, 45,* 50–57.

Dyson, A. Haas (1991). The word and the world: Reconceptualising written language development, or, do rainbows mean a lot to little girls? *Research in the Teaching of English, 25,* 97–123.

Dyson, A. Haas (1993a). *Negotiating a permeable curriculum: On literacy, diversity, and the interplay of children's and teachers' worlds.* Urbana, IL: National Council of Teachers of English.

Dyson, A. Haas (1993b). *Social worlds of children learning to write in an urban primary school.* New York, NY: Teachers College Press.

Dyson, A. Haas (1994). "I'm gonna express myself": The politics of story in the children's worlds. In A. H. Dyson & C. Genishi (Eds.), *The need for story: Cultural diversity in classroom and community* (pp. 155–171). Urbana, IL: National Council of Teachers of English.

Dyson, A. Haas (1997). *Writing superheroes: Contemporary childhood, popular culture, and classroom literacy.* New York, NY: Teachers College Press.

Dyson, A. Haas (2003). *The brothers and sisters learn to write: Popular literacies in childhood and school cultures.* New York, NY: Teachers College Press.

Dyson, A. Haas (2008). Staying in the (curricular) lines: Practice constraints and possibilities in childhood writing. *Written Communication, 25,* 119–159.

Dyson, A. Haas (2013). *ReWRITING the basics: Literacy learning in children's cultures.* New York, NY: Teachers College Press.

Dyson, A. Haas (2015). The search for inclusion: Deficit discourse and the erasure of childhoods. *Language Arts, 92*, 199–207.

Emerson, R., Fretz, R., & Shaw, L. (2011). *Writing ethnographic fieldnotes* (2nd ed.). Chicago, IL: University of Chicago Press.

Falchi, L. T. (2011). *Emergent bilinguals: Multiple literacies in changing contexts* (unpublished doctoral dissertation). Teachers College, Columbia University, New York, NY.

Falchi, L. T., Axelrod, Y., & Genishi, C. (2014). *"Miguel es un artista"*—and Luisa is an excellent student: Seeking time and space for children's multimodal practices. *Journal of Early Childhood Literacy, 14*, 345–366.

Fisher, T., Albers, P., & Frederick, T. (2014). When pictures aren't pretty: Deconstructing punitive literacy practices. *Journal of Early Childhood Literacy, 14*, 291–318.

Fountas, I. C., & Pinnell, G. S. (1996). *Guided reading*. Portsmouth, NH: Heinemann.

Fountas, I. C., & Pinnell, G. S. (2006). *Leveled books (K–8): Matching texts to readers for effective teaching*. Portsmouth, NH: Heinemann.

Freebody, P. (2003). *Qualitative research in education: Interaction and practice*. London, England: Sage Publications.

Freire, P. (1970). *Pedagogy of the oppressed*. New York, NY: Continuum.

Gallas, K. (1994). *The language of learning: How children talk, write, dance, draw, and sing their understanding of the world*. New York, NY: Teachers College Press.

Garcia, O., Kleifgen, J., & Falchi, L. (2008). *Equity perspectives: From English language learners to emergent bilinguals*. Retrieved from Teachers College, Columbia University, Campaign for Educational Equity: http://www.equitycampaign.org/i/a/document/6468_Ofelia_ELL__Final.pdf.

Geertz, C. (1973). *The interpretation of cultures*. New York, NY: Basic Books.

Genishi, C., & Dyson, A. Haas (2009). *Children, language, and literacy: Diverse learners in diverse times*. New York, NY: Teachers College Press and Washington, DC: National Association for the Education of Young Children.

Genishi, C., & Fassler, K. (1999). Oral language in the early childhood curriculum: Building on diverse foundations. In C. Seefeldt (Ed.), *The early childhood curriculum: A review of current research* (2nd ed.) (pp. 54–79). New York, NY: Teachers College Press.

Gort, M. (2012). Code-switching patterns in the writing-related talk of young emergent bilinguals. *Journal of Literacy Research, 44*, 45–75.

Graue, B. (2006). The answer is readiness—Now what is the question? *Early Education and Development, 17*, 43–56.

Gunter, H. M., & Mills, C. (2014, September). *Exploring and theorising consultants and consultancy in contemporary English schooling*. Paper presented at the Policy and Politics Conference, Bristol, England.

Hohmann, M., Banet, B., & Weikart, D. (1979). *Young children in action*. Ypsilanti, MI: High/Scope Press.

Hudelson, S. (1987). The role of native language literacy in the education of language minority children. *Language Arts, 64*, 827–841.

Kenya Institute of Education (2006). *English Primary Syllabus*. Nairobi, Kenya: KIE.

Kerkham, L., & Hutchison, K. (2005). Principles, possibilities and practices: Making the difference. In B. Comber & B. Kamler (Eds.), *Turn-around pedagogies: Literacy interventions for at-risk students* (pp. 109–123). Newtown, Australia: Primary English Teaching Association.

Kindig, J. (2012). *Choosing to read: Connecting middle schoolers to books*. Portsmouth, NH: Heinemann.

Kupchick, A., & Catlaw, T. (2015). Discipline and participation: The long-term effects of suspension and school security on the political and civic engagements of youth. *Youth & Society*, 47, 95–124.

Lindfors, J. W. (1999). *Children's inquiry: Using language to make sense of the world*. New York, NY: Teachers College Press.

Lisanza, E. M. (2011). *What does it mean to learn oral and written English language: A case study of a rural Kenyan classroom* (unpublished doctoral dissertation). University of Illinois, Urbana-Champaign, IL.

Lisanza, E. M. (2014). Dialogic instruction and learning: The case of one Kiswahili classroom. *Language, Culture, & Curriculum Journal*, 27, 121–135.

Lloyd, S., & Wernham, S. (1992). *The phonics handbook*. Chigwell, England: Jolly Learning Ltd.

Marsh, J. (2003). One-way traffic? Connections between literacy practices at home and in the nursery. *British Educational Research Journal*, 29, 369–382.

Marsh, J. (2013). Early literacy and popular culture. In J. Larson and J. Marsh (Eds.), *Handbook of early childhood literacy* (2nd ed.) (pp. 207–222). Thousand Oaks, CA: Sage.

Marsh, J. (2014a). The relationship between online and offline play. In A. Burn & C. Richards (Eds.), *Children's games in the new media age: Childlore, media and the playground* (pp. 109–131). London, England: Ashgate.

Marsh, J. (2014b). The discourses of celebrity in the fanvid ecology of Club Penguin machinima. In R. H. Jones, A. Chik, & C. A. Hafner (Eds.), *Discourse and digital practices: Doing discourse analysis in the digital age* (pp. 193–208). New York, NY: Routledge.

Marsh, J. (2014c). From the wild frontier of Davy Crockett to the wintery fiords of Frozen: Changes in media consumption, play and literacy from 1950s to the 2010s. *International Journal of Play*, 3, 267–279.

Marsh, J. (2015). "Unboxing" videos: Co-construction of the child as cyberflâneur. *Discourse: Studies in the Cultural Politics of Education*. Published online ahead of print June 25, 2015, doi: 10.1080/01596306.2015.1041457

Marsh, J., & Bishop, J. C. (2014). *Changing play: Play, media, and commercial culture from the 1950s to the present day*. Maidenhead, England: Open University Press.

Marsh, J., Hannon, P., Lewis, M., & Ritchie, L. (2015). Young children's initiation into family literacy practices in the digital age. *Journal of Early Childhood Literacy*. Published online before print June 8, 2015, doi: 10.1177/1476718X15582095

Martínez, R. A. (2010). Spanglish as literacy tool: Toward an understanding of the potential role of Spanish-English code-switching in the development of academic literacy. *Research in the Teaching of English*, 45, 124–149.

Martínez-Roldán, C., & Sayer, P. (2006). Reading through linguistic borderlands: Latino students' transactions with narrative texts. *Journal of Early Childhood Literacy*, 6, 293–322.

Massey, D. (2005). *For space*. Los Angeles, CA: Sage.

McNaughton, S. (2011). *Designing better schools for culturally and linguistically diverse children: A science of performance model for research*. New York, NY: Routledge.

Miller, P. J. (1979). *Amy, Wendy, and Beth: Learning language in South Baltimore*. Austin, TX: The University of Texas Press.

Mills, M. (2003). Shaping the boys' agenda: The backlash blockbusters. *International Journal of Inclusive Education*, 7, 57–73.

Ministry of Education, Task Force on the Re-alignment of the Education Sector to the Constitution of Kenya 2010 (2012). *Towards a globally competitive quality education for sustaining development*. Retrieved from http://www.vision2030.go.ke/cms/vds/Task_Force_Final_Report_Feb_20123.pdf.

Moll, L. C., Amanti, C., Neff, D., & Gonzalez, N. (1992). Funds of knowledge for teaching: Using a qualitative approach to connect homes and classrooms. *Theory and Practice, 31*, 132–141.

Nelson, K. (2007). *Young minds in social worlds: Experience, meaning, and memory*. Cambridge, MA: Harvard University Press.

New York State Education Department (2011). *New York state prekindergarten foundation for the Common Core*. Retrieved from http://www.p12.nysed.gov/ciai/common_core_ standards/pdfdocs/nyslsprek.pdf.

Ofcom (2015). *Children and parents: Media use and attitudes report*. London, England: Office of Communications. Retrieved from http://stakeholders.ofcom.org.uk/binaries/ research/media-literacy/children-parents-nov-15/childrens_parents_nov2015.pdf.

Paley, V. G. (1997). *The girl with the brown crayon: How children use stories to shape their lives*. Cambridge, MA: Harvard University Press.

Parkes, B. (1997). *Who's in the shed?* Pelham, NY: Benchmark Education Company.

Pennycook, A. (2010). *Language as a local practice*. New York, NY: Routledge.

Permentier, M., van Ham, M., & Bolt, G. (2009). Neighbourhood reputation and the intention to leave the neighbourhood. *Environment and Planning A, 41*, 2162–2180.

Peterson, S. S., & Parr, J. M. (2012). Gender and literacy issues and research: Placing the spotlight on writing. *Journal of Writing Research, 3*, 151–161.

Potter, J. (2012). *Digital media and learner identity: The new curatorship*. New York, NY: Palgrave Macmillan.

Precey, M. (2014, March 7). Minecraft gamer's YouTube hit more popular than Bieber's. *BBC News Hampshire*. Retrieved from http://www.bbc.co.uk/news/uk-england- hampshire-26327661.

Reyes, I. (2012). Biliteracy among children and youth. *Reading Research Quarterly, 47*, 307–327.

Reyes, I., & Esteban-Guitart, M. (2013). Exploring multiple literacies from homes and communities: A cross-cultural comparative analysis. In K. Hall, T. Cremin, B. Comber, & L.C. Moll (Eds.), *International handbook of research on children's literacy, learning, and culture* (pp. 155–171). Hoboken, NJ: Wiley-Blackwell.

Ricouer, P. (1981). *Hermeneutics & the human sciences*. Cambridge, MA: Cambridge University Press.

Robertson, R. (1995). Glocalization: Time-space and homogeneity-heterogeneity. In M. Featherstone, S. Lash, & R. Robertson (Eds.), *Global modernities* (pp. 25–44). London, England: Sage.

Rogoff, B. (2003). *The cultural nature of human development*. New York, NY: Oxford University Press.

Ruiz, R. (1988). Orientations in language planning. In S. L. McKay & S. C. Wong (Eds.), *Language diversity: Problem or resource? A social and educational perspective on language minorities in the United States*. New York, NY: Newbury House.

Rymes, B., & Anderson, K. (2004). Second language acquisition for all: Understanding the interactional dynamic of classrooms in which Spanish and AAE are spoken. *Research in the Teaching of English, 39*, 107–135.

Samway, K. (2006). *When English language learners write: Connecting research to practice, K–8*. Portsmouth, NH: Heinemann.

Sarroub, L. (2008). Living "glocally" with literacy success in the Midwest. *Theory into Practice, 47*, 59–66.

Simon, R. (2012). "Without comic books there would be no me": Teachers as connoisseurs of adolescents' literate lives. *Journal of Adolescent and Adult Literacy, 55*, 516–526.

Smitherman, G. (1986). *Talkin and testifyin: The language of Black America*. Detroit, MI: Wayne State University Press.

Soltero, S. W. (2004). *Dual language: Teaching and learning in two languages*. Boston, MA: Pearson.

Stern, D. (1985). *The interpersonal world of the infant: A view from psychoanalysis and developmental psychology*. New York, NY: Basic Books.

Stewart, W. (2011, June 3). Phonics expert on national curriculum review accused of "conflict of interest". *Times Educational Supplement*. Retrieved from http://www.tes.co.uk/article.aspx?storycode=6086551.

Van Manen, M. (1991). *The tact of teaching: The meaning of pedagogical thoughtfulness*. Albany, NY: SUNY Press.

Vygotsky, L. S. (1962). *Thought and language*. Cambridge, MA: MIT Press.

Vygotsky, L. S. (1978). *Mind in society: The development of higher psychological process*. Cambridge, MA: Harvard University Press.

Warwick, M. (2012, November 12). The new national curriculum made to order? *Guardian*. Retrieved from: http://www.theguardian.com/education/2012/nov/12/primary-national-curriculum-review.

Wohlwend, K. E. (2011). *Playing their way into literacies*. New York, NY: Teachers College Press.

Wu, J. (2008). Learning native language first helps students learn English. In J. D. Ginn (Ed.), *Bilingual Education* (pp. 25–34). Farmington, MI: The Gale Group.

Wyse, D., & Goswami, U. (2008). Synthetic phonics and the teaching of reading. *British Educational Research Journal, 34*(6), 691–710.

Zacher Pandya, J. (2011). *Overtested: How high-stakes accountability fails English language learners*. New York, NY: Teachers College Press.

SECTION 2

Thematic Threads of Continuity and Contrast

3

THE RELEVANCE OF COMPOSING

Children's Spaces for Social Agency

Barbara Comber

Researching alongside young children as they begin schooling is compelling as we observe them grappling with making meaning and making friends. Of the many accomplishments ahead, assembling semiotic repertoires for composing is perhaps the most challenging literacy practice. It is a life-long project as we work out what we know, what we can say, how we can say it, where and to whom. These are key elements of critical literacy. For children in the early years of schooling, learning to write coincides with learning how to read, learning how to do school, making new friends, negotiating the playground, managing the times and spaces of the classroom. The social, institutional, and academic experiences of schooling present both new affordances and demands. It is no wonder the literature on transition to schooling is so vast! Parents, grandparents, kindergarten teachers, developmental psychologists, and of course children wonder and worry about starting school. Today, as always, children take up the tools and technologies in their communities to make meanings with chalk, sand, charcoal, screens, paint, paper, pencils—wherever and however they can make their mark.

As I write there is renewed and animated discussion in the media, in the wake of the murders at the *Charlie Hebdo* office in Paris, about the age-old question as to whether the pen is mightier than the sword. *Charlie Hebdo* is a satirical magazine featuring the hard-hitting work of a number of world-leading cartoonists. Since the tragedy, cartoonists world-wide have reiterated the power of their work to speak to readers across national and language boundaries. When young children discover what they can do with their different semiotic resources—amuse, question, persuade, convey ideas, play, record, join events, and so on—they are repositioned as active citizens who can participate, and exercise power, in their communities and sometimes beyond.

The relationship between composing and agency has long been clear in the work of literacy scholars (Brandt, 2001; Burnett, 2010; Clay, 1975; Dyson, 1993a, 1993b, 2013; Fisher, 2012; Genishi & Dyson, 2009; Halliday, 1989; Ivanic, 1998; Kamler, 2001; New London Group, 1996), but we still know too little about how young children growing up in different places come to composing, what it means to them, and what they do with it. This is urgent as classrooms become even more multicultural and multilingual and children engage with an increasing range of meaning-making resources, semiotic repertoires, tools, and technologies. It is urgent too as spaces for composing shut down as a result of global educational reform which reduces children's learning opportunities (Berliner, 2011; Comber, 2012; Sahlberg, 2010).

The nature of early childhood learning environments, at home and at school, in preschools, kindergartens and early grade classrooms, varies internationally and regionally (Greishaber, Shield, Luke, & Macdonald, 2012; Jones, 2014). In some places the increased availability of new technologies for producing multimodal texts is changing the possibilities on offer and the physical dimensions of learning settings. Yet even in affluent communities, many classrooms remain in transition, with whiteboards and blackboards side by side, exercise books, pencils, and iPads together on student and teacher desks. In areas of high poverty children's access to the material resources for composing may remain minimal.

This chapter addresses the question of the relevance of composing for children in creating spaces for social agency. It begins with a working definition of agency, outlines forms of agency and what might constrain it. Referring to case studies of particular children, it then goes on to discuss key themes, which illuminate what is possible and what is at stake when children compose. These overlapping themes include identity (sense of self, belonging), positioning (helping, initiating, befriending, "being bright"), voices (made through sound effects, singing, language style, and appropriating from popular culture and digital worlds), play (appropriate, imagine, design, and create), and resistance (not participating, silence, moving). Two main cases are drawn upon, those of Ta'Von (Anne Haas Dyson) and Gareth (Jackie Marsh), who demonstrate agency in terms of finding spaces of belonging and meaning-making occasions in the classroom and playground. Vignettes from other children are referred to in order to illustrate common themes.

What Is Agency and How Might It Be Relevant to Children's Composing?

A sense of agency can be understood as feeling that we are able to act in the world and that those actions will be recognized and respected by significant others. In terms of writing, Janks (2010, p. 156) argues that "the ability to produce texts is a form of agency that enables us to choose what meanings to make," which she sees as akin to Freire's (1972) understanding of "naming the world." Approaches to multiliteracies also emphasize the importance of agency in the design aspects of composing (Janks, 2010; Kress, 2010). Following recent critical sociocultural approaches to literacy studies (Lewis, Enciso, & Moje, 2007, p. 6), agency is understood as "a way of positioning oneself so as to allow for new ways of being, new identities." As the case studies presented here demonstrate, agency is relational and dynamic; it requires constant negotiation as people encounter new and changing situations. For children starting school and simultaneously learning to read and write, this is particularly pertinent, as their frames of reference for the institution of schooling and its specific stratification systems may be limited. What worked for them in kindergarten may no longer be acceptable at school. The need to deal with the new rules about managing their bodies in time and space and displaying what are considered appropriate behaviors and expected writing skills at predesignated times is an international phenomenon (Comber & Woods, 2016; Dixon, 2011; Dyson, 2013; Fisher, 2012). For children growing up in relative poverty, as indeed are the children whose stories are included in this volume, being able to imagine, play, create, and design a better and fairer world is crucial (Greene, 1988; Katz, 2004).

Rather than an individual trait or accomplishment, agency can also be seen as collective practice; that is, social action with, and on behalf of, others. Locally children can be agentive in pairs, groups, classes, or cohorts. Employing communication technologies, their agency may also extend beyond the local when they produce texts in various modes and media that circulate more widely. Children's agency also relates to teachers' sense of agency (Comber, 2012; Dixon; 2011; Fisher, 2012). In other words the spaces for children to take action may be contingent upon the extent to which their teachers control or open up the classroom to negotiation. Of course teachers conduct their work in specific policy, institutional, and community contexts. As Fisher (2012, p. 302) has noted, it may be that, rather than teachers being unwilling to change, in the present time they may be "over-compliant" in terms of delivering a more fragmented and curriculum-led approach. Indeed our recent studies suggest too much time is given to the fragments, to what we have described as "fickle literacies" (Comber & Woods, 2016), where children display surface dimensions and elements of literate practices without necessarily making meaning. However, in other places teachers might form strong alliances with communities to take approaches which build on children's languages and funds of knowledge, as we see in Natalia's case (Iliana Reyes), situated in a Central Mexico village school with a bilingual curriculum model including the dominant Spanish and the local indigenous language, náhuatl. The point though is that teacher agency is itself somewhat contingent and must be negotiated locally.

Children's agency may be evident in a range of practices—moving, gesturing, making sounds, speaking, playing, helping, telling stories, making image laughing, and so on. We need to understand what they produce, do, situ, because we can only interpret agency in context. For example, si not necessarily mean passivity or a lack of agency. Failure to participate in recitation practices or routines may signal a form of agency or resistance, as is clear in Gareth's selective participation in classroom literacy practices. Children may decide (consciously or otherwise) not to participate in a required practice. Composing in various media and through different modes allows children to explore who they are in relation to others. Gareth, as discussed further below, has a strong repertoire of digital literacy practices, such as curating his preferred YouTube videos, indicating his agency as a viewer and participant in particular Internet sites.

Some constraints upon children's agency are produced by the school as an institution. These include the requirement to display particular forms of knowledge and practice at particular times in specific places using predesignated language and embodied stances and gestures (stillness, hands in laps, hands-up to speak, and so on). Some children, particularly those who have enjoyed, and/or need, the freedom to make noise and move frequently in their out-of-school lives, may find these restrictions on sound and movement particularly challenging. Indeed children may need to employ gestures, sounds, and movements to make meaning and social connections (Dixon, 2011; Fisher, 2012; Kliewer, 2012). Children do not always come to school already inducted into the institutional practices it may demand of their bodies for literate work. Becoming school-literate subjects is new work. Some children find it easier to make inroads into the world of schooling because they bring repertoires of practices which allow them to connect with the school as a social place; some bring academic resources that they can use to position themselves as pedagogic subjects. Whatever children bring, all need to negotiate the school as a particular kind of meeting place (Comber, 2013).

Identity: Making Meaning, Making Friends

All children come to school with a sense of who they are and want to be, as a legacy of growing up in particular families and communities. Their ways of knowing and relational practices mean that they bring already emerging identities.

In many situations Ta'Von exemplifies the relevance of composing for children to develop spaces for social agency. As Anne shows, Ta'Von is a "player"; at his table, he sings, he initiates ideas, he vocalizes humorous ideas as he draws and composes. His development as a writer goes hand in hand with his capacity for fostering relationships with his peers and his teacher. Ta'Von composes himself as raced and gendered and from a specific cultural grouping—that is, as a Black American working-class boy—in the very ways he draws and then names his pictures. Not only that, he populates his texts with selected classroom friends. While he works hard to belong, he does not do this at the expense of his sense of self. He stands up for his braided hair, his skin color, and his ways of speaking. He portrays his visible features in his drawings and labels and regularly uses preferred vocabulary, such as "dude."

One of the clearest examples of Ta'Von's agency as a composer occurs when he authors a permission letter to cover his attendance at the roller skating excursion, just in case his mother forgets to sign the permission form. Writing on behalf of his mother, Ta'Von appropriates elements of the correct discourse ("Dear Mrs. Norton") and indicates that he understands features of the permission letter genre ("It's OK to go"). More importantly perhaps, he demonstrates that he understands the social purposes of such a text and that he anticipates how writing might help him to solve a potential problem. He shows that he is prepared to work with the textual resources at his disposal to take action. He is not daunted in writing to his teacher despite the power differential; his social astuteness allows him to find the correct register to pitch his case.

Like Ta'Von, Urvashi Sahni's case study, Sheela, is not intimidated by the usual hierarchical separation and status difference that often prevents children initiating communication, moreover a letter, to a teacher. Sheela takes the opportunity when it presents itself to compose a friendship between herself and her teacher and declares this in her "story." These self-initiated composing acts indicate how attuned some children are to the social world and how it functions, and their readiness to exercise power. A social perceptiveness is evident here which can be seen as a form of critical literacy (Gee, 1993) and gives these children the confidence to act and alter relationships with adults through writing. The usual power relations are rewritten through children's textual practices. Ta'Von and Sheela both benefit from what Kliewer (2012, p. 164) describes as "thoughtful teachers . . . who foster development in rich environments" which allow children to engage with "visual-tactile, pictorial and orthographic sign systems" to make meaning through narratives. Urvashi, as teacher-researcher, and Mrs. Norton allowed Sheela and Ta'Von room to move in their composing and their relating, which promoted agency and positive identity work simultaneously. Such teachers allow a flow of literacy development driven by children meeting social goals (Kliewer, 2012).

Not only does Ta'Von employ writing to relate to his teacher, in another piece, he makes a play for his peer Vida's friendship as he portrays her on his page and declares that he likes to see her. On yet another occasion when he depicts his parents coming down a slippery slide and positions himself as changing his baby sibling's nappy, his unique humor is appreciated by peers at his table. His drawings and his namings of his drawing are frequently populated by people in positive relationships with each other and importantly with him. He actively uses the opportunities to write to communicate and connect socially.

We know that "belonging" is crucial in children's transitions to school and that serious consequences can occur when children do not make friends or feel they belong at school. Children's agency may be aligned with teachers' wishes, but often it may not. Children such as Ta'Von, Rafiki (Esther Mukewa Lisanza) and Sheela selectively appropriate aspects of school literacy to reposition themselves and in so doing artfully capture the respect of their teachers and peers. The social pay-offs Ta'Von in particular enjoys foster the determination to connect and the confidence to take risks in making meaning and producing strong and distinctive representations. His named drawings differ greatly from Gus's (Barbara Comber and Lyn Kerkham) largely unnamed figures. Ta'von's sense of who he is becomes visible on the page. In contrast in Gus's case, a lack of respect and recognition from a teacher and peers result in a sense of it all being too hard. Classroom identity work is necessarily children's priority. They need to be recognized and respected in order to belong and to undertake the work of school learning.

Positioning: Making a Place in the School World

New Zealand educational researcher, Graham Nuthall (2007, p. 37) argues:

> Difficult and unusual as it may seem, long-term successful teaching involves working with the peer culture. Teachers therefore need to know who is in which friendship groups, who wants to be liked by whom, who has status, who is rejected.

Ta'Von, Sheela, Rafiki, and Danti (Sophie Dewayani) were liked by their teachers and peers and knew that they were liked. Gareth and Miguel (Celia Genishi) had particular friends and regularly enjoyed specific forms of social play. That is not to say the social status of these children was a given. Classroom relationships must be negotiated and renegotiated. Nuthall (2007, p. 37) also claims that "social relationships determine learning" because what children do in class-rooms is contingent on their making meaningful connections with their peers. When teachers position children as separate individuals and reduce their capacities to communicate, or when a child finds making friends hard, their resources for learning are seriously reduced. In terms of learning to compose, Ta'Von, Sheela, Rafiki, and Danti were able to appropriate significant dimensions of classroom literacy practices and blend them with home and peer resources in the service of both social and academic learning. In other words they were able to position themselves successfully to use what they had already and to make use of what they were learning in their own interests.

Those children who enjoy teachers' approval can position themselves in different ways. For instance, Ta'Von, whilst he still was assembling his literate repertoire in terms of encoding, already offered to help his peers. Rafiki, as a teacher–pupil, enjoyed particular classroom rights and privileges, as he translated and explained tasks for his peers. Sheela worked to create an affinity with her teacher. Gus, on the other hand, in grade 3 remained help-dependent to a large degree when it came to composing and at a loss to reliably connect socially with his peers. While he worked hard to shift his status, sometimes through silly displays, sometimes by intervening in squabbles that were not his business, sometimes being the first to audibly greet a classroom visitor or bring particular objects to school (for example, sweet treats or a new costume for book week), he remained vulnerable and was often positioned as a loner (socially) and as a struggler (academically).

When teachers allow children to make use of their resources assembled from home and popular culture, they are repositioned as experts or at least as already knowing. Danti knew more about the Dora clapping routines than her teacher. Ta'Von knew about being a "dude." Rafiki and Danti and their peers shared songs from the radio and community. Gareth shifted his positioning during carpet time when the topic turned to superheroes, more aligned with his demonstrable expertise at home in curating his preferred video clips. Gus attempted to share his knowledge of the Royal Show and its rides through creating his "Death Train," but this contribution was rejected. The extent to which children can bring in and make use of knowledges assembled outside of the classroom remains contingent on how teachers assess their use, value, and appropriateness.

Ultimately it is the teacher who decides on a child's relative academic status. While Mrs. Norton really liked Ta'Von and allowed him considerable room to move in her classroom, she still did not see him as one of her "bright" students. While Urvashi, as a visiting teacher-researcher, opened spaces for Sheela to write a friendship with her teachers into being, she was aware that other teachers found this an inappropriate threat to the hierarchical power relations of the status quo. While Gus returned to school with a "clean slate," his teacher still doubted his intellectual capacity to understand complex texts and to contribute right answers. One's academic positioning as a particular kind of literate subject is difficult to shift.

However, children's shared knowledges and practices allowed them to communicate around the teacher as discussed below. As Nuthall warns (2007, p. 37), "When there is a clash between the peer culture and the teacher's management procedures, the peer culture wins every time." Gus and Gareth resorted to what counted (or they thought would count) in their peer world to imagine a world and to form affiliations and in so doing risked their teachers' displeasure. When Miguel's friends were placed in a different classroom in kindergarten he seemed driven by a kind of artistic desire to compose relationships with others, real and imagined, on paper. By second grade, with its no talking rule and its curricular disinterest in imagination and play, Miguel was left outside the achieving circle. Sheela, Rafiki, and Danti, and to some degree Ta'Von, on the other hand, were able to position themselves socially in ways accepted by their teachers and enough peers. Sheela, Rafiki, Natalia, and Danti had teachers who shared their cultural and linguistic heritage to some degree. Ta'Von as one of only a few children of color in the classroom had more work to do to position himself amongst his peers and find ways of relating to and with his teacher that did not deny his identity as a working-class Black boy. Positioning then is a complex activity that requires children's ongoing action and interpretation. Once labeled, or worse rejected, it can be hard to move or position oneself visibly in positive ways.

Voice: Interrupting Business-as-Usual

Throughout the cases there are examples of children's voices, authorized and unauthorized in various volumes, through different media, in a range of configurations and in different spaces—on the page, in the playground, in the classroom, in secret—speaking out. Over and over we hear of children singing, including songs from their communities and from popular culture, which they have accessed through radio, television, or through computers and other devices. Sometimes we hear of children grunting and growling as they make sound effects to accompany the narratives they are composing, either alone or with friends. Sometimes they speak when authorized by their teachers after bidding for a turn. Gareth found his school voice when the topic turned to superheroes, where he had knowledge to contribute. Danti re-enacted the Dora Clap in rehearsing her composing.

Ta'Von was a child who readily vocalized what was on his mind and what his intentions were. He was a confident communicator, whether speaking, drawing, or writing. We have already seen how he used his voice to initiate directions in the conversation, to provide commentary on his composing, and to make his characters speak and relate. Gareth also, when not under the immediate gaze of the teacher, initiated conversations and extended the narrative potential around the assigned task, including little dramatic role-plays and his own verbalized modifications in completing the story map with "X marks the spot." These children performed important functions in the group as they made available their ideas, entertained their peers, and rehearsed possibilities in relation to their assignment or reconfigured it entirely. Occasions for writing at the group table became performative stages for children where they could exercise influence in ways not often available in the whole class space and rarely when children were working alone (and/or silently).

However, when children are silenced by order of the teacher, their individual and collective voices are simply paused. As soon as they can make an opportunity, their sounds re-emerge, sometimes in secret whispers, sometimes in the freer spaces of corridors and playgrounds, and sometimes in concert where they might hum or sing, or produce an array of sound effects. Their voices, when not heard, are always lurking just below the surface—a kind of underground subliminal communication channel which is ever ready to be tuned in and the volume raised. As Esther Lisanza points out, children cannot resist talking with each other.

When children access digital communications of various kinds they build repertoires of practice that extend beyond their schools and neighborhoods into regional and even global networks through their shared interests in and knowledge of playworlds such as Lego, Dora the Explorer, superheroes, religious and popular songs. These collective voices allow agency as they appropriate, remake, and compose new narratives together in various modes and with different media.

Play: The Stuff of Meaning-Making

When children have permission to talk as they compose, they are able to make tasks relevant in their social worlds. Gareth, for example, was able to act out various elements as he sat with peers as they illustrated their story maps of the Little Red Hen. The children played with the task and performed for each other as well assessing each other's drawings. They drew on their knowledge of items from other contexts. They exercised agency in using the completion of task as an occasion for experimenting with and developing social relations. On this occasion the shared task created a conversational space as their drawings appeared on their pages. Gareth, in particular, was confident and vocal in this situation in a way that he was not during times on the carpet for formal question and answer or recitation-style literacy lessons. Here, what children thought counted as a "good spade" mattered. Here he could embellish the story and invite a friend to pretend with him; here he could initiate and use his sense of humor; here what he knew could emerge, rather than exposing what he did not know or could not do.

Play provides rich material for children to compose on paper. Their enacted play in the playground, out of school, and in imaginary and virtual worlds is fodder for narration and representations. When Gareth and his friend were able to engage in school-sanctioned superhero talk in the official literacy carpet time, as well as in free activity, the desire to make shared meaning and significant symbolic artifacts was triggered. In this situation we see a "permeable curriculum" (Dyson, 1993a, b) in action as he took up things he was learning in the school context and found ways of sharing these with his friend as they moved in and out of different spaces, including the privacy of their tire meeting place. At home Gareth was an agentive meaning-maker through, for example, his material, semiotic, and social engagement with Lego on and offline—playing with family members with the toys themselves, and watching YouTube accounts from other child Lego players. When he could take up a playful and expert position in the school context, making meaning on paper had different potentialities. He could bring his play world into the space of composing. As Jackie Marsh concludes (this volume, p. 27): "Gareth was not so much a reluctant writer as a child who was reluctant to align himself to the austerity literacy model."

Gareth did not respond on cue to the demands to produce phonics soun
The "success criteria" associated with conducting reading in a particular way not generate a response. When asked to participate in tasks that, as yet, h' meaning for him and routinized literacy practices, he appeared reluctar when given the space to create dramas and narratives in play, he was

participant. Gareth's case is a strong reminder that children's engagement and participation in literacy practices is contingent on how they understand what is on offer and what is required of them. The dangers of labeling particular children's literacy in terms of assumed traits are clear (Comber & Kamler, 2004).

Across the case studies we see children composing as they play. Whether with blocks, trucks, and dinosaurs, or recalling a chant from *Dora the Explorer*, or imagining a ride in a theme park, or dancing to a popular song, or imagining new friends, or seeing themselves as superheroes, the children create, adapt, imagine, remember, in various ways enacting and narrating their thoughts. If children are unable to make use of these resources which they co-produce in, and through play, their material for writing is seriously restricted.

Resistance Makes Sense

Children learn to exercise power and negotiate relationships long before they start school. In family and community situations they work to connect, influence, persuade, help, amuse, compete, share, and so on, in order to form affiliations and develop a sense of who they are in relation to others. When they come to school they need to expand their relations and do so in a new context with different boundaries and possibilities. The literacy classroom and its default interaction patterns around reading and writing may be unfamiliar to them. Hence children such as Gareth, who are positioned powerfully in their home context given their engagement with popular culture and with assembling a digital repertoire, need to discover what is possible in school. Their preferences and expertise, which may have been fostered and supported at home, may not count for much in official school literacy lessons.

Children's sense of what constitutes satisfying meaning-making may be very different from the practices they encounter in the classroom. Not surprisingly some children may respond to unfamiliar expectations with various forms of resistance. Sometimes they make this visible through gesture and bodily movements. Miguel makes truck sounds as he plays with toy vehicles alone or with peers, sometimes using the truck to initiate an imagined scenario with a friend. We see Gareth fiddling with his shoes, shooting imaginary guns, hiding behind his whiteboard, and Gus yawning and claiming that he cannot write. Both boys move around the room when they can.

Considering Gareth more closely, we see the demands of participation in school literacy practices are enmeshed with the disciplinary expectations of the institution—bodily dispositions, places, stillness, and timing. When Gareth could move, talk, and choose to occupy a space, his capacity for multimodal meaning-making and the ability to compose narratives became clear. When he was called to the carpet to sit still and display fragments of knowledge at specific times, his response was understandably one of resistance.

Dixon (2011) distinguishes between writing as scribing and writing as authorship. From her ethnographic work across early childhood grades in South Africa, she demonstrates how the official spaces for children to draw and write (with whom, what, when, and how) close down as they go up the year levels. Writing at school becomes more of an individual and predesigned activity. Dixon (2011, p. 124) argues that:

> The predominant means through which children's literate subjectivity is constructed is through their ability to complete prescribed tasks rather than creative, original texts. Docility is valued over creativity.

She goes on to show that the extent to which writing involves social negotiation and collaboration lessens and concludes that, "tasks that involve drawing or writing no longer have an element of classroom community but focus on the individual" (Dixon, 2011, p. 125). Internationally, teachers report being under pressure to have children perform on tests which often emphasize handwriting, spelling, punctuation, and grammar—facets of scribing which are relatively easy to test (Comber & Woods, 2016; Fisher, 2012). As Fisher (2012, p. 300) points out, "classrooms are complex places" that are shaped not only by the history of schooling as an institution, but also by "the history of the participants in the activity of the classroom—both teachers and students."

Those histories are evident in the ways in which different children are positioned and position themselves in classrooms as social, academic, and physical environments. While Gareth and Ta'Von appeared to negotiate the physical, social, and academic demands of the school writing context with resistance and bravado respectively, Gus, in contrast, demonstrated a lack of agency with respect to composing texts and composing a school self. He had not managed yet to compose a literate self or indeed a school self that reliably worked for him. Yet he worked hard to please his teacher and his peers when he could. Given that children's learning is very much contingent on what and how they are able to learn from and with peers, when Gus faced silent writing and was seated at a table without friends, he was left with only his own resources and storylines. These conditions continued to reinforce what he could not do as a writer. Resistance made sense.

Designing Spaces for Action: Composing Possible Classrooms

Schools, and indeed classrooms, can be positive and generative meeting places for children to learn to compose and to take social action (Comber, 2013) as the diversity of participants and their knowledges allow for the possibility of negotiating something new. Ta'Von composed himself differently in response to

Vida, with Brittany listening in, than he did in relation to Salvia. Rafiki enabled his friends to address the teachers' literacy demands, even as he created an imaginative space for himself. In order for teachers to capitalize on this potential, and design enabling literacy pedagogies, there must be room to move—both physically and psychically. Spaces for action need to be material, psychological, and social. Ideally children might have access to the kinds of space that Gareth enjoyed (including the tire, the mark-making area, and authorized outside zones), with different spaces fostering different learning and play possibilities. However, even if children are crammed into desks, as in Rafiki's classroom, or on the floor of a small classroom near a noisy street, as in Danti's, they need to be free to imagine and explore. The challenge for teachers then is to design curricular opportunities and activities that mobilize children's capacity to act as individuals, in pairs and groups, and as a class with collective interests.

Literacy lessons can be designed to align with children's interests, at the same time as teachers and peers introduce new resources, challenges, and information which extend thinking. In order to find the motivation to grapple with the work of scribing, children need to be invested in the potential of composing to work for them in the social world of the school. Natalia wanted to learn her grandfather's language (náhuatl) and uses some náhuatl vocabulary to compose her stories about her grandfather's band and her father's bread-making. Ta'Von wanted that permission to go roller skating; he wanted Vida and Salvia as his friends. Sheela wanted to form a friendship with her new teacher. Gareth needed to write "a message" as part of his superhero play with Stephen. Gus wanted to make a great poster of an imaginary side-show ride at the Royal Adelaide Show. After initial reticence, Danti populated her weather picture with an image of Dora. The teacher's encouragement to "add anything—people, parks, anything" provided another opportunity for Danti to bring her knowledge of Dora into the classroom and made the work of drawing more satisfying as she grappled with the meanings she intended. Miguel for his part made sense of assigned tasks the best way he could by incorporating his extensive repertoire of drawing to solve problems including designing a "character map." Children's inventiveness in the face of sometimes daunting tasks is impressive!

Learning to have a say and form relationships is crucial to children's academic and social well-being at school and beyond. Discovering the affordances of writing (or multimodal composing more broadly) allows children to exercise power in new ways either individually or in collaboration with others. Researchers have documented even very young children writing for their rights (Comber & Nixon, 2013; Vasquez, 2004). When they discover what can be done with composing, whether that be playful or pleasurable, the chore of scribing or drawing becomes worth it.

References

Berliner, D. (2011). Rational responses to high stakes testing: The case of curriculum narrowing and the harm that follows. *Cambridge Journal of Education, 41,* 287–302.

Brandt, D. (2001). *Literacy in American lives.* Cambridge, England: Cambridge University Press.

Burnett, C. (2010). Technology and literacy in early childhood educational settings: A review of research. *Journal of Early Childhood Literacy, 10,* 247–270.

Clay, M. (1975). *What did I write? Beginning writing behaviour.* Portsmouth, NH: Heinemann.

Comber, B. (2012). Mandated literacy assessment and the reorganisation of teachers' work: Federal policy, local effects. *Critical Studies in Education, 53,* 119–136.

Comber, B. (2013). Schools as meeting places: Critical and inclusive literacies in changing school environments. *Language Arts, 90,* 361–371.

Comber, B., & Kamler, B. (2004). Getting out of deficit: Pedagogies of reconnection. *Teaching Education, 15,* 293–310.

Comber, B., & Nixon, H. (2013). Urban renewal, migration and memories: The affordances of place-based pedagogies for developing immigrant students' literate repertoires. *Multidisciplinary Journal of Educational Research, 3,* 42–68.

Comber, B., & Woods, A. (2016). Literacy teacher research in high poverty schools: Why it matters. In J. Lampert & B. Burnett (Eds.), *Teacher education for high poverty schools* (pp. 193–210). New York, NY: Springer.

Dixon, K. (2011). *Literacy, power, and the schooled body: Learning in time and space.* New York, NY: Routledge.

Dyson, A. Haas (1993a). *Negotiating a permeable curriculum: On literacy, diversity, and the interplay of children's and teachers' worlds.* Urbana, IL: National Council of Teachers of English.

Dyson, A. Haas (1993b). *Social worlds of children learning to write in an urban primary school.* New York, NY: Teachers College Press.

Dyson, A. Haas (2013). *ReWRITING the basics: Literacy learning in children's cultures.* New York, NY: Teachers College Press.

Fisher, R. (2012). Teaching writing: A situated dynamic. *British Educational Research Journal, 38,* 299–317.

Freire, P. (1972). *Pedagogy of the oppressed.* Harmondsworth, England: Penguin.

Gee, J. P. (1993). *The social mind: Language, ideology, and social practice.* New York, NY: Bergin & Garvey.

Genishi, C., & Dyson, A. Haas (2009). *Children, language, and literacy: Diverse learners in diverse times.* New York, NY: Teachers College Press and Washington, DC: National Association for the Education of Young Children.

Greene, M. (1988). *The dialectic of freedom.* New York, NY: Teachers College Press.

Grieshaber, S., Shield, P., Luke, A., & Macdonald, S. (2012). Family literacy practices and home literacy resources: An Australian study. *Journal of Early Childhood Literacy, 12,* 113–138.

Halliday, M. A. K. (1989). *Spoken and written language.* Oxford, England: Oxford University Press.

Ivanic, R. (1998). *Writing and identity: The discoursal construction of identity in academic writing.* Amsterdam, Netherlands: John Benjamins Publishing Company.

Janks, H. (2010). *Literacy and power.* New York, NY: Routledge.

Jones, S. (2014). How people read and write and they don't even notice: Everyday lives and literacies on a Midlands council estate. *Literacy, 48,* 59–65.

Kamler, B. (2001). *Relocating the personal: A critical writing pedagogy.* Albany, NY: State University of New York Press.

Katz, C. (2004). *Growing up global: Economic restructuring and children's everyday lives.* Minneapolis, MN: University of Minnesota Press.

Kliewer, C. (2012). Creating literacy: Young children with and without disabilities constructing meaning together. In C. Dudley-Marling & S. Michaels (Eds.), *High-expectation curricula: Helping all students succeed with powerful learning* (pp. 162–175). New York, NY: Teachers College Press.

Kress, G. (2010). *Multimodality: A social semiotic approach to contemporary communication.* New York, NY: Routledge.

Lewis, C., Enciso, P., & Moje, E. B. (Eds.) (2007). *Reframing sociocultural research on literacy: Identity, agency & power.* New York, NY: Routledge.

New London Group (1996). A pedagogy of multiliteracies: Designing social futures. *Harvard Educational Review, 66,* 60–92.

Nuthall, G. (2007). *The hidden lives of learners.* Wellington, New Zealand: New Zealand Council for Eductional Research Press.

Sahlberg, P. (2010). Rethinking accountability in a knowledge society. *Journal of Educational Change, 11,* 45–61.

Vasquez, V. (2004). *Negotiating critical literacies with young children.* Mahwah, NJ: Lawrence Erlbaum.

4

RESOURCES FOR COMPOSING

Peggy J. Miller and Urvashi Sahni

Children's agency does not exist in a vacuum. The eight cases presented in Chapter 2 illustrate a fundamental premise shared by all sociocultural theories: Children live in particular contexts, participate in particular practices, and use particular cultural resources to create meaning and make their way in the world. The authors of these cases understand children and cultural resources to be interdependent; there can be no agency without something to draw upon and work with.

The term "cultural resources" shares a family resemblance with other terms in the sociocultural lexicon, especially "tools" and "artifacts." In *Cultural Psychology*, Cole (1996) defines artifacts as products of human history that are simultaneously ideal and material. This duality implies that artifacts are both public and private, inside the head and outside the head. The same is true of cultural resources. The television show *Dora the Explorer* is a cultural resource, with a distinct history. It exists in the social and material world, beamed into the homes of countless small consumers, some of whom, like Sophie Dewayani's Danti, find Dora irresistible. Before long, Dora is not just "out there" in the world; she has a new life in the hearts and minds of her young fans. Dora's personality, her plots, and her accessories fuel Danti's imagination. Like Dora, Danti is game: "I can do it!" And, indeed she can: She draws Dora, transforming a teacher-modeled scene of rain and rainbows into a backdrop for her heroine.

Another virtue of the term "cultural resources" is that it is capacious enough to encompass the wide range of appropriations made by the eight children in their far-flung locales. When children compose or talk about composing, they do so in one or more *languages*, using a variety of *technologies* (e.g., chalk and slates, pencils and paper, markers and white boards, computers, iPads) in a variety of *spaces* (e.g., desks, rugs for whole-group lessons, role-play areas, private corners of the playground, online communities) and use diverse semiotic tools (drawing, singing, talking, writing). They draw on *oral and written texts* (e.g., folklore, stories, textbooks, literature, religious texts) and *varied popular art forms* (e.g., film, television, popular music, graphic arts). While Danti drew Dora, Sheela (Urvashi Sahni) chose to write about Holi, an Indian festival of colors, which she embellished with drawings. *Social norms, practices, and relationships*, including those of the classroom, also serve as resources. In her composition, "My Story," Sheela claimed her teacher as a friend, rewriting the traditional norms that prescribe distance between teachers and students. When child writers collaborate, peer practices, such as peer play, may infuse the process of composing, enforcing, or transforming pedagogical practices (Dyson, 1993a; see also Jackie Marsh's case, Gareth, and Anne Haas Dyson's case, Ta'Von).

This chapter unfolds in four sections. We begin by mapping some key analytic distinctions as they apply to cultural resources in the classroom. Next we discuss the critical importance of the teacher–pupil relationship in realizing the educational potential of the resources that children bring to the classroom and in promoting children's growth as persons. When teachers construct a shared world with their students, learning happens on both sides. In the third section we focus on children's developmental trajectories and consider some of the complex contingencies on which they rise and fall. In the final section, we argue that the developmental trajectories of poor and minority children are disproportionately disrupted by educational "reforms" that enforce one-size-fits-all standards. This process reproduces inequality by systematically misconstruing children's resources as deficits. Throughout this chapter, we draw primarily on three case studies from Chapter 2: Sophie's Danti, who worked on the street and attended the Early Childhood Center in Bandung, Indonesia; Urvashi's Sheela, who attended a rural primary school in Uttar Pradesh, India; and Barbara Comber's and Lyn Kerkham's case, Gus, who attended primary school in one of the poorest urban areas in Australia.

Resources in the Classroom: Some Distinctions

Like many five- to seven-year-olds around the globe, the children featured in this book go to school. Although there are vast differences among the schools they attend, three similarities stand out: All purport to teach literacy, all are designed and controlled by adults, and all have an official view of what happens in the classroom. The *official version* is often enshrined in written documents, such as mission statements, disciplinary policies, and pedagogical goals, and it coexists with a plurality of *unofficial versions*. Peer culture is a rich reservoir of unofficial views of school and its purposes (Corsaro, 2011; Dyson, 1993a, 1997, 2013; Gilmore, 1986). Sometimes young students find the (official) literacy curriculum to be less interesting than the (unofficial) opportunities to play with other children and develop friendships. In her study of a Taiwanese kindergarten in a working-class community, Liang (2000, 2011) discovered that some children were very clever at finding moments in the official, highly structured classroom routine when they could talk to each other, share a joke, or extend a pretend script; she called these fleeting episodes "play on the fly." For the most part, these episodes went undetected by the teacher. Similarly, Esther Lisanza's Rafiki and his friends found ways to smuggle their indigenous language into the classroom despite the official ban, and to sing, dance, draw, and write despite a highly restrictive, test-based curriculum. Again, the children's unofficial uses of language and literacy operated beneath the teacher's radar; she either did not realize what they were up to or chose to look the other way. Sometimes teachers dismiss children's sub-rosa doings as "merely play," not recognizing that learning is taking place or that friendships fuel literacy development; sometimes they collude in children's "violations" of the rules because they disagree with the rules.

Under other circumstances, however, the consequences can be severe when children do not conform to the official order. This is illustrated most poignantly by the case of Gus, whose violations of the classroom rules of comportment led to his expulsion from school in the third grade. When Comber and Kerkham tried to figure out why Gus had disappeared from the classroom, they discovered that, in the second grade, he had a history of "low-level annoying behaviors," such as not following instructions, and lying and aggressiveness with peers. When these behaviors continued and escalated in the third grade, Gus was suspended from school on five occasions and then removed from the school and placed elsewhere for ten weeks. The severity of these punishments and the costs to Gus of repeated banishments from school are shocking, especially given his age and the nature of his infractions. Yet he is not an isolated case. In the US there is growing concern about the toll of out-of-school suspensions in public schools, often for nonviolent behaviors such as insubordination and defiance and for fighting with peers, and about the disproportionate suspension of African American students (Gibson & Haight, 2013; Gibson et al., 2014; Haight et al., 2014).

Gus's experience illustrates how much is at stake when children behave in ways that are at odds with the official rules and when those rules are enforced without taking the child's perspective into account. This leads us to ask, "What exactly was going on with Gus?" Did he deliberately flout the rules? Did he not understand what the rules were? Given his Reception and third grade teachers' perception that his mother had "problems," did he feel uncomfortable in school? Did his troubles with writing exacerbate his anxiety, noticed as early as kindergarten, and create other reactions (e.g., frustration, lack of confidence) that led him to cope in ways that did not accord with the rules? As the rate and severity of punishment escalated, did Gus become more anxious, less comfortable in the classroom, and less compliant? These kinds of questions arise whenever young children get defined as classroom miscreants.

One striking feature of Gus's case is that some adults had come to know a Gus who was quite different from the official miscreant-Gus. The ethnographers, who observed in his second grade classroom, were mystified by his expulsion because they had not witnessed the kinds of behaviors for which he was cited. The teacher in the school where he was placed reported no disruptive behavior in class and a single time-out during the ten-week placement. Several teachers, as well as the ethnographers, commented on Gus's positive engagement with reading and interpretation of texts. This leads us to ask, "What exactly was going on with the adults who suspended and ultimately expelled Gus?" Although it is hard to imagine that these steps could have been taken by the teacher alone, without the involvement of other staff and the approval of the principal, we do not know how these decisions were made or by whom. Nor do we know what the conditions were that supported such actions or precluded alternative strategies for engaging with Gus. Ironically, Gus's culminating punishment—placement in a different classroom—turned out to be a positive experience for him, however inadvertently (more about this later).

So far we have been working with the official/unofficial distinction primarily as it applies to pupil conduct, with only glancing reference to writing itself. Perhaps the most obvious lesson from Gus's case is that all questions about how writing is practiced and taught become moot when disciplinary suspensions deny children access to composing by excluding them from the classroom entirely. This serves as a powerful reminder that the development of writing is part and parcel of the development of the whole person, with his or her goals, anxieties, home life, perceptions of self, and relationships with others at home and in school. After all, it is the child who is being taught, not the curriculum.

With this caveat in mind, it is, nonetheless, important to recognize that the official/unofficial distinction also applies to writing per se. The official view of writing includes what writing is, how it should be taught, what kinds of materials children may use in their writing, and how they should conduct themselves vis à vis the teacher and fellow students while composing. Examples of official definitions of writing from Chapter 2 include copying lines of text from the textbook, copying words and sentences from the blackboard and filling in blanks without necessarily understanding the meaning of the words, writing phonemes in a decontextualized manner, and generating text in response to teacher-provided prompts and story maps. Schools vary in the extent to which teachers have the power to establish official definitions, practices, and rules of engagement. When policies and curricula are dictated by authorities at higher levels in the educational hierarchy (e.g., the headmaster, the district, the national department of education), teachers may enforce, bend, or subvert these prescriptions or follow them reluctantly and sometimes sullenly, even when they don't agree. But these macro-level complexities, these layers of authority that constrain and enable teachers, are unknown to the children. From their perspective, the teacher is the voice of authority, the arbiter of the right way to do things in school.

Apart from the official/unofficial distinction, cultural resources can also be *sanctioned* or *unsanctioned*. This distinction encompasses the official/unofficial distinction in the sense that the official version of what happens in the classroom is sanctioned by educational authority while unofficial versions are not. H cultural resources can also embody ideologies that circulate widely in t society, sanctioned by tradition and/or by a range of institutions; or they c embody ideologies that go against the status quo, unsanctioned by legitimating powers. Sanctioned ideologies are often deeply taken for granted and may or may not jibe with official school policies and practices. At the Early Childhood Center attended by Danti and her peers, the Ablution Clap was used to teach the children how to perform the Islamic ritual of ablution. School and religion were aligned in sanctioning this practice. The Dora Clap, on the other hand, was an unsanctioned outgrowth of peer culture, invented and sustained by the children themselves.

The case of Sheela illustrates a complex interplay of sanctioned and unsanctioned gender ideologies. Eight-year-old Sheela lived in a village where girls were married as soon as they reached puberty. Sheela's mother shared the prevailing opinion that education was of no economic value for girls. However, Sheela was an enthusiastic and resourceful student who participated avidly in all literacy activities. She used a variety of resources, including the interactive and dialogic support of her peers and the teacher-researcher (Urvashi), to inhabit the classroom on her own terms, surpass the curricular goals, and appropriate writing as a tool of empowerment. Over the course of the study, she developed her own voice as a writer, defying the dominant ideology that girls should be silent. Most remarkably, she rewrote "her story," imagining a world in which her mother embraced the value of educating her daughter. She treated the sanctioned gendered ideology as a resource: She turned it on its head. Instead of acceding to a view of other girls and women as enforcers of gender discrimination, she envisioned a host of female allies—her mother, her friends, and her teachers—who would support her in attaining her goals. It was the space for self-exploration provided by Urvashi as teacher-researcher that led to this redefining and reconstruction of herself. Urvashi seemed to free up the classroom from the sanctioned gendered ideology and to authorize Sheela's rewriting of it. Respected by Urvashi as one of her teachers, she learned to respect herself.

The foregoing discussion of analytic distinctions in cultural resources helps us get a grip on the complexity of classroom life. Because everyone, adult and child alike, brings cultural resources from multiple worlds into their literacy activities, these spaces teem with diverse perspectives. When classrooms are approached exclusively from the official vantage point, however, this diversity goes unrecognized, unappreciated, and unutilized for pedagogical purposes. Worse still, it may be regarded as a problem to be solved or an encroachment to be eliminated. This is especially apparent with respect to language variation. Many countries have a history of enacting draconian measures to stamp out children's use of indigenous languages and vernacular dialects in school. In the contemporary era there is a wide array of policies and practices pertaining to indigenous languages, as illustrated in Chapter 2: national policy that accepts indigenous languages but local schools that prohibit them (Esther's Rafiki in Kenya), recognition of children's bilingual-ism but use of benchmarks that do not take bilingualism into account (Celia Genishi's Miguel in New York City), and national policy that accepts indigenous languages, but without funding for educational programs, coexisting with local initiatives to revive indigenous languages (Iliana Reyes's Natalia in Mexico). (Language as a dominant theme in our cases is the major topic of Chapter 5.)

Learning from the Children

The authors of this volume believe that there is enormous educational potential in the multitude of resources that children bring to the classroom. But how can that potential be tapped? Two decades ago Anne Haas Dyson (1993) introduced the *permeable curriculum*, an idea that speaks directly to this question. Resting on the assumption that young writers pursue diverse social goals and draw on diverse cultural resources, rooted in home communities and peer culture, the permeable curriculum refers to ways in which teachers construct a shared world with their students, allowing for interplay between the teachers' and the children's experi-ences. The word "interplay" is critical. When a boundary is permeable, the flow goes both ways.

Permeability is not possible if the teacher's goals are unidirectional, as they were for Sheela's teacher; firmly wedded to the official curriculum, she focused on spelling, not ideas, and was not prepared to consider the children's develop-ment from their perspective. Similarly, adult-imposed rules of language use took precedence in Rafiki's school. Banning the children's native tongue not only devalued a local resource; it was tantamount to banning a large part of the child who spoke that language. Alienated from the teacher by an alien tongue, Rafiki and his peers focused on building relationships using their own resources.

Commitment to a permeable curriculum obliges teachers to look beyond official dictates and definitions and to widen the scope of what they are willing to count as resources. We might call these *sanction-able* resources; that is, resources that are brought by children and recognized by teachers as legitimate venues for com-posing, regardless of their official status. Examples from Chapter 2 include local languages, family stories, stories of personal experience, traditional music, love songs, church songs, dance steps, and children's television programs. Sometimes teachers encourage children to write about themes, such as superheroes, that they know will be appealing; when Gareth's teacher did this in the context of an otherwise highly constrained literacy curriculum, he became fully engaged in Ɪuperhero play and writing in a way that contrasted sharply with his resistance ꞮꞮe official literacy tasks. Dyson (1993) says, "Teachers as well as children must Ɪen, curious, and willing to imagine worlds beyond their own" (p. 9).

ꞮꞮral other educators featured in Chapter 2 exemplify these qualities. For ꞮꞮthe founder of the Early Childhood Center in Bandung, Indonesia sought to teach basic literacy skills in a home-like atmosphere; she made a concerted effort to devise learning opportunities that were attractive to the children, allowing them to incorporate love songs and television programs into their literacy activities. Danti's drawing of Dora occurred in the context of a teacher-led opportunity for composing but emerged out of specific negotiations between the teacher and Danti, negotiations that met the needs of both. Similarly, in the rural primary school in Uttar Pradesh, India, Urvashi as teacher-researcher responded with interest when Sheela mentioned her pet parrot, encouraging her to write about her parrot, which Sheela did. This seemed to mark a watershed moment for Sheela, empowering her to use writing to represent her personal experience. In both cases, the girls responded eagerly to their teachers' responsiveness to their perspectives. This kind of mutuality builds on itself, establishing writing as a personally meaningful activity and forging trust between student and teacher.

Indeed, it is impossible to overestimate the importance of the teacher–student relationship in building a permeable curriculum and creating a space where children can claim ownership of their own learning. When Urvashi took over in Sheela's classroom, her most far-reaching innovation was to restructure the teacher–student relationships. She configured the classroom into a circle of mutuality, defined by a relationship of respectful response, within which other circles proliferated. All the children, including Sheela, learned to write because they had someone to write for. They wrote because the relationship mattered to them. They used writing to nurture their relationship and, in turn, the relationship nurtured their growth as writers and persons. The curriculum was responsive because it emerged from and was grounded in a set of responsive relationships. Literacy was empowering, too, because of the special relationships in which it was embedded. However, the more important prior factor was the relationship, even more so than literacy, though both developed hand in hand.

Given its inherent power differential, the teacher–student relationship assumes special significance in terms of its empowering or depowering potential. This point can be illustrated by returning to the case of Gus, the child who was expelled from school in the third grade. Gus had three teachers during the span of the study. Two of the teachers apparently did not get to know Gus as a person despite his anxiety, his struggles with writing, and his repeated suspensions from school. They saw him primarily through the narrow lens of a learner who did not measure up. However, when Gus was expelled from school and placed in a different classroom, his new teacher devised an approach that worked extremely well. She helped him put his struggles into perspective, recognized that his mother wanted to help, and recruited her involvement on Gus's behalf. He thrived. It is almost as though he was a different child when seen through the eyes of the placement teacher. By taking a more holistic approach, by engaging Gus as a person in the larger context of his life outside of school, she helped him feel that he belonged.

It is poignant and yet hopeful to see what a difference one teacher can make in such a short period of time and how quickly a child can respond when a respectful relationship is offered. Perhaps we need to reconceive society and polities in terms of relationships, circles of mutuality based on mutual respect and response. Such a vision coheres well with a commitment to participatory democracy, defined by Dewey (1985) as "more than a form of Government—it is primarily a mode of associated living, of conjoint communicated experience" (p. 93). With specific reference to education, this implies that the institutional structure of education should be reconfigured in participatory terms of mutually responsive and respectful relationships between teachers, supervisors, planner, students, and communities. Teachers, as much as students, need to be responded to respectfully as *persons doing important work.*

Furthermore, we need to reconceive the role of schooling and literacy, taking a view of children as persons and ends-in-themselves having legitimate goals of their own. Oftentimes, educators, even critical educators like Giroux (1989), take too reductive a view of schools and learning. Critical educators have done invaluable work in pointing out that the political ideology underlying the institutional structure and practice in schools deserves scrutiny. Yet they should guard against the ideological trap of taking an exclusively political view of literacy and schools. Children are not national resources; they are persons, and the purpose of schooling is first and foremost to nurture their growth as persons, and to help them appropriate literacy for their own ends.

India is joining the testing-bandwagon, with its shrill demand for more and more testing. Aghast at the findings of an evaluation study (Annual Status of Education Report, 2013), which revealed that only 22% of children in grade 3 and about 50% of children in grade 5 can read grade 2 textbooks, the Gods of Education at the state and national level are crying out for more accountability from teachers, i.e., more standardized testing. The concern, unfortunately, is propelled by the "children-as-national-resources" argument rather than a "children-as-persons" one. In all the rhetoric about poor achievement and low literacy levels, there is no mention of increased responsiveness to children's lives or building upon the resources they already have, which is the way to improve children's literacy levels.

In arguing that children's growth as persons should take precedence, we also appeal to a trend in sociocultural theory that takes an expanded view of what is at stake in children's participation in cultural practices (Goodnow, 1990). Instead of focusing exclusively on the acquisition of knowledge or skill, this vein of theorizing holds that cultural practices provide the matrix within which children develop selves and identities, affective stances, modes of attention, moral agency, and ways of being in the world (Holland, Lachicotte, Skinner, & Cain, 1998; Miller, Fung, Lin, Chen, & Boldt, 2012; Rogoff, 2003). This holistic perspective breaks down the segregation of thinking from other aspects of life, envisioning children as acting, thinking, feeling, valuing, identity-constructing persons enter into relationships with others (Miller & Goodnow, 1995).

The cases presented in Chapter 2 suggest that young children would reconc school as a playground rather than a political arena and redefine literacy as "creative literacy," construing it as a tool with which to imaginatively construct a self related to others in the world and to imagine possibilities for their lives and consequently for the larger public sphere. Viewed from the perspective of young children, literacy is not for social and political revolution or national development or even for meeting benchmarks on standardized tests; it is for people to relate with each other in empowering ways. Natalia's curricular context allowed her to expand her composing resources—and to move into biliteracy—in ways that underscored her identity as a granddaughter whose heritage included náhuatl. Driven by the need for inclusion, Anne described Ta'Von as using writing to manage his relationships. To paraphrase her, he composed a classroom space in which he mattered.

Diverse and Contingent Developmental Trajectories

And so did Danti and Sheela. The case studies of these two girls reveal an auspicious moment in their young lives as students and writers. For the time being, they were flourishing under the shelter of permeable curricula. School was a comfortable place for them. They relished the literacy tasks and social opportunities that school afforded; they had strong relationships with their teachers, which relationships drove their development as writers and persons; and they commanded a host of personally meaningful resources for composing. It is hard not to be optimistic about their development as readers and writers. But that optimism has to be tempered by a critical fact about the nature of developmental trajectories: Developmental trajectories are socially, culturally, and historically contingent. Children do not unfurl their individual potential unaided or unmoored in time and place. Sociocultural theories posit that developmental trajectories are constituted in the interplay between the child and other social actors, mediated by particular cultural resources in particular contexts (Goodnow, Miller, Kessel, 1995; Rogoff, 2003). Thus, we must bracket our optimism for Danti and Sheela: If these fortunate circumstances persist—if, for example, the girls are allowed to continue their education, if school remains affordable to their families, if their teachers are able to sustain permeable curricula—then, we can be optimistic that they will continue to blossom as writers. But if not, their emergence as literate persons could be interrupted, compromised, or even reversed. Developmental trajectories can be fragile, especially for children whose families and schools have little power or cultural capital. Indeed, it turns out that Sheela was not allowed to continue school after grade 8 and was married off at age 15.

This way of thinking about developmental trajectories connects to two other insights from sociocultural theory and cross-cultural research. First, there is a large body of research that challenges the old idea of a single, universal developmental pathway; we now know that children navigate a plurality of pathways, reflecting the variety of sociocultural worlds that they inhabit and their own idiosyncratic inclinations and experiences (e.g., Briggs, 1998; Garcia Coll & Marks, 2009; Gaskins & Paradise, 2010; Göncü, 1999; Greenfield, Keller, Fuligni, & Maynard, 2003; Miller, Cho, & Bracey, 2005; Miller et al., 2012; Rogoff, 2003; Shweder et al., 2006; Weisner, 2002). Second, developmental trajectories are not necessarily progressive. Miller and Goodnow (1995) made this point in their discussion of development as change in children's participation in cultural practices. This broader definition of development is agnostic with respect to the direction of change. It recognizes that children may become more skilled, more fluent, more reflective, more responsible, and more confident as they participate in routine practices— telling stories, drawing pictures, composing texts. But it also recognizes that development may be curtailed when the practices available to children do not afford avenues for positive engagement and respectful negotiation. Children may not know exactly what the trouble is, but they know when they do not belong; they may become frustrated, discouraged, and alienated. Some of Danti's older peers dropped out of school in the fourth or fifth grade. Financial exigency was not the only reason: They were teased for working on the street, they felt ashamed, and they believed that they could not possibly pass the graduation exam in the sixth grade (Dewayani, 2013). They knew that even their teachers had no faith in their ability to succeed.

"At risk" children who do not succeed in school are often subjected to unflattering back stories: They were not prepared for school in the first place, they were not sufficiently motivated, they and their parents did not value education, and so on. The high-ranking educational official referred to in Danti's case touted the "Education for All" policy, while demeaning the children who worked on the street as lazy, irresponsible, and uninterested in education. This back story "explains" high drop-out rates as virtually inevitable. We might call this the flat-line narrative. In this account, children start out without the resources that educational authorities deem "necessary," they are unable to take advantage of the educational opportunities on offer, and they never catch up. This flat-line narrative was part of the macro-educational context that shaped the educational opportunities and experiences of Danti and her peers and shadowed their development.

However, an understanding of developmental trajectories as co-created and contingent allows us to imagine other back stories. Imagine a child who gets off to a strong start in school but whose prospects dim as she moves into other classrooms where conditions no longer support her development. This is exactly what happened with Zena, a low-income African American girl whose early years of schooling were documented by Corsaro, Molinari, and Rosier (2002). Zena thrived in Head Start with African American teachers and peers whose norms of speaking were compatible with her own. Her teachers were impressed by her academic skills. Her peers appreciated her narrative dexterity and verbal assertiveness; she was already adept at the kind of adversarial language enjoyed by older African American peers (Goodwin, 1990, 2009). She took a leadership role in dramatic play. Zena continued to excel in kindergarten, but in first grade she experienced a reversal. The verbal strengths for which she had been admired in Head Start and kindergarten now stigmatized her in the eyes of her White middle-class teacher and peers. Her verbal style was deemed offensive and she was perceived to be bossy and moody. Conflicts with her peers began to have a negative impact on her academic performance.

In "The Dismantling of Narrative," Michaels (1991) described a similar trajectory in the context of sharing time or show-and-tell, a narrative activity used in the early grades to provide oral preparation for literacy. Michaels' meticulous sociolinguistic analysis revealed a subtle but powerful mismatch between the middle-class narrative style used by the teacher and the narrative style that working-class African American children brought to the first-grade classroom. Following one such child over time, Michaels documented the progressive curtailment of Deena's narrative development by the well-meaning but counter-productive interventions of her highly experienced teacher. This same teacher was able to interact effectively with the middle-class children whose style more closely resembled her own, supporting and extending their narratives, but not with the African American children whose topic-associating style she regarded as pointless rather than different. Over time, Deena became more and more frustrated and annoyed with the teacher, and the teacher became more and more convinced of Deena's inability to produce coherent texts.

It is sobering to consider how quickly young students' fortunes can change. Despite their early successes in school, Deena and Zena got caught in linguistic and cultural clashes between the norms of home and community, on the one hand, and the norms of the classroom, on the other, clashes that were not recognized as such by educational authority. When interactions across boundaries of race, class, and gender went awry again and again, it was the girls themselves who paid the price; they were perceived, inadvertently, through the lens of negative stereotypes and stigmatizing discourses. This double jeopardy disrupted what might have been ascendant developmental trajectories in pretend play, language, narrative, literacy, enjoyment of school, sense of belonging, and identity as learners. A similar pattern of mismatch dogged the early school career of Miguel, a child of Mexican immigrants in New York City. Miguel scored low on grade-level benchmarks that failed to take into account his experience as an emergent bilingual, yet his imaginative composing, involving drawing and writing, exceeded curricular standards. When standards tightened further in the second grade, exacerbating the mismatch with Miguel's mode of composing, his creativity and identity as an artist diminished.[1]

The Costs of Ever Higher (One-Size-Fits-All) Standards

We have already alluded to the role that negative stereotypes and stigmatizing discourses play in disproportionately disrupting the developmental trajectories of children from low-income and minority backgrounds. This is a global phenomenon; all the children in Chapter 2 were members of groups who were vulnerable to negative stereotyping in their respective societies. In this final section of the chapter, we bring deficit perspectives into sharper focus and argue that such perspectives are implicated in current educational trends intended to boost children's achievement.

Deficit discourses have a long history in the American context. In the middle of the last century, the prevailing view in psychology and education was that low-income children suffered from a host of deficiencies—in culture, cognition, and even play—that originated in the inadequacies of their home environments. Best known was the language-deprivation position, which explained the underachievement of poor and African American children not in terms of underfunded schools or racial segregation but in terms of a language deficit caused by parents who failed to provide sufficient linguistic stimulation during the early years of life. As a result of this deficit, so the reasoning went, children were so ill equipped for the cognitive and linguistic demands of the classroom—in some accounts they were said to have no language at all—that they had to be taught to speak.

The language-deprivation position inspired devastating critiques by leading social scientists of the day, who took issue on both empirical and theoretical grounds (e.g., Baratz, 1973; Bernstein, 1972; Cole & Bruner, 1971; Labov, 1972; Leacock, 1971). They argued that children from less privileged backgrounds acquired linguistic resources—languages, dialects, communicative codes, ways of speaking—that have their own integrity as communicative systems yet differ systematically from those of their more privileged counterparts. This argument can be seen as an early version of the argument undergirding this chapter, namely that all children bring resources with them when they come to school and that the most successful teachers are prepared to meet them where they are.

Although one would be hard pressed to find present-day proponents of language deprivation, as originally promulgated, there is growing awareness that discourses of deficiency are very much alive today (Dudley-Marling & Lucas, 2009; Genishi & Dyson, 2009; Michaels, 2011). Two key differences should be noted, however: Discourses are now couched in euphemistic terms—children are "at risk," "disadvantaged," or "diverse" rather than "deficient"—and basic premises are largely unspoken and implicit in institutional practices (Miller & Sperry, 2012). Tacit assumptions of deficiencies are apparent in the use of highly punitive and age-inappropriate discipline for minor infractions, as in the case of Gus, and in teachers' misconstruals of children's strengths as weaknesses, as in the cases of Miguel and Sheela and, from earlier work, Zena, and Deena. The latter illustrate what Pierre Bourdieu (1991) calls "misrecognition," the process by which individuals come to view the ways of speaking commanded by dominant groups as inherently more desirable. Systematic misrecognition essentializes the authority of dominant speakers and the lesser legitimacy of other ways of speaking, becoming a major mechanism by which symbolic domination of poor and minority children is achieved and helping to explain how macro-level dominant "orders" are reproduced at the micro-level.

We contend that this process of misrecognition is exacerbated by educational "reforms" that are intended, ironically, to boost achievement. At the very moment when urban schools in the US are becoming more diverse, language and literacy curricula are becoming more standardized and regimented, not more spacious and variegated (Genishi & Dyson, 2009). This trend, with its enforcement of one-size-fits-all standards at earlier and earlier grades, is a global phenomenon, as illustrated by the cases in Chapter 2. This narrowing of standards, with concomitant high-stakes testing, promotes misrecognition of low-income and minority children's strengths at every age by delegitimizing the resources they command.

But it is especially damaging in the early grades. When kindergarten teachers are evaluated on the basis of their students' academic performance, the time-honored mission of kindergarten as a low-key transitional year—a time to adapt to school, form relationships with peers, and engage in play and self-paced learning—is undercut. Thus, it is perhaps not surprising that one of the most powerful cautionary tales of misrecognition comes from kindergarten. Although Ta'Von emerged as a remarkable writer in the early months of kindergarten, his low ranking on mandated assessments in the first week of kindergarten left an indelible mark. Nothing he did—no matter how clever, fluent, or imaginative—was sufficient to raise him into the ranks of the officially designated "bright" children. The fact that his teacher had the confidence and long experience to resist the district's mandates and that she appreciated Ta'Von's strengths makes this outcome all the more dispiriting.

Sometimes it seems like the demand for ever higher one-size-fits-all standards for ever younger children is an unstoppable juggernaut. The case studies presented in this book reveal that one of the most damaging consequences of this trend is to breathe new life into narratives that demean poor and minority children, narratives that sow alienation and undermine the very goals that educational reforms were intended to promote. Against this onslaught, we take heart in the children who reclaimed what was theirs and composed lives that mattered, the peers who imagined with them, and the teachers who met them where they were: aspiring to speak grandfather's language, determined to be a literate girl, enraptured by superheroes.

Note

1   Although children from poor and minority backgrounds are especially vulnerable to this kind of disruption, even children who come from positions of privilege are not necessarily immune. Comber's (2014) longitudinal portrait of Tessa, a daughter of educated, middle-class parents in Adelaide, South Australia, is illustrative. As a four-year-old Tessa was precocious in her language and literacy development, an avid participant in literacy-related play, and a star pupil in preschool. Because the resources that she brought from home fit the sanctioned resources, her teachers had no trouble recognizing her school readiness and academic talent. Other positive connections between home and school, such as the Greek heritage of her first teacher, which matched her own family's ethnic background, also supported her development. However, in the third grade, Tessa's exceptional progress and enthusiasm for school began to decline in the face of challenges from the peer group. In literacy tasks assigned to groups or pairs, she was ostracized or criticized by other capable girls, in part, at least, because she was not "girlie." As a result, Tessa no longer felt she belonged in school. Although Tessa continued to develop her repertoire of literacy practices in the context of her home and family, her status as a high-achieving student and popular peer came to an end.

References

Baratz, J. C. (1973). Language abilities of Black Americans. In K. S. Miller & R. M. Dreger (Eds.), *Comparative studies of blacks and whites in the United States* (pp. 125–183). New York, NY: Seminar Press.

Bernstein, B. B. (1972). A critique of the concept of compensatory education. In C. B. Cazden, V. P. John, & D. Hymes (Eds.), *Functions of language in the classroom* (pp. 135–151). New York, NY: Teachers College Press.

Bourdieu, P. (1991). *Language and symbolic power.* Cambridge, MA: Harvard University Press.

Briggs, J. (1998). *Inuit morality play: The emotional education of a three-year-old.* New Haven, CT: Yale University Press.

Cole, M. (1996). *Cultural psychology: A once and future discipline.* Cambridge, MA: Harvard University Press.

Cole, M., & Bruner, J. S. (1971). Cultural differences and inferences about psychological processes. *American Psychologist, 26*(10), 867–876.

Comber, B. (2014). School literate repertoires: That was then, this is now. *Learning and Literacy, 11,* 16–31.

Corsaro, W. (2011). *The sociology of childhood* (3rd ed.). Thousand Oaks, CA: Pine Forge Press.

Corsaro, W., Molinari, L., & Rosier, K. B. (2002). Zena and Carlotta: Transition narratives and early education in the United States and Italy. *Human Development, 45,* 323–348.

Dewayani, S. (2013). What do you want to be when you grow up? Self-construction in Indonesian street children's writing. *Research in the Teaching of English, 47,* 365–390.

Dewey, J. (1985). *Democracy and education.* Carbondale, IL: Southern Illinois University Press.

Dudley-Marling, C., & Lucas, K. (2009). Pathologizing the language and culture of poor children. *Language Arts, 86,* 362–370.

Dyson, A. Haas (1993). *Negotiating a permeable curriculum: On literacy, diversity, and the interplay of children's and teachers' worlds.* Urbana, IL: National Council of Teachers of English.

Dyson, A. Haas (1997). *Writing superheroes: Contemporary childhood, popular culture, and classroom literacy*. New York, NY: Teachers College Press.

Garcia Coll, C., & Marks, A. K. (2009). *Immigrant stories: Ethnicity and academics in middle childhood*. New York, NY: Oxford University Press.

Gaskins, S., & Paradise, R. (2010). Learning through observation. In D. F. Lancy, J. Brock, & S. Gaskins (Eds.), *The anthropology of learning in childhood* (pp. 85–117). Lanham, MD: Alta Mira Press.

Genishi, C., & Dyson, A. Haas (2009). *Children, language, and literacy: Diverse learners in diverse times*. New York, NY: Teachers College Press and Washington, DC: National Association for the Education of Young Children.

Gibson, P. A., & Haight, W. (2013). Caregivers' moral narratives of their African American children's out-of-school suspensions: Implications for effective family–school collaborations. *Social Work, 58*, 263–272.

Gibson, A., Wilson, R., Haight, W., Kayama, M., & Marshall, J. M. (2014). The role of race in the out-of-school suspensions of black students: The perspectives of students with suspensions, their parents and educators. *Children and Youth Services Review, 47*, 274–282.

Gilmore, P. (1986). Sub-rosa literacy: Peers, play, and ownership in literacy. In B. B. Schieffelin & P. Gilmore (Eds.), *The acquisition of literacy: Ethnographic perspectives* (pp. 155–168). Norwood, NJ: Ablex.

Giroux, H. A. (1989). Schooling as a form of cultural politics: Toward a pedagogy of and for difference. In H. A. Giroux & P. McLaren (Eds.), *Critical pedagogy, the state and cultural struggle* (pp. 125–152). New York, NY: State University of New York Press.

Göncü, A. (Ed.). (1999). *Children's engagement in the world: Sociocultural perspectives*. Cambridge, England: Cambridge University Press.

Goodnow, J. J. (1990). The socialization of cognition: What's involved? In J. W. Stigler, R. A. Shweder, & G. Herdt (Eds.), *Cultural psychology: Essays on comparative human development* (pp. 259–286). Chicago, IL: University of Chicago Press.

Goodnow, J. J., Miller, P. J., & Kessel, F. (1995). *Cultural practices as contexts for development: New directions for child development, No. 67*. San Francisco, CA: Jossey-Bass.

Goodwin, M. H. (1990). *He-said-she-said: Talk as social organization among Black children*. Bloomington, IN: Indiana University Press.

Goodwin, M. H. (2009). Girls as adversarial virtuosos. In R. A. Shweder, T. R. Bidell, A. C. Dailey, S. D. Dixon, P. J. Miller, & J. Modell (Eds.), *The child: An encyclopedic companion* (p. 751). Chicago, IL: University of Chicago Press.

Greenfield, P. M., Keller, H., Fuligni, A., & Maynard, A. (2003). Cultural pathways through universal development. *Annual Review of Psychology, 54*, 461–490.

Haight, W., Gibson, P. A., Kayama, M., Marshall, J. M., & Wilson, R. (2014). An ecological-systems inquiry into racial disproportionalities in out-of-school suspensions from youth, caregiver and educator perspectives. *Child and Youth Services Review, 46*, 128–138.

Holland, D., Lachicotte, W., Skinner, D., & Cain, C. (1998). *Identity and agency in cultural worlds*. Cambridge, MA: Harvard University Press.

Labov, W. (1972). *Language in the inner city: Studies in the Black English Vernacular*. Philadelphia, PA: University of Pennsylvania Press.

Leacock, E. (Ed.). (1971). *The culture of poverty: A critique*. New York, NY: Simon & Schuster.

Liang, C.-H. (2000). Play in a working-class Taiwanese preschool (unpublished doctoral dissertation). University of Illinois at Urbana-Champaign, IL.

Liang, C.-H. (2011). Life in the preschool: Fieldwork, adults, and children. Taipei, Taiwan: Wunan [in Chinese].

Michaels, S. (1991). The dismantling of narrative. In A. McCabe & C. Peterson (Eds.), *Developing narrative structure* (pp. 303–351). Hillsdale, NJ: Erlbaum.

Michaels, S. (2011). Déjà vu all over again: What's wrong with Hart and Risley and a "linguistic deficit" framework? Paper presented at the annual meeting of the American Educational Research Association, New Orleans (April 8–12).

Miller, P. J., Cho, G. E., & Bracey, J. (2005). Working-class children's experience through the prism of personal storytelling. *Human Development, 48*, 115–135.

Miller, P. J., Fung, H., Lin, S., Chen, E. C-H., & Boldt, B. R. (2012). How socialization happens on the ground: Narrative practices as alternate socializing pathways in Taiwanese and European-American families. *Monographs of the Society for Research in Child Development, 77*(1), Serial No. 302.

Miller, P. J., & Goodnow, J. J. (1995). Cultural practices: Toward an integration of culture and development. In J. J. Goodnow, P. J. Miller, & F. Kessel (Eds.), *Cultural practices as contexts for development: New directions for child development (No. 67)* (pp. 5–16). San Francisco, CA: Jossey-Bass.

Miller, P. J., & Sperry, D. D. (2012). Déjà vu: The continuing misrecognition of low-income children's verbal abilities. In S. T. Fiske & H. R. Markus (Eds.), *Facing social class: How societal rank influences interaction* (pp. 109–130). New York, NY: Russell Sage.

Pratham Education Foundation (2013). *Annual Status of Education Report*. Retrieved from http://www.prathamusa.org/sites/default/files/aser_2013.pdf.

Rogoff, B. (2003). *The cultural nature of human development*. New York, NY: Oxford University Press.

Shweder, R. A., Goodnow, J. J., Hatano, G., LeVine, R. A., Markus, H. R., & Miller, P. J. (2006). The cultural psychology of development: One mind, many mentalities. In W. Damon (Series Ed.) & R. M. Lerner (Vol. Ed.), *Handbook of child psychology: Theoretical models of human development* (6th ed., vol. 1) (pp. 716–792). New York, NY: Wiley.

Weisner, T. S. (2002). Ecocultural pathways, family values, and parenting. *Parenting: Science and Practice, 2*, 325–334.

5

THE POWERS OF LANGUAGE

Toward Remixing Language Policy, Curricula, and Child Identities

Celia Genishi

> *Yo quiero hablar como mi Tata, su lengua.*
> (I want to speak like my *Tata*, his language.)

To open this chapter on the broad-ranging theme of language, I appropriate the words of Natalia, Iliana Reyes's six-year-old case study participant in Nealculiacán, Mexico. Natalia's pithy expression of desire to speak like her grandfather *Tata* in his indigenous language, náhuatl, alludes to multiple facets of language as it unfolds in the daily life of children and will unfold in this chapter: namely, language policy and language arts curricula, with their undergirding elements of power, choice, and identity.

The powers of language are ever present, in daily interactions, multimodal expressions of culture, popular and otherwise; esoteric systems of symbols manipulated by computer programmers or code-breakers. Language in its everyday form—that is, spoken language or talk—is placed in the foreground here, not standing alone but accompanying other forms of language that our case study participants draw upon as they go about the pleasure and business of composing themselves and elaborating upon their language identities.

The foundations of the chapter are framed historically by the research of psycholinguistic and sociolinguistic pathbreakers who created new boundaries around disciplines like psychology and sociology, by incorporating into them language, its development, and its variations in use (Brown, 1973; Ervin-Tripp & Mitchell-Kernan, 1977; Labov, 1970). Since the 1970s the primacy of social worlds and the dominant role of social situations (Cazden, 1970; Nelson, 2007) have at times melded with postmodern and critical stances that assert the fluidity of power (Foucault, 1980) and of individual and group language and racial/ethnic identities (hooks, 1994; Valenzuela, 1999). Despite the spread of theories to challenge inequities in schooling, national and school-based policies have continued to make power in education appear static, often fixed in standardized test scores and the curricular policies they shape (Genishi & Dyson, 2012).

Within an ever broadening disciplinary framework, research related to young children and their language and literacy appears bimodal, that is, there is a persistent vein of research that perpetuates deficit discourses about children from low-income families who are often of color (Bereiter & Engelmann, 1966; Fernald, Marchman, & Weisleder, 2012; Hart & Risley, 1995). Countering these discourses have been researchers in classrooms for young children who have described in detail the sociolinguistic abilities and flexibility of children who are often from low-income families of color (authors in this volume; Dyson, 1993b, 2013; Genishi & Dyson, 2009). Despite these careful studies, those who enact education policies continue to place children in risky situations where, like Miguel (Celia Genishi), they encounter a mismatch between their strengths and curiosities and insistent mandates, especially those related to language and literacy curricula.

In this volume the theme of *language* is most prominent as it is woven through the three case studies focusing on Rafiki (Esther Mukewa Lisanza), Natalia (Iliana Reyes), and Miguel, calling to mind complex layers of meaning. Language, which I define broadly as any system of symbols that convey meaning, varies in its uses, as well as in its practical manifestations. It is often used in partnership, as in *language choice, language curriculum, language policy*. These terms are relevant to groups of children and sometimes whole schools, communities, or countries. But language is also internal to individuals who use language, sometimes according to rules of the classroom and communities and sometimes according to their own creative rules. In this chapter I trace the different manifestations of *language* across the three case studies and then seek connections to the five other case studies and to the overall themes of the book. The fluidity of these phenomena, such as policies or identities, makes it hard to separate them from each other. Further, it is hard to separate them from the other broad themes of *agency* and *resources*. Agency, for example, seems integral to language choice, resistance to the use of a particular language, and specific interpretations of policy. Language is also a prime resource, which may be sanctioned or unsanctioned within and across social situations. All three broad themes (i.e., agency, resources, and language) are interwoven or instantiated in the lives of the case study children and those around them as they compose themselves through multiple modes and multiple languages.

Official and Unofficial Language Policies: Making Space for Local Interpretations

In the contrasting sociocultural contexts of the three case studies, there were important school-driven policies that theoretically determined children's and teachers' experiences in school. Although the public perception of a *policy* may be that of a fixed guideline—even a law—that shapes what students learn, in

Rafiki's, Natalia's, and Miguel's schools, classroom data showed that policies were not fixed, but fluid. In this section I consider the different ways in which policies were locally interpreted in particular communities in Kenya, Mexico, and the United States, three settings that were divergent geographically, socioculturally, politically, and educationally.

Rafiki's Classroom in Kenya: Children Blur the Borders of Language Policies

The national language policy in Kenya has declared the student's home language, Kamba, to be the language of instruction. However, in the particular rural primary school that Esther studied, Kamba was forbidden once Swahili was made the language of instruction. After Swahili was also banned, English became the language of instruction, in large part because the curriculum was test driven, and examinations were given in English. Moreover, although English was declared to be the official language, relatively few people spoke it. Children were not observed to speak it at home or in their communities. Thus school staff appeared to be in an uncertain place in terms of enforcing the official policy. How the official policy defined the curriculum and how children and teachers enacted it is considered next in light of Esther's observations.

Both the writing and reading curricula reflected the increasing pressure of tests and national examinations on teachers. In addition to national examinations, students took tests at the end of the month and term. As Esther noted, the National Syllabus states, "Specifically, the learner should acquire writing skills to be able to express own feelings and ideas meaningfully and legibly in correct English structure" (National Syllabus, p. 4). Examples of specific objectives emphasized form and not content, and they included the following:

- writing letters of the alphabet clearly and correctly
- writing patterns clearly and correctly
- writing names of objects
- drawing patterns and items
- writing simple sentences about things.

Objectives on the complete list were similar and thus, as Esther observed, there was virtually no room in the official curriculum for child expression or invention in speech or writing. The focus on writing was linked to a parallel focus on reading, despite the challenge of a very limited supply of textbooks to read. The school principal in fact told Esther that students were expected to read by the end of their third term (Lisanza, this volume, p. 101). We see next, though, how children and teachers were able to interpret and enact the constrained official policy in intriguingly flexible and creative ways.

Indeed children in Rafiki's classroom found their own curricular niches where they could deviate from the official English-only policy. Thus Esther had not only documented the official curriculum but also observed the occasional interactions when child-initiated spoken language was clearly heard. One example showed Rafiki to be in his role of teacher-pupil with two peers Mbula and Kasuku, who asked for his help while Mrs. Simba, their teacher, was at her desk apparently unaware of the children's talk. Mbula and Kasuku asked questions about the cloze task (e.g., "Drinking water makes us_____ (healthy, sick)"). In this short excerpt (Lisanza, this volume, p. 103), note that the three speak Swahili about the items written in English:

Mbula: *Rafiki hii tunafanya nini?* [Rafiki, what are we doing here?] (she points at the first blank: Drinking water _____)

Rafiki: *Unaandika sentensi na* answer [You write down the sentence and the answer].

Mbula: (to Kasuku in a singing tone) *Nimeelezewa na Rafiki* [I was explained to by Rafiki].

The dialogue continued as Rafiki comfortably helped his peers, and they happily accepted his explanations, as if help from Rafiki lent them a special status. The bilingual exchange demonstrated the constant overlap of talk, reading, and writing, as well as the efficacy of drawing on an officially forbidden language to complete their lesson. After they finished their collaboration, the three took their work to Mrs. Simba for grading.

There were also interactions that were unofficial and off-task, such as a musical one that children engaged in after completing an official task. Here is a summary of a memorable interaction (Lisanza, this volume, p. 104) that I'll call the "*kavuli* improv" or improvisation: Rafiki saw a dove near the classroom door and said softly "*kavuli, kavuli*" ("little dove, little dove") in Kamba; Amani followed by singing in Kamba a tune she appeared to invent about "*kavuli*"; and Titu then began a song in English about Jesus. Next Amani started a pop song in Swahili, and Kambua and Mhariri stood up to make dance-like movements. Children seated nearby said in Swahili that the two girls were learning to dance. In a short span of time the children softly and ingeniously improvised and expressed themselves in three languages, through speech, song, and then through dance.

Adults unfamiliar with this setting who hear conversations occurring largely in Kamba and Swahili may ask, "Are the teachers out of the room?" With a group of 89 children, teachers could easily be out of earshot, allowing children to use sanctioned and unsanctioned languages captured in song and reflected in dance. Esther offered an additional explanation when she described the sociocultural context experienced by the children and their families. The African Inland Church was the spiritual sponsor of the school, as well as a frequent and regular presence in the community. In fact families attended church on Thursdays and Sundays; and children attended assembly on Monday and Friday mornings at school, where they sang gospel songs, heard readings from the Bible, and prayed. Thus the song called "Jesus You Are a Winner," which Titu began to sing for his friends, was probably familiar to all. Note that this spontaneous multilingual ensemble event took place with no adult initiation or intervention. Thus the interaction illustrates the power of the children themselves to occasionally choose which languages to use in their chosen modes, within the context of conflicting school and national language policies. Given the large class size and limited materials, the human resources on display were remarkably impressive. Next we see a contrasting school and policy in Iliana's case study, while we also see the reappearance of music, this time in the sanctioned setting of school–community dialogues.

Natalia's School in Nealculiacán, Mexico: Awakening to Linguistic and Musical History

Iliana's case study of first grader Natalia is part of a larger ethnographic study focused on a small rural community and its bilingual school. The language arts curriculum provided a contrast to that of Esther's school because community members, some of whom knew the indigenous language, náhuatl, were invited to participate in classroom activities. The community members' relationship to language policies was complicated by national and local stances toward the many indigenous languages of Mexico, of which náhuatl is one of the most widely spoken.

According to its constitution Mexico recognizes all its indigenous languages. In practice the Spanish language dominates in schools, leading to the subtraction of indigenous languages like náhuatl from students' linguistic repertoires. As Iliana pointed out, success in school often came at the expense of their home languages and cultures. The observed school, however, was not typical, in that it was supported by both the SEP (*Secretaría de Educación Pública*, or Secretary of Public Education) and the Indigenous Secretary of Education. Moreover, the teacher Mariana and the school principal were strong supporters of Bilingual Indigenous Education.

Indeed Mariana, the teacher-researcher collaborating with Iliana, spoke about "awakening" the indigenous language among school and community members. In this welcoming environment it was no surprise that Natalia aspired to speak náhuatl, the language of *Tata,* her grandfather. Still, as in Esther's school in Kenya, there was conflicting evidence of support or lack of it for the everyday use of náhuatl. As Iliana pointed out, the school's sign was written boldly in Spanish and not in náhuatl. Such demonstrations of linguistic hegemony are visible in many locales, including the English-saturated United States.

As a participant in the Community Literacy Canasta project, Mariana collaborated to awaken children to the possibilities of their indigenous language by inviting community and family members into the classroom and curriculum, something the teachers in Esther's school in Kenya were not able to do. Music was a common thread that children happily took up, according to Esther's and Iliana's data, however; and Mariana incorporated it historically and personally into the curriculum by inviting Natalia's mother to share stories about her father, Natalia's grandfather *Tata*, with the group. *Tata* was the sole surviving member of a well-known band from the 1960s that played traditional instruments and created their lyrics in náhuatl. Interestingly, band members translated the lyrics into Spanish (few knew written náhuatl) largely so that the whole community could understand them. The twenty-first-century interest in awakening the community to its heritage language was not present decades earlier. Thus children with indigenous roots had grown up within a porous, non-rigid sociolinguistic context, where they became used to negotiating among generations, between their two languages. In this school, in collaboration with the teacher, participants developed their own linguistic policies and practices under a national policy affirming indigenous groups' rights.

Miguel's Classrooms in New York City: Where Language Policies Are Fluid but the Curriculum Rules

Like Esther's and Iliana's case studies, mine was embedded in a larger study in a complex sociocultural and political context. The public schools of New York City serve over a million students in five boroughs, including Manhattan, where my collaborators and I collected data (Falchi, Axelrod, & Genishi, 2014). We documented Miguel's language use from his days in Head Start until he completed second grade in a public school. Language policies appeared in many ways to be as open to interpretation in New York City as they were in Kenya and Mexico, despite differences in school size and organization. That is, administrators and teachers were aware of dominant linguistic and curricular policies, at the same time that they enacted their own interpretation of those policies at the local or school level.

The United States does not have an official language even though some states may designate English to be such. In practice English functions as the official language, and this practical reality influences curricular policies at every level of education. State governments have significant influence over local school districts, and individual schools have more or less autonomy, depending on the state and district. Within districts administrators in schools serving affluent students who have satisfactory test scores, for example, may allow or encourage curricular flexibility. As for Miguel, he had experienced several language policies by the time he completed the second grade. In his Head Start center the overall policy was to encourage children to use the language(s) they already knew, as well as the language(s) they did not know. Miguel heard and understood Mixteco at home, spoke Spanish at home and at the Head Start center, and began to speak English in his second (four-year-olds') year at that center.

In kindergarten Miguel became part of a public school dual language program that differed significantly from a monolingual English program. New York State provides instruction in English as a Second Language or bilingual instruction, depending on a public school's structure, parental preferences, and a complex assessment process. In Miguel's dual language program two days of the week were "Spanish days," two days "English days," and the fifth day was half Spanish and half English. As at the Head Start, however, in practice the language policy was fluid, and at the public school children and teachers were heard to use both languages, sometimes switching back and forth, rather than speaking only the language of the day. We observed that there was more flexibility—that is, practices were more child centered—in the kindergarten and first-grade years. By the second grade, the content became more academic more of the time, as if in preparation for the standardized tests to be administered at the end of the third grade. In addition that year the rule *"Trabajar en silencio"* ("Work in silence")— often openly disobeyed—was posted on the classroom wall.

Expectations for Miguel's classroom performance differed notably from those of Rafiki and Natalia in terms of language policy and the content of the language arts curriculum, which was highly prescribed. Like that of Miguel's classroom, the curriculum that Rafiki experienced was highly prescribed, but its straightforward content contrasted with the more elaborate, genre-oriented expectations of Miguel's school. Thus if Miguel had been a model student, he might have produced examples starting in the kindergarten, written in Spanish and English, of prescribed genres such as "personal narrative." Because he often took his own path toward (literacy) learning, however, Miguel resembled Rafiki and Natalia in one important way: He took an artistic and expressive path toward school learning, incorporating drawing rather than music into his distinctive work. Indeed his first-grade teacher, Ms. M, declared, *"Miguel es un artista"* ("Miguel is an artist").

By the time he became a second grader, narratives were less multimodal and less self-initiated because they were more regulated by the reading/writing curriculum. For Miguel the artist, the lack of fit between curricular demands and his written narratives increased to the point where the word *mismatch* best described his situation; and according to curricular benchmarks, he was consistently assessed as "low." The phenomenon of mismatch is relevant to other case study children and will be taken up again below.

Before moving on, I consider the underlying motif of curricular permeability (Dyson, 1993b) and some teachers' role in its enactment. Recall the notable instances of teachers who seem to be out of earshot or out of the vicinity of unsanctioned language interactions, for example, the multilingual *kavuli* improv or the use of Spanish and English in Miguel's classroom when only one of the languages was supposed to be used. Teachers may have been busy grading or working with other children, but they were probably aware of children speaking at unsanctioned times in unsanctioned languages. Perhaps the teachers were engaging in what we researchers at the conference called the "wink"; that is, a giving of unofficial permission. Winks allowed time and space for children to communicate, even invent, alone or with each other in the language or mode of their choice. (This phenomenon seems less nuanced but related to the sometimes mocking use of "wink" by ethnographers [Ryles, as cited in Geertz, 1973, p. 6]). Of course children are attuned enough to "observe" the wink and may even have a wink of their own. For example, when four-year-old Miguel very audibly said, "Thank you, Pat!" he may have been declaring that he knew more about English than he had let on, or he may have been gently mocking the Head Start teachers' routine push for polite displays. Thus subtle communicative choices, with or without spoken language, may be reciprocal and made by both teachers and children. How children's subtle or obvious official and unofficial language performances influenced their identities is considered next.

Language and Curricular Remixes: Choice and the Assertion of Identity

Policy has traditionally been thought of as a static predetermining entity. *Identity,* however, has not been considered static for a number of years (Grieshaber & Cannella, 2001; Martínez-Roldán, 2003). Identity circulates and shifts and may be constructed by others and/or by oneself. Still, curricular mandates may constrain children who find official lessons to be difficult. For these children official school identities are narrowly conceived.

Rigid Boundaries: Identities Fixed by Reading/Writing Curricula

Miguel, Natalia, and Rafiki captured a broad and intriguing range of identities in school, shaped not only by their individual personalities and propensities, but also by the respective language curricula of their schools. With the exception of Natalia's distinctively open curriculum, almost all of the schools of the eight case study children required teachers to follow curricular mandates. Each child, then, might develop, or their teachers might develop for them, an "official identity" related to their performances within the official curriculum. Unlike Natalia and Rafiki, Miguel seemed to be consistently constructed as a "low" performer, based on his inability to achieve curricular benchmarks; thus he was a mismatch with the official reading/writing curriculum in his primary school. Similarly Gareth (Jackie Marsh) and Gus (Barbara Comber and Lyn Kerkham) were also viewed as not matching or meeting narrow curricular criteria for success in their classrooms. Five-year-old Gareth, for instance, was expected in his school in northern England to master synthetic phonics according to the Read Write Inc. program, adopted as part of the new national literacy curriculum. In 2013 Australian schools also adopted a national curriculum incorporating literacy, so that Gus experienced a program in writing that was similar to Gareth's in degree of prescriptiveness. The program seemed to engage Gus so little in grades 2 and 3 that he was identified not according to his official performances but by his behavior issues (Comber & Kerkham, this volume, p. 59) In short, in their three geographically distant locations, the three boys could be described as mismatches bumping up against prescriptive curricula, and their officially constructed identity was "unsuccessful student."

Blurred Boundaries: Identities Expanded within Permeable Curricula

The boundary between official and unofficial curricula and identities is decidedly blurry. By looking beyond rigid time and curricular boundaries, we are able to focus on children like Natalia whose classroom experiences contrasted with the other case study children, most especially with Gus's. Mariana, Natalia's teacher, told the class to write about what they had heard regarding Natalia's *Tata*—she assigned a retelling that they could illustrate by imagining how the band looked as they performed many years ago. Encouraged by Mariana to use Spanish and náhuatl, Natalia began to write her *Tata*'s language, borrowing some náhuatl words and inserting them into her mostly Spanish text. Thus began the biliterate expansion of her language identity to include some ancestral words. Indeed the Community Literacy Canasta project was an ongoing and open invitation to children and adults to identify more with their indigenous language and culture and less with dominant Spanish/colonial forms of expression.

In his classroom in Kenya, Rafiki's indigenous language and culture made their appearances, alongside the official curriculum that structured most of the children's school experiences. Rafiki enjoyed multiple identities that bordered on official and unofficial. For example, there was his hyphenated identity as a "teacher-pupil." Of course his own behaviors were key to his being constructed as helpful or, as Esther pointed out, as a "more capable peer" (Vygotsky, 1978, p. 86). Moreover, the classroom context, with 89 children, was one in which pupils who could help teach would be clearly identified and valued.

Continuing to look beyond rigid curricular boundaries, we are able to see "unsuccessful students" Gareth, Gus, and Miguel display looser, more fluid identities. For example, in the prekindergarten years Miguel began to compose his identity as a bilingual speaker who seemed comfortable code-switching (Blom & Gumperz, 1986; Martínez, 2010) by the time he was five years old. Then in the primary grades, he was known by some as Miguel the artist. Like Miguel, Gareth appeared to be more comfortable with drawing than writing. Fortunately his teacher Miss Fairweather made Read Write Inc. lessons permeable enough to allow Gareth to be an artist, to draw a story retelling and make playful child-initiated conversation along the way with his friends. Indeed the children in his class had opportunities for play of all kinds before and after their math- and literacy-focused times on the carpet. To add to his classroom identity as a playful artist, Gareth was becoming an expert in digital literacies at home on the iPad. This was an identity that did not permeate the Read Write Inc. curriculum but that Jackie came to know outside Gareth's classroom.

Second grader Gus, in contrast, was more comfortable reading than drawing or writing. In fact he was especially uncomfortable with writing. Thus his official identity as a literacy learner was partial at best. In year 2 Barbara and Lyn observed him participating in reading lessons and drawing on his oral language abilities as he contributed to group discussions. In fact his teacher Heather was pleased with his oral participation. By year 3, however, Gus lacked confidence in both reading and writing and, sadly, also in social interactions. The researchers learned during the first term of year 3 that Gus had acquired a new official identity, that of a student with behavior issues (Comber & Kerkham, this volume, p. 59), certainly not an identity he would have desired for himself. In fact he was expelled for ten weeks because of his behaviors, not because of weak performances in reading and writing. Thus his opportunities at that time to compose a reading/writing self in the classroom were nil.

Offering a striking contrast to Gus, kindergartner Ta'Von (Anne Haas Dyson) sought and built classroom experiences marked by "respectful inclusion and playful companionship" (Dyson, this volume, p. 30) via a playfully animated and sociable self. In a classroom where he was one of two African American boys, Ta'Von stood out. He occasionally used features of African American Vernacular English (AAVE), often burst into spontaneous song, and had hair styles that included braids and "meatballs," from Ta'Von's perspective. With all of his distinctiveness, after just a few months he succeeded in reading and writing within the mandated curriculum. According to his teacher Ms. Norton, he was "amazing" (Dyson, this volume, p. 29).

Ironically, this informal assessment of his work, which sounded like a synonym for "really high performing," did not gain him entry into the group of children that Ms. Norton termed "bright." To those of us who came to know him through Anne's case study, Ta'Von seemed like the very definition of "bright"—motivated, eager to be a friend to all, distinctive in his modes of expression, able to complete his assigned tasks and then some. Anne posited that even a teacher with a permeable curriculum may be influenced by societal views of race and class and their potential intersection with varied mandated assessments. It appeared that most of Ta'Von's peers easily identified him as a playful and competent companion, but his teacher did not extend to him the identity of the highly respected group called "bright"; those "bright" children were so identified through their scores at school entry on mandated assessments (e.g., naming letters, identifying letter sounds). Such were the politics of an otherwise welcoming classroom, at the nexus of curricular and assessment mandates and a local form of informal assessment.

Reflecting on Ta'Von's story led me to step away from the sociopolitical context of schools where the curriculum rules and think about inclusiveness in contrasting sites where "bright" is not a defining category, yet where children seem undeniably bright.

Sheela (Urvashi Sahni), for instance, was a second grader in the state of Uttar Pradesh, India, whose experience with the official curriculum was defined by the act of carefully and beautifully copying letters, words, and short sentences in Hindi from a textbook on to a wooden slate. Child-initiated composing was not an option. Still Urvashi observed Sheela going beyond the borders of the official curriculum, by copying poems from scraps of newspaper discovered by Sheela and her friend.

During Urvashi's teacher research project, Sheela moved beyond her narrow official identity as a compliant student, occasionally creating stories while looking at pictures in textbooks with a peer. Sheela also "began to write and draw her worlds" (Sahni, this volume, p. 71) with Urvashi providing opportunities to draw, speak, and write about her experiences and curiosities. Eventually Sheela crossed the border into reflecting on the self she was composing, declaring her friendships with peers and with Urvashi as well, despite her classroom teacher's caveat that teachers like Urvashi, called *Mamiji* or "aunt," are not students' friends. In this new unconventionally inclusive space Sheela began to construct a "permissible" self (Bruner, p. 91, cited in Sahni) who within the boundaries of story could change where the cultural divide between teacher and student fades. Sheela invented stories as well when she imagined how her daily life might be transformed. In one such story her mother approved of her going to school, rather than rejecting the idea, which she did in conversation with Urvashi. By means of this teacher research project, Urvashi, Sheela, and her friends demonstrated their collective agency and expanded the life spaces of their permissible selves, thereby composing multiple and expanded identities.

In yet another contrasting sociopolitical setting, Danti (Sophie Dewayani) lived in a locale in Bandung, Indonesia, where four- and five-year-old children spent time on the streets singing and performing to contribute to their families' incomes. To provide an education so that children could learn the curriculum of classrooms, the Indonesian government offered the program called Education for All, an aspirational name for an inclusive program. One consequence of this program was the opportunity for children like Danti to attend an Early Childhood Center for part of the morning. The founding teacher Bu Sri taught reading, writing, and math skills in enjoyable ways to prepare the children for school, where on entry they would be expected to know basic skills. Some child-oriented and child-welcomed ways included popular culture and are considered in the next section.

> 's exciting to think, write, talk about, and create art that reflects passionate engagement with popular culture, because this may very well be "the" central future location of resistance struggle, a meeting place where new and radical happenings can occur.
>
> (hooks, 1994, p. 427)

Classrooms are usually constrained places, lacking in passion; yet across our case studies we have seen that children find spaces where they expand their identities through multiple symbolic modes. As hooks (1994) notes, popular culture may be the irresistible site for change and, from our perspective, for education reform that incorporates "flex" and not the rigidity of test scores. Almost all of the eight child study participants demonstrated a strong interest in popular culture, whether it was through enthusiasm for Dora, a popular song, video game, popular hairdo, superhero, or cartoon. To conclude this chapter on language, I look across children and settings and imagine how the children might contribute their own reforms on a stage with enough room for creativity.

Returning to Danti's early childhood center in Indonesia, we saw that it fell outside an official curricular boundary. Bu Sri created a permeable curriculum with many points of entry for child discourse about characters and topics that appealed to the children. As Sophie discussed, Dora the Explorer was part of the scene, via televised episodes in Indonesian. (The original videos in English and Spanish were not played because there was a special fee for those.) The presence and popularity of television characters like Dora and SpongeBob and the added joy of singing local pop songs made the preschool year playful and full of language, spoken, heard, and sung. Danti's classroom was not conventionally multilingual, but it was clearly multimodal. Thus it served as a reminder that early childhood classrooms are most vibrant when children's preferences are not only allowed but encouraged. It is also a reminder that curricular boundaries that constrain children and create the heartrending practice of officially identifying students as "low" or unsuccessful in their first years of schooling are of adults' making and should be erased in favor of permeable and inclusive curricula.

Whether our case study children worked in the streets while not in school or went home to play in a cramped or ample space, they all sought spaces where they could engage in their own cultural practices. Music was the most frequent and spontaneous mode for that engagement. So how appropriate that the theme of this chapter has been language. Children can play with language like a musical theme; they can transform its tempo, melody, volume, or medium. And in fact there were events like the *kavuli* improv of Rafiki and his friends when children playfully created multilingual, multimodal social moments that made a constraining official curriculum permeable.

Imagine how the eight children might create an educational remix, their own theme and variations. Imagine how they might cross sociolinguistic and geographic boundaries to locate a curriculum that matched their ways of composing through language and other modes of expression. What if Gareth, Gus, or Miguel found themselves in a community-linked curriculum similar to Natalia's where their family members' cultural practices were jumping-off points for learning? And what if modes of expression could be oral, written, or read; musical or artistic; electronic or not? What if Sheela and Ta'Von were able to relocate to a school like Danti's for school-aged children where the teacher might allow border-crossing friendships of all kinds and literacy lessons that incorporated child-chosen elements of popular culture? What if Danti found herself in a kindergarten classroom like Ta'Von's where school-like lessons shared the curricular stage with child-oriented play and children's inventions? What if Rafiki and Natalia were able to participate in a multilingual program something like Miguel's that was permeable enough to include the use of indigenous languages, alongside a curriculum spacious enough for multiple modes of child improvisation? Imagine the eight children presented in this volume on a vast stage together, where they each find the time and space to express themselves, play, and befriend each other. Here their fluid choices of expressive modes and their developing identities would be valorized in sanctioned and unsanctioned moments, pushing through in a permeable curriculum.

Over a hundred years ago, philosopher John Dewey (1959/1897) wrote about education not as test-driven curricula but as experience, describing children as "social individuals" who had their own interests and aimed to be part of a classroom community. Ironically in the United States, the purported birthplace of child-centered, progressive education, there is now a federal policy called Race to the Top (US Department of Education, 2014), which relies heavily on standardized tests to measure success in schools and thus leads to many instances of mismatch between children and curricula. Curricula that supposedly prepare students for these tests often emphasize the need for independent learners, children who do not share and do not peek at their friends' work. Yet the data in our case studies have revealed that children in widely separated schools across the globe insisted on their own powerful language-based practices, so that they could be social individuals composing their productions in creative and unique ways. Children everywhere can do this—given more time and space, they can continue to compose themselves on an expanding global stage.

References

Bereiter, C., & Engelmann, S. (1966). *Teaching disadvantaged children in the preschool.* Englewood Cliffs, NJ: Prentice-Hall.

Blom, J.-P., & Gumperz, J. J. (1986). Social meaning in linguistic structures: Code-switching in Norway. In J. J. Gumperz & D. Hymes (Eds.), *Directions in sociolinguistics: The ethnography of communication* (pp. 407–434). New York, NY: Blackwell. (Originally published in 1972.)

Brown, R. (1973). *A first language: The early stages.* Cambridge, MA: Harvard University Press.

Bruner, J. S. (1990). *Acts of meaning.* Cambridge, MA: Harvard University Press.

Cazden, C. B. (1970). The neglected situation in child language research and education. In F. Williams (Ed.), *Language and poverty: Perspectives on a theme* (pp. 81–101). Chicago, IL: Markham.

Dewey, J. (1959). My pedagogic creed. In M. S. Dworkin (Ed.), *Dewey on education.* New York, NY: Teachers College Press. (Originally published in 1897.)

Dyson, A. Haas (1993). *Social worlds of children learning to write in an urban primary school.* New York, NY: Teachers College Press.

Dyson, A. Haas (2013). *ReWRITING the basics: Literacy learning in children's cultures.* New York, NY: Teachers College Press.

Ervin-Tripp, S., & Mitchell-Kernan, C. (Eds.). (1977). *Child discourse.* New York, NY: Academic.

Falchi, L. T., Axelrod, Y., & Genishi, C. (2014). "*Miguel es un artista*"—and Luisa is an excellent student: Seeking time and space for children's multimodal practices. *Journal of Early Childhood Literacy, 14,* 345–366.

Fernald, A., Marchman, V. A., & Weisleder, A. (2012). Socioeconomic status differences in language processing skill and vocabulary are evident at 18 months. *Developmental Science, 16,* 1–13.

Foucault, M. (1980). *Power/knowledge: Selected interviews and other writings 1972–1977.* New York, NY: Pantheon.

Geertz, C. (1973). *The interpretation of cultures.* New York, NY: Basic Books.

Genishi, C., & Dyson, A. Haas (2009). *Children, language, and literacy: Diverse learners in diverse times.* New York: Teachers College Press and Washington, DC: National Association for the Education of Young Children.

Genishi, C., & Dyson, A. Haas (2012). Racing to the top: Who's accounting for the children? In G. Boldt & B. Ayers (Eds.), Occasional Paper #27, *Challenging the politics of the teacher accountability movement: Toward a more hopeful educational future.* New York, NY: Bank Street College of Education. http://bankstreet.edu/occasionalpapers/op27/part-ii/whos-accounting-children/.

Grieshaber, S., & Cannella, G. S. (2001). *Embracing identities in early childhood education: Diversity and possibilities.* New York, NY: Teachers College Press.

Hart, B., & Risley, T. R. (1995). *Meaningful differences in the everyday experience of young American children.* Baltimore, MD: Paul H. Brookes.

hooks, b. (1994). Postmodern blackness. In P. Williams & L. Chrisman (Eds.), *Colonial discourse and post-colonial theory: A reader.* New York, NY: Columbia University Press.

Labov, W. (1970). The logic of nonstandard English. In F. Williams (Ed.), *Language and poverty: Perspectives on a theme* (pp. 153–189). Chicago, IL: Markham.

Martínez, R. A. (2010). Spanglish as literacy tool: Toward an understanding of the potential role of Spanish-English code-switching in the development of academic literacy. *Research in the Teaching of English, 45,* 124–149.

Martínez-Roldán, C. (2003). Building worlds and identities: A case study of the role of narratives in bilingual literature discussions. *Research in the Teaching of English, 37(4),* 491–526.

Nelson, K. (2007). *Young minds in social worlds: Experience, meaning, and memory.* Cambridge, MA: Harvard University Press.

U.S. Department of Education (2014). *Race to the Top Fund*. Retrieved from http://www2.
ed.gov/programs/racetothetop/index.html.

Valenzuela, A. (1999). *Subtractive schooling: U.S.–Mexican youth and the politics of caring*. Albany,
NY: State University of New York Press.

Vygotsky, L. S. (1978). *Mind in society: The development of higher psychological processes*.
Cambridge, MA: Harvard University Press.

SECTION 3

On Composing Childhoods

6

MAKING SPACE FOR MISSING CHILDHOODS

Implications for Theory, Policy, and Pedagogy

Anne Haas Dyson

> When I was a child I used to play a game, spinning a globe . . . and jabbing down my finger without looking where. If it landed on land I'd try to imagine what was going on "there" "then." . . . My knowledge was extremely rudimentary but I was completely fascinated by the fact that all these things were going on now, while I was here in Manchester in bed.
>
> (Massey, 2005, p. 14)

Like the social geographer Doreen Massey, I have vivid childhood memories of thinking about space as filled with "a simultaneity of stories-so-far" (p. 9). When I was about eight or nine, I would spend Saturday afternoons in our two-room village library, often down in the basement. The attraction was old *National Geographics*. My school had some copies of that magazine . . . with many missing pictures, cut out by adults who thought we children had never seen a human body. I would sit on the floor of the dimly lit basement, pull a stack of magazines from a cardboard box, and thumb through each page by page, looking for kids. One image, and the feelings it elicited, has stayed in my memory through these many decades. It is a photo of a child, living somewhere on the African continent; the child is alone, the frame close in as he stands by a tree, dry land stretching off into the distance.

Where, I wondered, was the child's family? Did he have a mother? Did he have any friends? The child was beautifully decorated, which suggested a careful adult hand. Still, the child was all alone and not smiling. I worried about that child. I searched through the boxes of magazines, trying to find a later issue where he might be featured again. The child as subject of someone else's agency was in the picture; but there was no person there, no agentive being steeped in human connections, no intentional actor participating in the daily practices—or special events—that make a meaningful life. Looking back now, as an adult, I realize that, since I knew nothing of what that child did with whom, I also knew nothing of what the child knew—what he had gleaned from participating in daily practices and, thus, his accumulating resources. He was just a figure alone, staring ahead, perhaps at the adult calculating the settings necessary for the desired image. Given his placement in a *National Geographic* article, he was no doubt a representative of his time and place, of "his people."

As argued in this book, intentional children too often disappear into essentialized categories, like the "at risk," their school identity calculated through formal and informal test scores. Such a label often is linked to an "unflattering back story" (Miller & Sahni, this volume, p. 186). As was particularly vivid in the cases of Gus and Danti, these back stories extend to children's families and to parents, who may be perceived as failing to properly support—or even send—their children to school, given a flaw in their value system. Such stories draw a picture frame tightly around an unknown child, as assumptions about family life echo in the distance. Poverty, migration, racism, classism, sexism—larger societal structures that influence a child's life—are outside the frame (Noguera, 2013); so too is the child's potential identity as friend, player, singer, drawer, and, highlighted herein, composer with images and words.

Within a society, poor children, disproportionately children of color, may be "other" to the dominant group; within a global view, as terms of comparison shift, they may be "other" to children of more privileged nation states. To counter the power-infused, distancing discourse of "other" children, this book has offered case studies of young school entrants and their composing; the cases, drawn from larger ethnographic studies, are filled with the particulars of children's lives (Abu-Lughod, 1991).

Despite the tremendous variation in the sociopolitical, economic, and curricular situations of children's schooling, comparative study revealed commonalities as well. All children brought to school resources, among them, their language(s), their knowledge of their home places—their markets, their churches, their physical surroundings, their daily rituals—and the images, songs, and stories important to them. Depending on available and appealing technologies, all children used symbols—they talked (whether or not they were "supposed to"), they sang, most drew, and all played. And, finally, for all, their experience of school was tied to relationships, real or longed for, with peers and teachers. Amid relationships and symbol-making of all sorts, children's intentional use (or avoidance) of writing took shape. In these stories of child composing, issues of identity and power also took shape, wrapped around the themes of provision for child agency, for child-valued resources, and for access to an expanding repertoire of languages.

Collectively, then, the authors of these cases have uncovered how and under what circumstances young children are likely to find writing relevant to their lives as children. These processes and circumstances, and their interwoven issues, are what Erickson (1986) might call "concrete universals" (p. 130). Even given great variation in children's schooling circumstances, to become composers with written language, all children need to find relevance in, and a comfortable symbolic home for, written language in their communicative repertoire; and this relevance may be found in official or unofficial child worlds or even in the intersection of the two.

In the remainder of this chapter, I conclude our group's reflective and collective scrapbook, as it were, by discussing the implications of the project for literacy theory, educational policy, and everyday pedagogy.

Complexities of Studying the Written Language of School Children: Finding Relevance

Children as just that, *children*, are usually missing from grand theorizing about literacy and social lives. On that intellectual playground, the big kids—the teenagers, the undergraduates—*have* emerged as major players (e.g., Fisher, 2007; Jocson, 2006; Kirkland, 2013). But if young children appear at all, they are viewed through the life worlds of adults; those adults are theoretically located in culturally distinct, separate communities. Children are the apprentices, the not-yet fully functioning members (e.g., Barton & Papen, 2010; Heath, 1983).

However, the major theoretical issues that dominate writing studies are all there in children's worlds and, indeed, have been threaded throughout this book. Among those issues are (a) the potential for composing to deliberately and critically mediate ideological tensions, formed at the intersections of structural dynamics in local places (e.g., issues of gender, class, race, age, religion); (b) the situated nature of multimodal design and its ramifications for literacy development; and (c) the politics of a multilingual repertoire.

Below, I provide samples from the case studies of these issues. As has been so throughout the book, understanding the case studies and their potential for informing theory requires approaching children not simply as learners, but as agents in life spaces shared with other children (Wells, 2009). Moreover, any classroom space entails both official and unofficial or child-controlled worlds, which may or may not inform each other. Finally, the issues must be embedded in the materiality of local spaces (e.g., their organization of people, the presence and nature of official and unofficial tools and texts, the valued channels of communication), which are themselves infused with structural dynamics (e.g., consumer marketing, language ideologies, and educational and political mandates). So, as the discussion unfolds, the children are portrayed within a dynamic "frame" in which they are highlighted but neither alone nor static. The discussion will leak into matters of policy and pedagogy, matters to be stressed in major sections to come.

Critical Mediation of Ideologies and Identities:
Sample Child Voices

Among the pertinent cases of critical mediation are those of Sheela and Ta'Von.
They each had teachers who allowed for child agency, and important relationships
with others. Sheela's agency as a writer evolved within her relationships with
her friends, with whom she shared copied bits of poetry in the unofficial world.
A key relationship in supporting Sheela's encoding of her *own* words was her
loving, encouraging relationship with Urvashi herself. Within that teacher–student
relationship, Sheela wrote her right to be an agent in her world, a "friend" to
her teachers as well as her peers, and a person who was worthy of being supported
by women who believed in her education, even if that worthiness was
problematized by poverty, gender, and village tradition.

Ta'Von, in a relatively more affluent school, nonetheless found aspects of his
racial, cultural, and gendered self questioned in his classroom. From the very
beginning of his kindergarten year, he thus found composing a relevant tool;
through its use, he claimed his identity through images of his physical features—
the braids on his head, the color of his skin—and of his relational self, as his
represented image was alongside family or friends. Indeed his talk during
composing revealed his efforts to reach out to peers through composing and,
thereby, to become someone who belonged, who was not an "other" to his
classmates.

Sheela and Ta'Von were literally worlds apart. Yet, the comparison of their
stories suggests what matters in young children's grappling with critical (power-
related) issues in their own lives. First, for both, these issues were crystallized for
them in the classroom: Sheela's gender and caste were experienced in an education
initially limited in its lack of space for child voice and in its precarious future
for a village girl; Ta'Von's racialized self, symbolized by his hair, was marked as
out of bounds for a proper little boy. Second, both found ample support in the
classroom as well; their ventures into composing were linked to relationships that
mattered. Finally, for these small children, imagination and symbolic tools—
composing through images and words—mattered in envisioning and even
demanding social recognition and respect from others.

The Situated Nature of Multimodal Design: Sample Artists,
Singers, and Talkers

In children's official worlds, written text could be disconcertingly set apart from
other symbolic media. For example, Rafiki's official writing curriculum had
him, and his 88 peers, copying words and sentences from the board. There was
no composing at all in writing class. But, unofficially, in the cracks in the official
curriculum, Rafiki and his peers found agentive space; they drew, wrote, sang,
recited and wrote poems, stories, and accounts of special happenings. These

symbolic tools were not kept separate but intermingled in individual
social events.

This easy movement among, and "weaving" of, symbols (Dys
evident in many children's cases in official and/or unofficial wor
example, Danti's child-invented Dora the Explorer clapping g
she appropriated that game to bring agentive energy and even joy to an official
composing task. (Readers might imagine how thrilled Danti might be to share
her "D" with "Dora.") Or recall Gareth, who, with his talk, transformed a teacher-
assigned story map into an unofficial dramatic encounter with his friends. And
then there was Miguel, an absorbed player, a fan of animals, and an artist; his
visual artistry could contextualize his writing in first grade. In second grade, though,
the rigidity and complexity of the assigned writing tasks seemed to leave Miguel
with no official recognition of his intentional, even intense, artistry.

In sum, case comparison allowed us a multilayered examination of symbol
use in the classroom, itself a multilayered world. Intentional symbol-weaving
could occur in the unofficial world; that world provided potential companions
and child-controlled space for valued resources, be they popular media images
or church songs. Symbol weaving could also occur in unofficial transformations
of official tasks into more relevant ones. Finally, it could occur in a "permeable"
official curriculum (Dyson, 1993); children could bring their intentions and
resources into the official world, where they were recognized by the teacher.
That permeable curriculum could disappear, though, if narrow, inflexible curricular mandates took over; at the same time, unofficial space could be squeezed
by disciplinary regulations (e.g., "no talking").

Children, then, tended to engage in multimodal composing, given time and
space (however unofficial) for child agency in choosing to use familiar symbolic
tools and valued resources. This tendency makes sense, first, because in at least
some ways, there was textual multimodality in children's lives, be it the arrangement of image and word in textbooks, the design of print and image on food
cartons and public buildings, or children's potential awareness of digital media
(featured in Gareth's case, in the data from his home); still, most children may
have been aware of the ubiquitous family cell phone, with its communicative
tool kit of talk, image, and sound [present in the homes of Esther's Kenyan village,
though televisions and computers were not (personal communication)]). Second,
developmentally, children tended to contextualize early explorations of print in
familiar symbol systems—play, drawing (if materials were available), and, of course,
talk (Vygotsky, 1978). Readers might recall Gareth's "X marks the spot," Ta'Von's
"reading" of the numbers 5 and 6, and Natalia's intense interest in biliteracy
embedded in her relationship with her grandfather *and* in learning about his
traditional music. Multimodality is not a school-imposed curricular trend; it is,
in fact, how the very young approach the new medium of written language.
This approach to written language through familiar and appealing media could
be problematized by the narrow focus of literacy programs on benchmarked skills,

even in classrooms for five-year-olds, if not younger. Gus, as readers might recall, avoided drawing and felt helpless about writing. We might wonder what symbolic tools he *was* comfortable with. Did he like to build with construction blocks, or did he dramatize scenes with play figures? Such activities can necessitate signs or lead to enacted, dictated, and co-written stories. Was he interested in family members' names, or those of favorite media characters or popular singers? We participants knew what five-year-old Gus could not do, but the school frame around him was so narrow, we now can only imagine possibilities to counter our worries.

The topic of multimodality *should* open up children's pathways into composing. At the same time, it should change the end goal of school composing, from one solely concerned with written text to one valuing children's deliberate use of multiple semiotic systems, including languages and language variants, to produce a text appropriate for the situation (Dyson, 2013; The New London Group, 1996). This latter point leads us to our last issue, the politics of multilingualism.

The Politics of a Multilingual Repertoire: Sample Language Performers

As detailed by Celia in Chapter 5, children in our collective group included those with multilingual repertoires, all of whom had the potential to stretch their repertoires and add new communicative ways . . . if those ways were both accessible and relevant in their daily lives. All languages in a multilingual repertoire, though, were not equal; their very existence bespoke a political history that affected geographic sites, children, and children's families as well (e.g., through war, colonialism, immigration). Insight into the impact of colonialism on children's language lives and a means for countering it are suggested by cross-case comparison.

To begin with just two of the three featured cases, Spanish was the imposed language of power for Natalia, and typically it dominates in Mexican schools. Náhuatl, however, was the indigenous (i.e., pre-colonial) language spoken by Natalia's beloved grandfather, understood by her mother, and included in the communicative repertoire of her teacher. Iliana, Natalia's teacher, and other teachers and community members, particularly Natalia's mother, joined together to revitalize the indigenous language through stories, songs, and traditions. Despite the lack of material resources, Natalia saw náhuatl as indeed part of her heritage, a language she wanted to learn and one featured in her official curriculum.

An opposing school situation existed for Rafiki. He spoke Kamba, the indigenous language of his village. Far from being promoted by the school, Kamba was banned, despite a national policy allowing use of children's native languages in the early grades. Rafiki also spoke Swahili, another indigenous language and a lingua franca of southeastern Africa. There was one class in his school in Swahili, which was banned too after the early grades. The colonial language was English, although it was not the language spoken by the multilingual Rafiki and his peers.

The children's schooling, however, emphasized English, since it was the language of important exams. The children's use of other languages was officially seen as subtracting from their achievement in English.

What is dramatized through these two cases is children's differential dependency on school and community for fostering potential languages in their repertoire. Rafiki's indigenous language was a vibrant part of his village life; in that village, multilingualism was the norm. This was seen in the unofficial world, in which children moved among languages, including English, shaped, as it could be, by memorable rhymes and songs from nursery school or church. However, the children were dependent on school for English and for learning literacy and other content taught in this language they did not understand; this did not bode well for their academic futures (Trudell & Piper, 2013).

For Natalia, the indigenous language was disappearing, overwhelmed by the dominance of Spanish in schools and out. Natalia's key relationship in that language was with her grandfather, who lived some distance away. Thus, she needed the support of the school and, through teachers' and Iliana's efforts, the community to fulfill her potential to become bilingual and biliterate. We learn language if it is a relevant, accessible tool in our lives. It is not a singular achievement.

If Rafiki and Natalia are in quite contrasting situations, Miguel is in the middle, in terms of becoming multilingual and multiliterate. Living in a Spanish-speaking family and a Latino neighborhood in New York City, and attending schools that allowed and furthered his emergent bilingualism, Miguel's Spanish and English seemed well supported in school and out. By the age of four, his code-switching skill was evident. (Miguel also had receptive skills in his heritage language, Mixteco, spoken by his parents, but that language played no role in schooling; we do not know how the language fared in Miguel's repertoire.)

Miguel's bilingualism, including his bilteracy, did not coexist underneath the official school curriculum like Rafiki's, nor did it seem to be a world-expanding aspect of official schooling, as did Natalia's. His school challenges in composing were not related to some sort of mythical "at riskness" due to his language flexibility, nor even to schooling in a language he did not control. As Celia details, Miguel's challenges were related to an increasingly rigid and confusing writing curriculum, even in a language he controlled. A thoughtful artist when approaching valued tasks, Miguel's intensity and creativity were no match for the linear, text-centered march of a complex writing curriculum; that curriculum explicitly demanded genres that had no particular relevance, no particular sense in Miguel's life, nor was there an official effort to make them relevant.

The relationship between languages and schooling in a child's history is complexly related to power, history, geography, personal disposition, and school policy and curriculum. There is no one story, just a complex narrative that, we hope, will build on a child's already existent repertoire. Although I have concentrated here on our bilingual/multilingual cases, the same is true for a child's particular version of a societal language. African American Vernacular, for example (evident in Ta'Von's case), arose from an oppressive history, is popular among the hiphop generation, and often dismissed as "not school language," much like Kamba. But, like Kamba, it is a vibrant language with relevance in individual and community life; as such, it will be sustained even as it evolves (Smitherman, 2006). Thus, vibrant languages that are part of children's everyday lives are potential rich resources for children's composing.

Policy Support for an Appropriate Education for the Young: Arranging for Relevance

Educational policy is not a decontextualized document, a "disembodied thing," as Teresa McCarty explains (2011, p. xii); rather, it is a situated and dynamic process, enacted through practices and imbued with ideologies and attitudes that influence people's arrangement for, and choices about, children's use of language, including their composing. As illustrated most vividly in Celia's Chapter 5, there are the policies seemingly fixed at the macro level by federal or state mandates; those may be reinterpreted by a district or individual school, which has its own policies, perhaps those that are imagined to yield higher test scores. In the end, policies are embodied in the moment-to-moment decisions made by teachers who are accountable to their supervisors but also, of course, to their children; moreover, in unofficial worlds, children may have their own ways of working underneath and around enacted policies.

Perhaps most troubling to our group were those policies set at the macro level by legislative mandates or Boards of Education that stressed accountability as defined by achievement test scores. In urban areas of the US, those scores might be a potential key to a school's survival and a teacher's paycheck. Among our case study children, most had curricular lives informed by national objectives and varied kinds of exams; these tended to fragment literacy actions into skills to be mastered in each grade level, as children climbed the ladder of success.

Adult motivations, of course, are not those of small children. Throughout this book, an important aim has been to look at school from the viewpoint of those small children and, having done so, to figure out how composing becomes a relevant tool for the very young. As a collective, we have not thought of children narrowly as a set of testing scores, but as complex people situated in the daily practices of their worlds as they understand them. Like us all, school children need relationships that matter; in school, those key relationships are with teachers and peers. Within the relationships, children may use their resources (if they are deemed acceptable) to engage in recurrent practices as they investigate, talk about, and play out their worlds. All children need access to symbolic tools, including written language—comprehensible written language—to negotiate, sustain, and manage relationships, to replay scenes and imagine encounters, to capture the music of language, and to reconstruct and reimagine their worlds; energized by participation in a composing practice, children have reasons to grapple with the details of the writing system. As fragmented skills, writing tasks do not grip children's attention except, perhaps, as races to see who can finish first.

If educational policies declare unimportant children's key symbolic tools—their drawing, talking, singing, playing, building—children lose important composing tools that may couch their engagement with written language. Snip away children's relational ties, and they are left without people to compose for and with. Push their interests, say, in animals or superheroes off stage, and children are left without energizing fuel for their narrative imaginations. Sweep under the rug children's needs to confront the injustices of daily life, and they are left deprived of a potential means of growing as a person. Imagine now a small child, deprived of relationships and resources, inside a picture frame built with test results. Such a child can no more be known than that young boy inside the tight frame of the *National Geographic* picture.

So, given our view of children as intentional, active agents, as people with resources that allow them to progress, in the preceding chapters we have spoken out against policy mandates that determine young children's, and teachers', futures through test scores; so much more can be learned by paying attention to, and talking with, our children and seeking to understand their frames of reference. There may be some useful curricular guidance to be had from a common understanding of expected skills, but to distribute those skills in a linear order, organized not by a child's pathway but by the institutional structure of grade levels, makes little sense; children have diverse paths into composing, and those paths are configured mainly by practices, not just lonely skills. We can work toward children having some flexibility in their use of written language by the end of the early grades (i.e., by age eight or nine), but narrowing our view of children to a list of skills is harmful. As Jimmy Britton said years ago (1989, p. 217), we can't "teach children we do not know."

Our view of positive schools for children is fully compatible with the basic policy guidelines put forward by UNICEF (http://www.unicef.org/education/bege, 2012) on "Child Friendly Schools." There is no one way to provide such schools, nor do all countries face the same challenges. Hence school policies will vary. For many, schools will need to partner with communities and institutions that can attend to children's basic needs: Children cannot learn well if their nutrition is poor, their medical needs unattended to, their daily lives threatened by violence. In the words of UNICEF:

> Imagine a textbook written in an indecipherable language, or a blackboard without chalk. Imagine a class being held in a loud concert hall [or an alley way filled with the daily clatter], or a child trying to do homework in the midst of a hurricane [or the sound of distant gunfire]. Clearly, when key components of the learning process and context are lacking, education itself is doomed to fail . . .

> (http://www.unicef.org/education/cfs, n.p.)

For this reason:

> Child-friendly educational environments must be safe, healthy, and
> protective. They must be provided with trained teachers, adequate resources,
> and appropriate physical, emotional, and social conditions for learning.
> Within a child-friendly school, children's rights are protected and their voices
> are heard . . . their identities and varied needs are respected . . .)

These conditions must hold "whether [children] attend school in a building, in
a tent, or under a tree." Thus, national governments should ensure that enrollment is free, textbooks provided, corporal punishment prohibited, local languages
respected and used, and all children are welcomed, including the disabled and
those with HIV and/or AIDS. The school, then, should be inclusive and promote
gender equality, the dignity of all children, and personal and social empowerment.
Moreover, in such a program, there is no one way to learn; educators must
"build on the assets that children bring." Key to building on children's assets is
time and space for children's compositional agency and, also, for teacher agency,
as argued by Barbara in Chapter 3. In the closing major section of the current
chapter, I reiterate the power of the teacher.

Teachers as Improvisational Enablers: Responding for Relevance

As citizens of our respective nation-states and, also, of the earth, we as child
advocates are responsible for taking action for children's quality of life; Caregivers
need jobs and livable wages; families need access to healthcare and good nutrition;
all need nontoxic environments, and, children especially, places to play and explore
the outdoors. As educators, though, we have a particular responsibility for the
worlds we negotiate with children in the classroom. In order to see and hear our
children, we have to push back the picture frame and transform our image of a
child into a figure in motion. Our understandings of children as persons and as
composers are linked to the configuration of practices on offer in our rooms
and to those composing practices they instigate with their peers. When we see
and hear our children as social participants and intentional beings, we find it easier
to recognize their resources, build on their assets, and simply learn their daily
doings (Comber, this volume; Genishi & Dyson, 2009; Yoon, 2013).

Certainly all teachers are not as free to negotiate curricular activities to best
engage their students. This may be particularly hard in schools serving low-income
and minority children. In the US, teachers in such schools may have relatively
more restrictive and more closely monitored curricula; indeed, in kindergartens,
teachers in schools serving primarily low-income children have had such pressures
for a longer period of time than teachers in schools serving more affluent children
(Bassok & Rorem, 2012; Dyson, 2013, 2015; Pandya, 2011). In our project cases,

a restrictive curriculum, focused on the mechanics of writing, dominated (but not exclusively so) in the children's schools, and this was particularly so as they moved up the grade levels.

Nonetheless, even in crowded classrooms with a paucity of materials, teachers can create agentive space for child voices. They may do so by making interactive space for, and responding to, their children in dialogue, be it in whole-class or small-group lessons, or one-to-one encounters; and they also do so by valuing talk among peers (Lisanza, 2014). Talk is particularly important for composing, since a composer is engaged by an anticipation of a response from some valued other (Bakhtin, 1986). That anticipation can fuel one's manipulation of symbols, exploitation of resources, and seeking out of help, so strong may be the desire to socially connect through a certain kind of text.

In addition, a teacher can create agentive space by acknowledging a child's resources. In this regard, the most disconcerting case was Gus. We read of a little boy who struggled to become a composer. His desire for guidance, perhaps of the type Urvashi offered Sheela, was not met and, by third grade, it became a feeling of despair; in his view he simply could not write unless someone just told him what to do. In third grade, sitting by Barbara's colleague Lyn, Gus imagined a scary ride at a theme park. He drew and wrote . . . only to be told by his teacher that his ride made her uncomfortable. Her response was understandable but ill timed. His words would not do; his teacher wrote her words. Gus's feeling that he could not write was reinforced.

In sum, no matter where children went to school, the teacher mattered. If materials and monitoring did not allow space for children to climb into the practice with their intentions and their resources, then superficial participation occurred in the official world, although unofficial but intentional multimodal composing may have proceeded. Still, the latter was lost to the official world.

Sometimes, after I've published a study that has something to do with child culture as transformed by child literacy (and vice versa), someone will write that the work is all very well and good but that teachers have no time to get to know their children in ways that a participant observer might. This is a faulty sentiment. Many teachers know their children very well from spending their days with them. They know their social leanings, their preferences for symbolic tools, their play inclinations. The problem comes, I think, in seeing all this information about the child as relevant for teaching. By presenting and comparing the classroom lives and representational and communicative efforts of young children spread around the globe, we have aimed to illustrate that literacy is not some decontextualized skill; even as the children experienced school in varied material and curricular circumstances, to compose, they all needed a sense of agency and a confidence that they had "the right stuff"—the right resources, including the "right" languages.

Too often, the desire to bring poor children up to snuff, as it were, has reinforced a curriculum that treats composing as a fixed line of skills to be mastered, rather than a situated means for establishing a dialogic relationship with an addressee (Bakhtin, 1986). Children may be urged to march through a curriculum to a drum beat that is out of sync with the zig-zagging, out-of-line children, who, in our cases, stop to inspect a ladybug in the window, "varoom varoom" an imaginary truck, or daydream about having tea with the teacher. I hope our collective efforts have illustrated that no child should be reduced to her or his test results, nor should any child be assumed to be known because of the house they live in, the neighborhood they call home, or their physical features and home languages.

Our trip with each other to our respective geographic homes is now drawing to a close. In one sense, this book is a scrapbook of sorts. May it become a living record of our responsibilities to all our children.

References

Abu-Lughod, J. L. (1991). Writing against culture. In R. G. Fox (Ed.), *Recapturing anthropology: Working in the present* (pp. 137–162). Santa Fe, NM: School of American Research Press.

Bakhtin, M. (1986). *Speech genres and other late essays.* Austin, TX: University of Texas Press.

Barton, D., & Papen, U. (Eds.). (2010). *The anthropology of writing: Understanding textually-mediated worlds.* London, England: Continuum International.

Bassok, D., & Rorem, A. (2012). *Is kindergarten the new first grade? The changing nature of kindergarten in the age of accountability.* Working paper. University of Virginia-Charlottesville, VA (cited with permission).

Britton, J. (1989). Writing and reading in the classroom. In A. Haas Dyson (Ed.), *Collaboration through writing and reading: Exploring possibilities* (pp. 217–246). Urbana, IL: National Council of Teachers of English.

Dyson, A. Haas (1989). *Multiple worlds of child writers: Friends learning to write.* New York, NY: Teachers College Press.

Dyson, A. Haas (1993). *Social worlds of children learning to write in an urban primary school.* New York, NY: Teachers College Press.

Dyson, A. Haas (2013). *ReWRITING the basics: Literacy learning in children's cultures.* New York, NY: Teachers College Press.

Dyson, A. Haas (2015). The search for inclusion: Deficit discourse and the erasure of childhoods. *Language Arts, 92,* 199–207.

Erickson, F. (1986). Qualitative methods in research on teaching. In M.C. Wittrock (Ed.), *Handbook of research on teaching* (pp. 119–161). New York, NY: Macmillan.

Fisher, M. (2007). "Every city has soldiers": The role of intergenerational relationships in participatory literacy communities. *Research in the Teaching of English, 42,* 139–162.

Genishi, C., & Dyson, A. Haas (2009). *Children, language, and literacy: Diverse learners in diverse times.* New York, NY: Teachers College Press and Washington, DC: National Association for the Education of Young Children.

Heath, S. B. (1983). *Ways with words: Language, life and work in communities and classrooms.* Cambridge, England: Cambridge University Press.

Jocson, K. M. (2006). "There's a better word": Urban youth rewriting their social worlds through poetry. *Journal of Adolescent & Adult Literacy, 49* (8), 700–707.

Kirkland, D. (2013). *A search past silence: The literacy of young black men.* New York, NY: Teachers College Press.

Lisanza, M. E. (2014). Dialogic instruction and learning: The case of one Kiswahili classroom. *Language, Culture, & Curriculum Journal, 27*, 121–135.

Massey, D. (2005). *For space.* Los Angeles, CA: Sage.

McCarty, T. L. (2011). Entry into conversation: Introducing ethnography and language policy. In T. L. McCarty (Ed.), *Ethnography and language policy* (pp. 1–28). New York, NY: Routledge.

Noguera, P. A. (2013). The achievement gap and the schools we need: Creating the conditions where race and class no longer predict student achievement. In M. Katz and M. Rose (Eds.), *Public education under siege* (pp. 180–193). Philadelphia, PA: University of Pennsylvania Press.

New London Group (1996). A pedagogy of multiliteracies: Designing social futures. *Harvard Educational Review, 66*, 60–92.

Smitherman, G. (2006). *Word from the mother: Language and African Americans.* New York, NY: Routledge.

Trudell, B. & Piper, B. (2013). Whatever the law says: Language policy implementation and early grade literacy achievement in Kenya. *Current Issues in Language Planning, 15*, 4–21.

UNICEF (2012). *Inequities in early childhood development: What the data say.* Retrieved from http://www.unicef.org/lac/Inequities_in_Early_Childhood_Development_LoRes_PDF_EN_02082012%281%29.pdf.

Vygotsky, L. S. (1978). *Mind in society: The development of higher psychological process.* Cambridge, MA: Harvard University Press.

Wells, K. (2009). *Childhood in a global perspective.* Malden, MA: Polity Press.

Yoon, H. (2013). Rewriting the curricular script: Teachers and children translating writing practices in a kindergarten classroom. *Research in the Teaching of English, 48*, 148–174.

Zacher Pandya, J. (2011). *Overtested: How high-stakes accountability fails English language learners.* New York, NY: Teachers College Press.

CONCLUDING COMMENTARY

Peggy J. Miller

Don't make up what you could find out.

Howard Becker (1996, p. 59)

The genius of the interesting teacher consists in sympathetic divination of the sort of material with which the pupil's mind is likely to be spontaneously engaged, and in the ingenuity which discovers paths of connection from that material to the matters to be newly learned.

William James (1899/1992, p. 775)

This book places eight young children front and center. We encounter them, first, as rendered by people who knew them and their circumstances up close and over time. Then we are invited to revisit them and ponder the meaning of their lives in school. This organization is brilliantly simple. It models a mode of inquiry for understanding children from poor and minority backgrounds: pay attention to each child's story on its own terms, then step back and take another look and another, using a variety of conceptual lenses.

It may seem superfluous to urge attentiveness when the genre at hand is the case study. Case studies are almost as arresting as the living, breathing children in our lives. Many of us claim a scholarly lineage of case studies to which we gratefully add Danti, Gareth, Gus, Miguel, Natalia, Rafiki, Sheela, and Ta'Von. For my part, I claim (among others) Chubby Maata, the three-year-old navigator of emotionally provocative dramas in Jean Briggs' (1998) *Inuit Morality Play* and Reeny, the kindergartener who developed a passion for the stories of Leo Lionni in Vivian Gussin Paley's (1997) *The Girl with the Brown Crayon*. These case studies, one by a psychological anthropologist and one by a teacher and writer, deepened my understanding of what it means to say, "culture and development are full·

entwined" or "persons and cultures are co-created." I learned that socialization is an astonishingly dynamic process and that the meaning-making that lies at its heart would not be possible without children's agency, without, that is, the play of individual perspective on the cultural resources at hand.

Why is it that cases are so good to think with? One answer to this question can be found in the methods from which they arise. Each researcher in Chapter 2 followed the focal child over a period of months or years in the classroom and sometimes in the home or community as well. They spoke the child's language (at least one), had long-term ties to the local community, and could situate the child and his school within the larger society, including relevant historical, political, and educational trends. This made it possible to form an in-depth picture of the child. When I say "in-depth," I mean that the understanding that emerged was multifaceted, constructed out of multiple temporal and spatial vantage points. As against this complexity, consider what an inaccurate impression we would have of Gareth if we saw him only in the classroom, not at home; or of Sheela if we saw her only with her teacher, not with Urvashi; or of Gus if we saw him only with his regular teachers, not with his replacement teacher, or of Ta'Von if we saw him only at his prekindergarten assessment. These methods also made it possible to trace the ways that macro-contextual factors impinged on children's lives, how good-sounding educational policies were used against children (Danti, Miguel), how national language policies were reversed at the local level (Rafiki) or undermined though lack of funding (Natalia). In short, these methods allow readers to see children as persons, who are up against some tough realities, and whose lives are subject to a host of unpredictable contingencies.

Case studies are good to think with because they counter the fiction that there is a generic low-income child or a generic child-member of a culture or an ethnic group or a community (see Göncü, 1999), and they resist the tendency to reduce children to variables or test scores. Not that there is anything wrong with variables or numbers per se. The problem is that debates about low-income and minority children are often unbalanced in the number/variable direction. The case studies in this book say: Look what else you can find out when you study children *this* way.

One other thing about variables: It is hard to identify with a variable. But it is easy to identify with the children in Chapter 2. This points to another reason why cases are good to think with: They invite reader identification. Recently, I a°¹ colleague about the cases he returns to again and again. He cited Tionna, ·l whose case was documented by Anne Haas Dyson (Dyson, 2013; Dyson, 2009). Tionna's favorite story as a first grader was written by nerican author in AAVE. But when Anne revisited Tionna in the his book was no longer her favorite because she now believed ιny wrong words in it. This case is especially poignant because ice of children trying so hard to do what is correct in school, ιnd again that they are wrong. My colleague identifies with

Tionna because, as a working-class speaker of a non-mainstream dialect, he too was subject to constant correction in school but without any explanation of what was actually happening or even of what the rules of the game were.

Why is this kind of identification important? Aspiring scholars and educators who grew up in low-income or minority communities often cannot find their experience reflected in the pages of scholarly works. They get tired of seeing people like themselves represented on the losing side of invidious comparisons with dominant groups. Opportunities for identification with low-income and minority children may be even more vital for readers who grew up in privileged circumstances, with no first-hand experience of poverty or stigma. By inviting reader identification within and across perilous demographic boundaries, case studies enlarge everyone's capacity to imagine each other (see Shweder, Bidell, Dailey, Dixon, Miller, & Modell, 2009). Without that capacity, it will be virtually impossible to improve education for the most vulnerable.

The cases in Chapter 2 attest that the kind of situation that Tionna encountered in school obtains in a wide variety of classrooms in far-flung corners of the world, sowing confusion and discouragement, especially among the most vulnerable. The costs to children are magnified by classroom practices that enforce very narrow definitions of what it means to be "correct"—practices such as draconian discipline, one-size-fits-all standards, and high-stakes testing. Whatever else these practices might do, they place poor and minority children at risk of being slotted into the hoary deficit narrative.

They also violate a time-honored principle of how to educate children: Start where the child is. I don't know where this idea originated, but I do know that William James endorsed it in *Talks to Teachers on Psychology*, published in 1899. James admitted that it is not easy to put this principle into practice. But he was confident that American teachers, determined to educate children for life in a democracy and equipped with tact, earnestness, and ingenuity, were up to the task.

This principle may matter most when children are beginning their educational careers, impressionable newcomers to the whole business of school. Teachers of preschoolers, kindergarteners, and first and second graders know that children of a given age exhibit tremendous individual variation in their enthusiasms and in their cognitive, social, and emotional development. They know too that an individual child may exhibit uneven growth across domains, ahead of his peers in social skills but behind in literacy or vice versa. In short, because teachers cannot assume uniform interests or a uniform starting point even within demographically homogeneous classrooms, they need to start where the child is.

But, of course, more and more classrooms are not homogenous. Children come to school with different languages and from different cultural, ethnic, religious, and socioeconomic backgrounds. This diversity makes it more challenging —and even more vital—to start where the child is. The good news is that far more is known now than ever before about the lives and development of diverse children; these advances come not only from education and developmental psychology but also from anthropology, the sociology of childhood, and a host of interdisciplinary fields. There are even good sources of information written for a general audience (Lancy, 2015; Shweder, et al., 2009). Even more to the point, the case studies in this book, as well as the literature cited in this volume, provide many examples of teachers starting where children are and creating permeable curricula that support their development. The bad news is that many teachers are dealing with policies and curricula that disregard tried-and-true pedagogical principles as well as new bodies of knowledge, making it very difficult for them to start where the child is.

How will this tension between the good news and the bad news be resolved? It is impossible to say because the outcome depends on unforeseeable political calculations. Despite that reality, this volume concludes with the hope that readers will abide with these eight children and that their unruly, haunting, and exuberant stories will inspire and unsettle in ways that make a difference.

References

Becker, H. (1996). The epistemology of qualitative research. In R. Jessor, A. Colby, & R. A. Shweder (Eds.), *Ethnography and human development: Context and meaning in social inquiry* (pp. 53–71). Chicago, IL: University of Chicago Press.

Briggs, J. (1998). *Inuit morality play: The emotional education of a three-year-old.* New Haven, CT: Yale University Press.

Dyson, A. Haas (2013). *ReWRITING the basics: Literacy learning in children's cultures.* New York, NY: Teachers College Press.

Genishi, C., & Dyson, A. Haas (2009). *Children, language, and literacy: Diverse learners in diverse times.* New York, NY: Teachers College Press and Washington, DC: National Association for the Education of Young Children.

Göncü, A. (Ed.). (1999). *Children's engagement in the world: Sociocultural perspectives.* Cambridge, England: Cambridge University Press.

James, W. (1899/1992). *Talks to teachers on psychology and to students on some of life's ideals.* In *William James: Writings 1878–1899* (pp. 705–887). New York, NY: The Library of America.

Lancy, D. (2015). The *anthropology of childhood: Cherubs, chattel, changelings* (2nd ed.). Cambridge, England: Cambridge University Press.

Paley, V. G. (1997). *The girl with the brown crayon: How children use stories to shape their lives.* Cambridge, MA: Harvard University Press.

Shweder, R. A., Bidell, T. R., Dailey, A. C., Dixon, S. D., Miller, P. J., & Modell, J. (Eds.) (2009). *The child: An encyclopedic companion.* Chicago, IL: The University of Chicago Press.

ABOUT THE CONTRIBUTORS

Barbara Comber is Research Professor in the Faculty of Education at Queensland University of Technology. Her research interests include teachers' work, critical literacy, and social justice. She has conducted longitudinal ethnographic case studies and collaborative action research with teachers working in high-poverty and culturally diverse communities. Her research examines the kinds of teaching that make a difference to young people's literacy learning trajectories and what gets in the way.

Sophie Dewayani is Head of Litara (Indonesia Children's Literacy), in which she helps develop materials for children's literacy education in Indonesia. In addition, Sophie teaches in Bandung Institute of Technology and, also, does research on children's construction of identity in literacy learning and children's responses to multicultural children's literature. Her current research focuses on the use of children's literature in Indonesian classrooms. Sophie is herself a published author of children's books.

Anne Haas Dyson is a former teacher of young children and currently Professor in the College of Education, University of Illinois at Urbana-Champaign. A fellow of the American Educational Research Association, she has spent 35 years studying the childhood cultures and literacy learning of young schoolchildren. Among her recent book publications are *The Brothers and Sisters Learn to Write*; *Children, Language, and Literacy: Diverse Learners in Diverse Times* (with Celia Genishi); and *ReWRITING the Basics: Literacy Learning in Children's Cultures*.

Celia Genishi is Professor Emerita at Teachers College, Columbia University. She is a former secondary Spanish and preschool teacher and has taught courses related to early childhood education and qualitative research methods in the Department of Curriculum and Teaching at Teachers College. Her books include *Ways of Assessing Children and Curriculum; Diversities in Early Childhood Education* (with A. Lin Goodwin); and *Children, Language, and Literacy: Diverse Learners in Diverse Times* (with Anne Haas Dyson). Her research interests include childhood bilingualism; children's language use, play, and early literacy in classrooms; and collaborative research and assessment with teachers.

Lyn Kerkham is a Research Associate in the School of Education at the University of South Australia. She has worked and researched in and with schools located in poor and culturally and linguistically diverse communities for more than two decades. Her interests include the affordances of place and space for innovative literacy curriculum, the effects of mandated literacy assessment on teachers' work, teachers as researchers, and critical literacy.

Esther Mukewa Lisanza is Assistant Professor in the Department of Liberal Studies, Winston-Salem State University. She is also a Visiting Scholar at the African Studies Center, University of North Carolina-Chapel Hill. Her teaching and research interests are in language and literacy development, the politics of language in education, and African indigenous knowledge and education.

Jackie Marsh is Professor of Education, University of Sheffield. Jackie undertakes research on young children's digital literacy practices in homes, schools, and community spaces. She is an editor of the *Journal of Early Childhood Literacy*. Jackie's latest book is *Changing Play: Play, Media and Commercial Culture from the 1950s to the Present Day* (with Julia Bishop).

Peggy J. Miller is Professor Emerita, Department of Communication and Department of Psychology, University of Illinois at Urbana-Champaign. Peggy is a developmental cultural psychologist who has written extensively on socialization through everyday talk in diverse communities. She is an expert on young children's narratives and on ethnographic and qualitative methods.

Iliana Reyes is a Research Scientist at CINVESTAV, Mexico City, and associated faculty in Language, Reading and Culture at the University of Arizona. Her areas of expertise include early literacy, bilingualism and biliteracy, and language socialization in immigrant communities. She has published extensively in the top journals of literacy education and psychology of language in the US and internationally, including *Reading Research Quarterly*, the *Journal of Early Childhood Literacy*, *Bilingualism: Language and Cognition*, and *Cultura y Educación*.

Urvashi Sahni is Founding President and CEO of Studyhall Educational Foundation in Uttar Pradesh, India, a Non-Resident Fellow at the Center for

Universal Education at the Brookings Institute, and a member of several international networks for girls' education. For the last 30 years, Urvashi has been a social entrepreneur and educationist. She is committed to reaching high-quality education for children in rural and urban India, mainly in the state of Uttar Pradesh. She has been focusing on educating girls from very poor communities, using a strong rights-based approach and the practice of critical feminist pedagogy. She works closely with the government at the state and national level, advising them on policy and collaborating with them to strengthen their schools and teacher-training institutes.

INDEX

Note: illustrations are indicated by *italicised* text, tables by **bold**.